What Is Not Sacred?
African Spirituality

Laurenti Magesa

ORBIS BOOKS

Maryknoll, New York 10545

ORBIS ⊕ BOOKS
Maryknoll, New York 10545

Fathers and Brothers
MARYKNOLL™

Founded in 1970, Orbis Books endeavors to publish works that enlighten the mind, nourish the spirit, and challenge the conscience. The publishing arm of the Maryknoll Fathers and Brothers, Orbis seeks to explore the global dimensions of the Christian faith and mission, to invite dialogue with diverse cultures and religious traditions, and to serve the cause of reconciliation and peace. The books published reflect the views of their authors and do not represent the official position of the Maryknoll Society. To learn more about Maryknoll and Orbis Books, please visit our website at www. maryknollsociety.org.

Copyright © 2013 by Laurenti Magesa

Published by Orbis Books, Maryknoll, NY 10545-0302.

Manufactured in the United States of America
No part of this publication may be reproduced or transmitted in any form or by any means, electronic or mechanical, including photocopying, recording, or any information storage or retrieval system, without prior permission in writing from the publisher.

Queries regarding rights and permissions should be addressed to: Orbis Books, P.O. Box 302, Maryknoll, NY 10545-0302.

Library of Congress Cataloging-in-Publication Data

Magesa, Laurenti, 1946-
    What is not sacred? : African spirituality / by Laurenti Magesa.
      pages   cm
    Includes bibliographical references and index.
    ISBN 978-1-62698-052-5 (pbk.)
    1. Christianity and other religions—African. 2. Christianity—Africa. 3. Africa—Religion. I. Title.
    BR128.A16M34   2013
    261.2096—dc23
                                                        2013013925

"We desire to bequest two things to our children—
the first one is roots; the other one is wings."

For this and subsequent generations of Africa—
especially the children—
that we may remain faithful
to the Divine Inspiration in the Continent

Contents

Foreword

In writings about African spirituality and prayer life, there is no study that to my knowledge has yet tried to show in depth the vivacity and vitality of these two aspects of modern African societies. This study by Laurenti Magesa does not limit its considerations to an academic discourse but deals to a greater extent with the concrete life of the African people today. Magesa's intention is to go beyond appearances in order to discover how the traditional concept of life shapes the whole behavior of man and woman in a world of so-called modernity and a time of globalization. Is it true that the words and traditions of the ancestors have totally lost their influence in today's world, characterized as it is by Western thought and technology? Magesa demonstrates how false such a supposition can be. On the contrary, many modern Africans, even among those who are generally considered intellectuals, do not hesitate to go back to their ancestral roots, to that which shapes them and nurtures their whole life. This is evident in the belief of witchcraft, in the practice of traditional medicine, and in the thriving of charismatic movements today in Africa, to mention but a few examples.

However, it is important to emphasize that the purpose of our author is not at all the "christianization" of African customs. Rather, he aims to show the dynamism of African elements in daily life which lead to God through the world by the involvement of the whole of creation in the process of spirituality and prayer. At that same time, this means that the encounter between African Religion, Christianity, and other religions should be viewed not from the perspective of conversion but rather from the viewpoint of a dialogue that includes special attention to the dignity of others. This supposes that one does not exclusively claim the monopoly of "truth" but is ready to listen and be enriched by the other. Magesa began this theology of dialogue in his important book *African Religion: The Moral Traditions of Abundant Life* (Maryknoll, NY: Orbis Books, 1997). More clearly and decisively, he elaborates this concept in his recent work *African Religion in the Dialogue Debate: From Intolerance to Coexistence* (Berlin: LIT Verlag, 2010). This new work again stresses the view that African spirituality has its own autonomy and inherent dignity, independent of contact with Christian and other models of spirituality.

Christianity and other religions need to respect the African religious concept and experience because God was already with our ancestors from the very beginning. Their experience of life is in reality the experience on the way to Emmaus: full revelation occurs, of course, in Christ's breaking of the bread, as he did at the Last Supper, but a real encounter with him already takes place on the way. Here, I see the importance of Magesa's gathering of several experiences across Sub-Saharan Africa in trying to show convincingly how African people did and still do overcome many difficulties, thanks to a traditional way of life that gives them energy and a spirituality of hope. The examples taken from *ubuntu* (Sotho, Xhosa), *ubupfura* (Rwanda), and *ubushingantahe* (Burundi) among others highlight this reality.

All Africans, men and women alike, who lived according to the African spiritual ideal can be considered as "Christians before Christians" (*chrétiens avant la lettre!*). It is legitimate to apply to them the teaching in the Apostles' Creed that "He descended to the dead" to redeem "the just ones." This famous teaching should not be limited to Adam and Eve and to the believers of the Old Testament ("the just ones") whom Jesus is believed to have redeemed. From the African perspective, all our ancestors and ancestresses of good will who followed the ideal of their traditions that were/are in accordance with God and the Risen Christ on the way to Emmaus can be counted among "the just." Magesa's emphasis on this point is seen when he states that Africans had particularly valid principles in their tradition to reach peace and reconciliation.

The recent past has witnessed some peoples putting aside their enmity to embrace brotherliness, sometimes after ethnic clashes and or genocides, including such examples as in Rwanda and in the Democratic Republic of Congo. The *gacaca* court system of community justice in Rwanda, the blood pact, and other traditional reconciliation practices have contributed immensely to this success. Magesa knows that not all is perfect and that there are many abuses of traditions. Therefore, what he pleads for is the keen reconsideration of the ideal in African traditions and the development of the positive in them, thereby abolishing their negative aspects as well. If Africans, particularly younger generations, become aware of this, the black continent might rediscover the pure spirituality that inspires and redynamizes the future and gives hope to our people.

The content of the study of our author is intended not only for Christians. It is also of interest to all those who want to understand Africans and their concept of life in any area, be it economic, political, or religious. May this book receive the attention it deserves in all the theological and catechetical schools in Africa and beyond, including non-Christian faculties and institutions.

Bénézet Bujo
Fribourg, Switzerland

Acknowledgments

"A person cannot dance well on one leg only."

A critical step in the process of writing this book was a seminar I facilitated for some graduate students and staff at Tangaza College, a college of the Catholic University of Eastern Africa (CUEA) in Nairobi, Kenya, in March 2006. The encouragement I received at this gathering strengthened my resolve to commit the ideas, then free-floating in my mind, to paper.

Among those who participated in the seminar and contributed invaluable support, I wish to mention with gratitude Fr. Steven Payne, Fr. Modest Inyait, Sr. Loretta Brenan, and Br. Denis Katusiime, faculty members of the Institute of Spirituality and Religious Formation (ISRF) at Tangaza College, all of whom gave me exceptional encouragement. Professor Michael C. Kirwen, Director of the Maryknoll Institute of African Studies of St. Mary's University (MIASMU) at Tangaza, goaded me not to relent when my spirits were drooping and offered generous assistance throughout the project. He also read part of the manuscript and offered invaluable suggestions. This book, like several previous ones, owes its existence to his unfailing support.

I am grateful to the Africa desk of the Dutch-based Advisory Board of Missionary Activities, *Adviescommissie Missionaire Activiteiten* (AMA), which provided funds in 2005 for the initial research for this book. Time constraints did not allow me to begin writing immediately. This, as Providence would arrange it, had to wait until 2011–2012 during a research fellowship granted by the Woodstock Theological Center in Washington, DC.

My colleagues at Hekima College, Rev. Joseph G. Healey, M.M., Dr. Gabriel Mmassi, Dr. Protas Opondo, and Prof. Aquiline Tarimo, facilitated the successful process of obtaining the fellowship with letters of reference cheerfully written whenever I needed them. My friend and *ndugu*, Gina Schneider, and her family, my brother Dr. Evaristi Magoti, his son Michael Magoti, and my bishop, the Right Rev. Michael Msonganzila of the Diocese of Musoma, Tanzania, smoothed some of the other obstacles that appeared along the way.

At Woodstock, unstinting assistance came from so many quarters it is difficult to list them entirely. At the great risk of omitting some, I must mention

Laura Michener and Maria Ferrara, the International Visiting Fellowship administrators; Thomas Reese, S.J., Raymond B. Kemp, John Haughey, S.J., Gaspar LoBiondo, S.J., and all the members of the Ignatius-Lonergan (Ig-Lon) study group; John Endres, S.J., Cristina Vanin, and Joseph Selling, who were International Visiting Fellows like me at the time; and librarian J. Leon Hooper, S.J., who showed great interest in my work. In a word, Woodstock provided an excellent environment in which to work.

My hosts during my time at Woodstock were Frs. Paul Langsfeld, Klaus Sirianni, and Gregory Shaffer. I will not attempt to describe their hospitality and the friendliness of their parishioners at St. Stephen Martyr Catholic Church. The mark of the genuine fellowship they accorded me will forever remain etched in my heart.

Jay Stirpe (whom by mutual agreement I christened "The Gentleman from Ohio") and I became fast friends. Throughout my stay in Washington, DC, he and Ms. Branka Slavica acted as my guides in the city. Jay also read and edited some chapters of this book. Dr. Jordan Nyenyembe suggested some indispensable literature for the effort.

At very short notice, my colleagues Fr. David John Ayotte, S.J., at Hekima College and Dr. Richard Rwiza at CUEA agreed to read the final draft of this project. I cannot thank them enough for sparing their time. They will notice that I have incorporated many of their suggestions.

I must recognize and acknowledge in a special way the crucial and generous assistance of Ms. Ndanu Mung'ala. Despite being deeply immersed in her own work, Ms. Mung'ala very graciously offered to read and edit the entire manuscript, taking upon herself full editorial license and responsibility. She has instructed me to state here that all questions concerning the style of the book be directed to her. What a relief for me!

I must admit that I agonized over how to title this book until I came across a saying from Mali in West Africa, contained in Mrs. Annette Miller's collection of African proverbs (Nairobi: Paulines Publications Africa, 2008) that I thought captures succinctly the essence of the work: *What Is Not Sacred?* I feel it is necessary and appropriate to thank Mrs. Miller for the insight.

"A person cannot dance well on one leg only." In ballet, ice-skating, bolero, salsa, twist, bongo flava, kwela, or any other variety of dance, one employs both legs to perform well. The people and institutions I have mentioned were for me the second leg that enabled me to "dance" this book into life. How well my own steps have been executed in the dance, however, is not a reflection on them. And, obviously, it is not a matter for me to judge.

Part I

*Encounters:
The Phenomenology of African Spirituality*

Spirituality Matters

"The cock drinking water raises its head to God in thankfulness."

This book addresses the worldview or spirituality of the peoples of Africa *south* of the Sahara desert, sometimes called black Africa. It is, therefore, important to note from the start that in this work the designation "Africa" is generally used as shorthand for this part of the vast continent, whose peoples are racially black and spiritually guided by a perception of life that is fundamentally neither specifically "Christian" nor exclusively "Muslim." Thus, Africa, as used in these pages, with only very few occasional references, generally excludes the populations of the northern region of the continent, which is predominantly racially Arab and religiously Muslim. The qualifier "predominantly" in this context, I must insist, is important and crucial for a proper appreciation of the validity of my general geographical option for consideration: in both the south and the north of the continent, people of either race and faith can certainly be found, but in very unequal numbers and influence, specifically in terms of (spiritual) worldview.

The book consists of two parts. The first attempts to explore systematically and in some depth the structures and meaning of African spirituality in order to understand the genuine religious identity of the majority of the black peoples living in the southern part of the continent. It is an effort to appreciate and articulate black Africa's struggle to be in touch with the mystery of life. The discussion is principally inspired by the lives of the Africans I have known, observed, and lived with for many years, although I suspect that some of them would not directly recognize themselves in the following pages. They have been and are members of different faiths and churches currently thriving on the continent, but in their daily lives all have represented for me the spirituality of indigenous black Africa as a whole.

I am aware that my view may appear as an enormous generalization, extrapolating from the experience of comparatively few people to make statements about the way of life of millions of people in an entire subcon-

3

tinent. Yet I have no reservation at all in making the claim because it is generally justifiable. Apart from my own admittedly limited observation, there is now a huge corpus of literature by numerous reputable scholars all over the world who have made similar observations and make the same claim about the peoples of this part of Africa. It is encouraging that among them are Africans. (The limited extent of the literature I have consulted on the subject provides an idea of this general consensus, despite the usual academic idiosyncrasies.)

Our rather bold claim to speak about "Africa," "African culture," "African Religion," or "African spirituality" in an apparently monolithic, undiversified sense requires further explanation. Many people appreciate the fact that Africa is not a country; it is a continent. It is comprised of literally thousands of ethnic groups and, consequently, cultural expressions. Even within individual African countries, there are numerous such cultural groupings and expressions; in Tanzania alone, for example, with a population of about 45 million people, there are over 120 ethnic groups. This is what leads many critics of "generalizing" works such as the present to ask skeptically: "What is *African* about Africa?" The implication of the rhetorical question is that it is difficult, if not impossible, to find anything culturally unitive in Africa; that one can speak meaningfully about Africa only in a piecemeal approach, not globally, and certainly not in terms of culture! But clearly, as Curtis Keim titled his book, this is one of the numerous cases abroad of unconscious or deliberate "mistaking Africa" (Keim 2009).

Although there are obviously different expressions of religious belief, as I shall note below, there exists an underlying basic similarity or sameness of spirit and intention in the different cultural-religious expressions in Africa and among Africans. This is what justifies the qualification "African" applied to many of these expressions, which is something I do in this book. In the final analysis, it is really a matter of emphasis. If emphasis is placed on the differences of practical expression, then one will justifiably speak in terms of African cultures; but if one underlines the similarities of inner meaning of the religious worldview and ethical values contained in the expressions, as is my intention in this book, the terms African culture, religion, philosophy, and spirituality (in the singular) are perfectly legitimate and justifiable. Incidentally, this is as true of Christianity and Islam as it is for many other religious traditions identifying themselves by a common name. Thus, while in places I will add qualifiers such as "in many African cultures" when describing some cultural religious practices, having in mind the differences and distinctions among them, it is not to deny the similarity of their core meaning and spiritual implications among the peoples of the subcontinent.

I am interpreting and summarizing a wide range of personal observations and academic research findings of numerous students of Africa here. I do so while sharing the awareness of many of them, particularly those reflecting from a religious faith background, as well as the perception of the African peoples themselves, that God is ultimately a mystery—one impossible to capture entirely in intellectual notions. There are some things in human life that are beyond completely rational or logical and terminological or empirical grasp or demonstration, and in that category of human reality lie many dimensions of religious life and belief.

Explicitly religious or not, most people tend to live their highest ideals without seeing the need to define them in particularly clear terms. Why? Their major preoccupation is to conduct their lives according to what their principles require, not to question them, much less to know their exact sources. The point here is that for most people and communities, the experience of living is more important than notions about it. Concepts and notions are useful in academic discourse to describe the various ways of experiencing life, but these are different concerns from those that occupy the thoughts of the average person in daily existence.

In terms of holistic existence in the world, human preoccupation in general involves physical preservation of self and community on the one hand, and faith in and devotion to a power or powers outside of and higher than the perceptibly human on the other. In practice, both require self-discipline in terms of work, managing personal emotions, and constructing relationships. This should be the primary level of meaning when we make reference to "spirituality." As the motor of human existence, spirituality is an inescapable reality. Walter Principe describes spirituality as three-tiered, with the first and most basic tier "the real or existential level." The other two levels derive from this and involve, on the one hand, "formulation of a teaching about the lived reality," and on the other, "study by scholars of the first and especially of the second levels" (Principe 2000, 47-48; also Schneiders 2005a, 19-29). As critically important as the latter may be, they are inferences or extrapolations from lived reality.

It is quite unfortunate, however, that the notion of spirituality in institutional religion has often been reduced to the level of teaching and study at the expense of the generic, existential one, "the way in which a person understands and lives within his or her historical context that aspect of his or her religion, philosophy or ethic that is viewed as the loftiest, the noblest, the most calculated to lead to the fullness of the ideal of perfection being sought" (Principe 2000, 48).

Thus it is that in many an institutional approach, students may undertake to study in the field of spirituality the thought, contemplative methods, or prayer forms of certain saintly persons, living or dead. This is sometimes done in a rather abstract way, quite independently from other concrete aspects of the lives of the people in question, even despite the fact that some of these individuals were or are very much involved in the life of their societies. The question for spirituality from the point of view of academic institutional methodologies is how the "spiritual masters" achieved union with God, almost apart from, or in spite of, their social environment and interactions. And if these engagements are brought into the picture, as they sometimes inevitably must be, they are paradoxically regarded as almost peripheral to the "spirituality" of the individual in question, not an intrinsic part of it.

Even in an academic approach, students need to pay great attention to the lived experience, the fundamental dimension of shared human existence. But since lived experience is differently expressed by different people and communities, it is legitimate to speak of various spiritualities: for example, English, German, American, or African spirituality. Further, it is possible and perhaps necessary at times to consider Catholic, Anglican, Presbyterian, Hindu, or Buddhist approaches to life as distinct spiritualities. Additionally, there are Franciscan, Ignatian, and Vincentian spiritualities, among many others. Within African spirituality one may further distinguish Chagga, Hausa, Igbo, Xhosa, Zulu, or Bobo spirituality, for example. Without losing sight of their essential inner unity, we must acknowledge that each of these ethnic groups constructs a spirituality within the larger whole of its own traditions and customs according to its own immediate environment. These traditions may be "independently" evaluated to see whether they are "good" or "bad" in relation to the "best interests" of universal existence. A criterion for judgment may be framed thus: How does a particular philosophy of life or ethic of an individual or group affect other human beings and the rest of creation on which humanity depends for survival? It is already clear from the criterion how tentative any approach will be.

Again, a bird's-eye view of the academic description of African existential spirituality in conversation with its "spiritual masters," notably the elders and other religious professionals, is the ultimate goal of the discussion that will follow. It is a narrative of the ideal that African communities strive for and individuals are instructed or socialized in: unity of spirit or the sense of identity of a people; trust and openness, which arise from and lead to interdependence; love and mutual care, which are expressions of participation; and respect for elders, nature, and the ancestors. The latter expresses African recognition of the essential role "supernatural" existence plays in natural existence (Some 1993, 70).

WORDS OF ADVICE FROM THE ELDERS

"It is not for you to call profane what God counts clean."

One of the earliest official statements of the Roman Catholic Church against cultural transplantation in the name of evangelization is the seventeenth-century instruction from the Congregation *De Propaganda Fide* (now known as the Congregation for the Evangelization of Peoples). It described the practice as "absurd" and distinctly criticized the propensity of European missionaries in China to equate the expression of gospel values with their own cultures. Anything that was not "openly opposed to religion and good morals," the instruction insisted, had to be left alone; people should not be compelled "to change their rites, habits and customs" just because these were different from what the missionaries knew and were accustomed to in their own lands (*De Propaganda Fide*, 1659).

The fact that the statement was issued suggests that there must have been resistance from converts against this mode of conducting the mission. Since the cultures of the peoples of the Far East, whose religious philosophies such as Taoism and Confucianism in China, Buddhism in India, and Shintoism in Japan are very strong, and all predate Christianity by at least five hundred years, this is not surprising. These religions and philosophies, so deeply rooted in the cultural consciousness of the people, could not be easily uprooted by foreign cultural expressions of the gospel among converts or potential converts. But since insistence on cultural conversion dominated, it is no wonder that up to this day there is only a small percentage of Christians in these lands compared to the total population. Enlightened missionaries attempted, with very limited success, to correct this error and adopt a form of evangelization that respected and incorporated elements of these cultures in the interpretation and practice of the gospel. Classic examples include Jesuit Fathers Matteo Ricci (d. 1610) and Roberto de Nobili (d. 1656) in China and India, respectively.

Both Ricci and de Nobili made a point of thoroughly studying the local languages of their host places. Ricci approached the Chinese language, culture, and religious customs not as innately profane phenomena but as fundamentally good entities whose perfection, as he taught, was to be found in Christ's gospel. De Nobili similarly adopted many Indian customs and, in a most original way, used local symbols to explain Christian doctrine. Ironically, however, both missionaries met with opposition for their evangelization approaches from many of their colleagues, who were apparently concerned that such methods adulterated Christian purity. Although in the

Constitution *Romanae Sedis Antistes* (1623) Pope Gregory XV upheld some of the ideas de Nobili was advancing, the "anti-inculturationists" of the time eventually managed to persuade the church authorities in Rome to ban the initiatives.

The triumph of the restorationists in China and India has been widely blamed for the failure of Catholic Christianity to spread in these regions of the East. Incidentally, current estimates put the total number of Christians in China at between seventy and one hundred million out of a population of approximately 1.4 billion people. What is interesting to note is the shift in Christian demographics before and after Mao Tse-tung's regime in 1949. While Catholics were twice the size of Protestants before 1949, following China's recent opening to the West under Deng Xiaoping, the reverse is now the case. The number of Protestants, Evangelicals, and Pentecostals is twice that of Catholics.

Since the statement of *Propaganda* and Gregory's Constitution of the seventeenth century, church authorities have intermittently revisited the inculturation issue in the contexts of particular churches, perhaps an indication of how central the cultural issue is in the process of evangelization. On the world stage, Pope Pius XII's position was significant. Although formulated as a reaction to the postures of European philosophies and ideologies of racism and racial superiority as well as the violence engulfing that continent at the beginning of his pontificate during the second quarter of the twentieth century, Pope Pius XII in his encyclical *Summi Pontificatus* of 1939 nevertheless touched upon the universal necessity for respect of "the unity of the human race," part of which is their diverse cultures. All peoples possess a heritage important to them that has to be respected, the pope affirmed, and the church must not set out to belittle any aspect of any culture that is not manifestly immoral; it must instead encourage and help improve anything of value inherent in the culture (Pius XII, *Summi Pontificatus*, 1939, no. 44).

But who is to determine at any given time which aspects of culture are or are not "inseparably bound up with religious errors?", as the pope put it in *Summi Pontificatus* (see also *Sacrosanctum Concilium* [SC], no. 37). Who is to judge which customs are or are not "in contradiction with the divine law"? This indeed remains the question of inculturation up to this day. Nevertheless, it is no longer in doubt that the label "profane," so liberally attached in the past to practically all but European cultures, was by these statements starting to be not only officially questioned but also rejected. "The missionary is an apostle of Jesus Christ," Pope Pius emphasized in his address. "His task is not to propagate European civilization in mission lands," he cautioned. "Rather, it is his function so to train and guide other peoples, some of whom glory in their ancient and refined civilization, as to prepare them for the willing and hearty acceptance of the principles of Christian life and behavior" (Pius XII, "Address to Directors of Pontifical Mission Works," 1944).

Much of the residual conceptual ambiguity about this matter was substantially removed by the Second Vatican Council, which in its various documents explicitly acknowledged the beauty of God that shines in every culture and language and in various religions. The Pastoral Constitution on the Church in the Modern World (*Gaudium et Spes* [*GS*]) sees the nature of the gospel of Christ not as being alien to any culture, but as assuming "the spiritual qualities and endowments of every age and nation, and with supernatural riches it causes them to blossom, as it were, from within; it fortifies, completes and restores them in Christ" (*GS*, no. 58). With Vatican II vernacular languages are accepted as important vehicles for meaningful worship (*SC*, nos. 36, 54); esteem for other religions is promoted (*Nostra Aetate*, no. 2); and religious freedom affirmed (*Dignitatis Humanae*, no. 9).

The conviction that cultural values are in a real sense the springboard of the gospel and of its genuine interpretation is a fundamental theme of the consciousness of the council. This is why Pope Paul VI could write in 1967, in reference to Africa, that the teaching of Jesus Christ does not abrogate but complements and perfects the positive values of African tradition. "And that is why the African, who becomes a Christian, does not disown himself, but takes up the age-old values of tradition 'in spirit and in truth'" (Paul VI, *Africae Terrarum*, no. 14).

Since the council, the message has been reiterated by subsequent popes, synods, and individual bishops, and elaborated by many theologians from the southern hemisphere in the inculturation branch of the theology of liberation. Both Pope John Paul II and Pope Benedict XVI have spoken and written extensively on this issue. With regard to Africa, respect for the values of African culture, traditions, and religion seems to be the constant thread of papal and episcopal pronouncements, to the extent that Pope John Paul II, echoing the recommendation of the bishops from the first Assembly on Africa of the Synod of Bishops (the first African Synod of 1994) states firmly that every future priest in Africa should study African culture and religion and understand their implications in people's lives (John Paul II, *Ecclesia in Africa*, 1995, no. 67).

Pope Paul VI enumerated in 1967 some of the values in African tradition to be cherished and cultivated so that they might not be lost: a sense of the sacred, respect for life and esteem for community and family, the view of existence as spiritual and sacred, and the rich symbolism in worship. Similarly, Pope John Paul II, speaking to some African students in Cote d'Ivoire in 1980, underlined this. He amplified the treasure of the African tradition: "respect for life, family solidarity and support for relatives, respect for the old, the sense of hospitality, judicious preservation of traditions, the taste for feasts and symbols, attachment to dialogue and palaver to settle differences." The pope voiced his conviction that a genuine African civilization in the modern world must be built on the foundation of these values. Pope Benedict XVI, for his part, writing in the wake of the second African Synod, sees "grounds for hope in Africa's rich intellectual, cultural and religious heritage," which Africa "wishes to preserve . . . to deepen . . . and to share . . . with the world" (*Africae Munus*, no. 9).

The African church itself has not lacked in sentiments and statements to the same effect. From the African cultural perspective, all of this constitutes advice from the elders; to disregard it implies lack of wisdom and entails sure descent into tragic situations. "He who does not listen to the advice of an elder breaks his leg." The above insights, and many others which need not be repeated here, provide a clear incentive to engage in conversations between African spirituality and the historical and current forms and expressions of Christian spirituality that have originated and developed elsewhere in different situations and cultures. Nevertheless, it is necessary to clarify one thing: official statements encouraging or even authorizing inculturation recognize a prior fact; they do not create inculturation. Even if official authorization had not been given, the process would not be eliminated. The reality of inculturation precedes and is far greater than the theology of inculturation. The attempt to articulate African spirituality presumes and is founded on the sensibility and activity of African peoples for millennia in relation to God, a relationship that forms their religious identity.

1

Accepting African Spiritual Identity

"A child does not laugh at the ugliness of its mother."

A constituent element of the human condition is beauty, in nature and in human beings and their cultures. However, another inescapable component of the same human condition is, well, ugliness. Alongside beauty, we are surrounded by unattractiveness of every kind on the personal, social, physical, and moral levels. Everywhere on earth, we find material imperfection in spite of many attempts to cover it up. Worse still, we also encounter among human beings dreadful cruelty, the natural and religious imperative to love notwithstanding. Moral deficiencies present themselves as viciousness, hatred, jealousy, selfishness, anger, pride, crimes against humanity and nature; in one word: evil.

All human beings, as individuals and societies, are situated in this ambivalence of a good but imperfect world. Of course, we might regret the lack of complete beauty in our physical reality and often denounce unethical inclinations and behavior in our societies. But our environment, beautiful or ugly, exerts a fundamental influence on us. This applies most basically to our cultures; their imperfections justify no attempt at their destruction, especially from external sources. While cultural transformation is desirable and often necessary, any attempt to eradicate any culture, with the most wicked expression of this being genocide, is both reckless and foolish.

I was born in the mid-twentieth century in a small, remote village of Tanzania, a country straddling the Indian Ocean on the east coast of Africa. The elders, in the literal sense of respected aged people, exercised a great deal of influence in Mabuimerafuru, my village. Christian schools and churches were gradually being established there. The schools taught the "three Rs": reading, writing, and arithmetic; and the churches preached Jesus Christ as the savior of the world. Together, both institutions insisted that people adhere to certain moral standards. For all practical purposes, what they meant by "moral standards" concerned almost exclusively sexual behavior, or what they referred to as proper relations between the sexes. Though it did not have as strong an influence as Christianity, there was also an Islamic presence in the village. I remember that at least one of my uncles was Muslim, having converted to the Islamic faith in the district's major town. It was barely fifty miles away, but for us, at the time, it seemed "far away." For the Muslims in my village, the idea of morality meant attending Friday prayer *(salat)* and giving alms to the poor *(sadakat)*.

Regardless of educational standards, which for the village youth typically meant four to six years of formal school instruction, and in spite of some conversions to Christianity and much fewer to Islam, the principal agents of instruction in morals in the village remained the elders, older men and women whom everybody acknowledged possessed knowledge of the affairs of the community and clan and to whom everyone showed deference. Individually and collectively, they imparted the wisdom they held in formal and informal settings during the celebration of different rites of passage, through stories, songs, proverbs, and riddles, and in enumerating taboos and behavior to be avoided if life was to run smoothly. The elders were responsible for handing traditions down to the community through the generations. In the village, morality meant something broader than the sexual mores that the churches and schools insisted on, or the prayer and almsgiving that the Muslims emphasized. It encompassed the entire spectrum of life and its concerns. It touched on matters of life and death and explored the grandest of affairs as well as the minutest.

So it was that whenever a number of young boys, all around sixteen to eighteen years of age or occasionally younger, underwent the rituals of initiation at the same time, they were instructed in issues of sexual propriety or morality. Sexual education was indispensable; marriage was the most fundamental of requirements to assure the continuation of the clan. But sexuality was not the only concern during the initiation period; the age-set was also educated in other issues concerning the broader realities of life using short, memorable epithets. Among them was the absolute value of identifying with the community: "A person is a person only with other persons, alone one is an animal"; deference toward seniors: "An adult squatting sees farther than a child on top of a tree"; and cooperative participation and togetherness for success: "A fly that has no one to advise it follows the corpse into the grave." And so, the elders insisted, "to be a human being is to affirm one's humanity by recognizing the humanity of others and, on that basis, establish humane relations with them" (Ramose 2002b, 231). All of this was recognition that to find fulfillment, the individual person's life has need of something that only others, the human community, can provide.

Such was the grand objective of what custom referred to as *full or perfect humanity*. It went by various names among different ethnic groups, but all describing the same value of ultimate or accomplished humanness: *Ubuntu* (among the Zulu, Xhosa, Ndebele—South Africa), *Botho* (Sotho, Tswana—Botswana), *Umunthu* (Chewa—Malawi), *Obuntu* (Ganda—Uganda), *Utu* (Swahili—East and Central Africa), *Unhu* (Shona—Zimbabwe), *Obunu* (Kwaya/Jita—Tanzania), *mutumin kirki*, the good man (among the Hausa people of Nigeria), and so on. The essence of all of these summed up the quality of being human: "A person with *Ubuntu* [with full humanity] is open and available to others, affirming of others, does not feel threatened that others are able and good" (Tutu 1999, 34). A person with *Ubuntu* embraces these qualities in others, "for he or she has a proper self-assurance that comes from knowing that he or she belongs in a greater whole and is diminished when others are humiliated or diminished, when others are tortured or oppressed" (Tutu 1999, 34-35; see also Kirk-Greene 1998, 121-29). What *Ubuntu* underscores is "the vital importance of mutual recognition and respect complemented by mutual care and sharing in the construction of human relations" (Ramose 2002a, 329). *Ubuntu* is manifested in self-giving and readiness to cooperate and communicate with others.

Two broad categories of moral virtues therefore constitute *Ubuntu*. They are both relational in nature, having to do with interpersonal as well as intrapersonal relationship. In interpersonal relationships, what is expected is respect and care for others, manifested as "tolerance, patience, generosity, hospitality and readiness to cooperate." Within the individual, *Ubuntu* calls for "integrity, a solidity or wholeness of character and spirit that is present in one's judgements, one's decisions and one's feelings." In a real sense, these give personality to the individual, not only in the psychosocial sense of personal worth and dignity, but in tandem with it, in the more important sense of the spiritual depth of communion with the whole of life and the entire creation (Shutte 2009b, 98).

From Burundi, Congolese theologian Bénézet Bujo explores the notion that implies the way of being perfectly human. This involves *Ubupfura* or *Ubushingantahe*, "the fundamental quality that ought to characterize every person." Among the Barundi (the people of Burundi), as among many African peoples, "this 'nobility of the heart' is an ideal toward which every member of the community should strive in order to enrich the others." It can be translated simply as profound kindness, "the state of being so thoroughly humane . . . that one makes oneself all things to all persons." It implies that in everything one does, one should strive to "give life to the other in such a way that each one gives birth to the other" (Bujo 2011, 148-49). Without this quality of heart, an individual is anything but human. Thus it is that anyone who cultivates full humanity, that is, *Ubupfura* or *Ubushingantahe*, the person "who is generous and hospitable, who welcome strangers to her house and table and cares for the needy, increases in vital force. Such a person builds up an identity that is enduring, that will not disintegrate—even in death—but continues to be a centre of life for all" (Shutte 2009b, 92).

In the political organization of the Barundi, Bujo describes the advisor to the king, a kind of prime minister, as a person of the character of *Ubushingantahe*, of intense humanness. Indeed, called *Mushingantahe*, or one possessed of *Ubushingatahe*, he was not only expected to be uniquely truthful and just, but he also had to be a hard worker, responsible, and exemplary in every way. He acted as a conciliator and pathfinder for peace in interpersonal, interethnic or intertribal conflict, a supplier of peace. He was looked upon as promoter of the social, political, and economic prosperity of society as a whole, the "father of all" (Bujo 2009b, 392).

No less important in an individual were the techniques to acquire social skills, such as public speaking, courting, proper feminine and masculine behavior, singing, or dancing. In its common and less common elements, all tradition was important, and the elders were its earthly guardians. But gradually with Western education, things began to change. This was not unexpected; the people of the village desired and prayed for it. Every self-respecting father wanted to send his sons (and at that time, it was unfortunately literally "sons," rarely daughters) to the mission school. I was one of the beneficiaries in my family. But the elders soon realized that the education they so much wanted for their children came with an unexpectedly high price. Frequently, when I proudly flaunted some of my newly acquired knowledge before my father on coming back home from college for the yearly holidays, he would remark with a note of sadness and disapproval (the reason for which I could not understand at the time): "Is that what they are teaching you at school?" Fairly conversant with current social and religious developments as he was (he was a religious instructor in established Catholic stations as far back as I could remember), he found some things were definitely intolerable to him, and, in so many ways, he let me know it. I was severely reprimanded when I failed to greet an elder first along the path, for example, or when I handed something over to an older brother or sister with my left hand. Yet these things incurred no censure at school. On the contrary, my peers and I at college considered their neglect as a sign of social progress.

The Nigerian novelist Chinua Achebe describes a similar situation in the fictional village of Umuru, where wished-for education influenced life in not only unexpected, but also unquestionably negative ways. Previously, when Umuru was still a small, self-contained village, the youth, at the behest of the elders, used to take care of the cleanliness of the market square every market day. But the rapid growth of the village, brought about by new educational socialization and the influx of strangers who held different customs, outlooks, and values changed all of this, altering many of the customs and expectations of the village. The villagers of Umuru had indeed, like everyone else, desired the education of their children and growth of their village, but the consequences of both had taken them by surprise. Some of them portended elements that were destroying the village, not symptoms of health to build it up (see Daley 2006, 227).

In Umuru, as in Mabuimerafuru, Western Christianity and education had the effect of changing the attitude of the youth toward the village traditions, fueling "the timeless complaint of the aged in any society" (Knighton 2005, 106). But this, to the elders of Mabuimerafuru and Umuru, was the equivalent of a child laughing at its mother. So the elders shook their heads at this rebelliousness of their children, seeing it as a perversion of their hopes. Even as the elders' influence waned visibly, however, the old values and perceptions of life of the village were not defeated; they sometimes (re)asserted themselves. In Umuru, the foreign and educated young clerk, Julius Obi, noticed their resilience in the general belief in Kitikpa, "the incarnate power of smallpox." When smallpox attacked Umuru, life there changed dramatically for everyone, young and old alike, because the disease represented the power of an evil spirit for the entire population. People would say of the epidemic, "'Kitikpa is in that village,' and immediately it was cut off by its neighbours" (see Daley 2006, 228). Apparently the elders had lost power, but their influence was real in the old ideas and beliefs, which no one dared to question.

Belief in the essence of what the primal African worldview stood for still lives on. In this sense, African spirituality is not something of the past; it is current and real. Every African of whatever gender, education, faith, or social status who dares tap into his or her own well of memory and life-experience will surely find it there. The search may entail a deliberate recall of this experience and the subtle but inexorable impact of veiled or evident rites and rituals since one was born on which an adopted faith such as Christianity or Islam has been superimposed. At any rate, to the honest searcher or observer, the everyday life of the African person, in all spheres and dimensions, testifies unmistakably to its existence.

Reports gathered from sixty-seven people from different parts of the continent on African attitudes to sickness and poor health illustrate this. Asked how he felt when unwell, a Kamba (from Kenya) said: "When I am sick, I take it as normal unless the doctor is unable to treat it. If this is the case, then I visit a diviner to determine the next direction." A Bemba (Zambia) confessed: "If I fall ill in the village, some family members feel it is from people because I am educated. Some would suggest I use traditional medicine but I would go to a diviner." From Ethiopia, a Tigrinya remarked that, although he himself does not think of witchcraft when he falls ill, "for some members of my ethnic group, the idea of bewitching is still operational. As such the idea of visiting a diviner is contemplated and sometimes performed." Finally, a Dinka (South Sudan) states: "When I am not well . . . I may feel that the sickness is the result of something I did not do right. The community will want to find out what mistake I have done and there are also feelings that someone is behind my sickness. A . . . diviner is consulted to find out the cause of the sickness" (Kirwen 2008, 57-65).

Since the early 1980s, one of the most disturbing illnesses in Africa has been HIV/AIDS. When one is struck with the disease, his or her sexual behavior is seen as the proximate and apparent reason for it, because educational efforts by governments and non-governmental organizations have impressed on people that HIV is transmitted mostly through sexual activity. However, this does not offer a satisfactory answer for many. The general judgment is that "the power of witchcraft" or "my bad behavior" toward some "unknown power" is the ultimate cause of the affliction. According to a Tutsi (Rwanda), "traditionally, I would feel that I have been bewitched or I have annoyed the ancestors. The community feels like the ancestors are angry and causing trouble." A Luo (Kenya) respondent says, "Sickness . . . [in his community] is attributed to witchcraft or the victim may have broken a moral code" (Kirwen 2008, 58). Some communities in East Africa give a specific name to the spirit of illness, especially that of bodily wasting away; they call it *Chira*. Among the Luo of Kenya, the ever-watchful *Chira* spirit visits punishment automatically upon all those who break a serious community taboo. Afflictions like epilepsy would fall into the same category. All this shows that, inasmuch as the elders may no longer be in open control of the mores of society, old mentalities have not been obliterated.

In the current context, where everyone is talking about the world as a global village, it is important to undertake an exploration into the particularities of the indigenous worldview of Africa. We wish to sample them because they have implications for the wider purpose of the discussion on the relevance of African spirituality in the contemporary world.

Perhaps the most compelling and inclusive reason to undertake this study is that there is a global need for an alternative ethic, a different approach to living life as opposed to the technologically controlled kind that we are familiar with today, an ethic that emphasizes the good and is not content only with what is right. At the very least, it now seems necessary to construct and inculcate a new "technological ethic." Many observers point out that unbridled technological development does not and cannot adequately provide for the survival of humankind and the comprehensive good of the universe. There seems to be something more to life than modern science and technological progress. While it serves no purpose to paint a caricature of the contemporary condition of the world, it must be said that humanity has a crisis on its hands, and one largely of its own making. The general description of the crisis is that we live in times that tend to be defined by a kind of individuating revelry, leaving serious disfigurement of human and universal relationships in its wake. The domination of the earth, excessive materialism, and negation of the identity of the weak mark these human relationships. Although the danger is not acknowledged by everyone, there is enough accumulating evidence to make it credible and to consider those who dismiss it as either ignorant or irresponsible (see Berry 1988; 1991; 1999; 2006; Berry and Swimme 1992).

This situation might be characterized as the contemporary dominant "religion," if the term is understood as the fundamental beliefs and consequent practices people live by. It originated in Europe but has spread to Africa and elsewhere, mainly through the globalizing of Western civilization. Based on consumerism, it has become a source of social contradictions of extreme wealth and poverty in local and universal social arrangements and has gradually eliminated any other relational consideration. The consequences so far have been conflict and violence, in short, "bad growth." This situation makes considerations for alternatives an urgent task.

Perhaps the alternative(s) might be found in the original spirituality of humankind that can be traced to the African savannas, forests, and valleys, as far back as 100,000 years ago (Stringer and McKie 1996). Some archetypal values, in terms of the original human attempt to make sense of human life and the universe, must have developed there. Conceivably, they survive in the wisdom of the people of Africa. Might it not be possible, then, that aspects of the hope that all humanity fundamentally and inwardly holds can be found in African indigenous spirituality? At any rate, in light of what the world is facing, is it not worth the effort to investigate it?

Mircea Eliade narrates a story that is relevant to this attempt. A pious rabbi had a dream telling him to travel to another country to find a treasure hidden under a bridge. Arriving at the bridge, the rabbi met a guard who wanted to know what he was after. The rabbi narrated the dream, at which point the guard burst out laughing in contempt at what he saw as the naiveté of the rabbi. He too had had a dream, he said, telling him to go find a treasure hidden in a certain corner of the house of Rabbi Eisik, son of Jekel. This happened to be our rabbi's very name! But being a "reasonable" man, the officer said, and being proud of this, he had dismissed the dream. However, "The rabbi, with a deep bow, thanked him and made haste to return . . . [home]; there, he dug in the neglected corner of his house and discovered the treasure; which put an end to his poverty" (Eliade 1960, 244-45).

Might humanity, if it dug deep enough into its heart, discover this treasure that would put an end to its poverty of relationships? More to the point, might Africans, if they dug deep enough, find in their culture treasure that would put an end to their spiritual poverty? Pope Benedict XVI, in his Apostolic Exhortation *Africae Munus*, was convinced of this: "A precious treasure is to be found in the soul of Africa, where I perceive a spiritual 'lung' for a humanity that appears to be in a crisis of faith and hope, on account of the extraordinary human and spiritual riches of its children, its variegated cultures, its soil and sub-soil of abundant resources" (*Africae Munus*, no. 13).

An unfortunate trait of human psychology is that one can turn what one wants to use into an object. The African continent has suffered at the hands of others because they saw it as a source of "commodities" to use, including the slave traders and colonialists who objectified Africa. In seemingly clear conscience, they used it for their own selfish political, economic, and social ends. Most of "the strangers who came to . . . [Africa] came for trade and money, not in search of duties to perform, for they had those in plenty back home in their village which was really home" (see Daley 2006, 227-28). An exploitative view of Africa has profoundly shaped the history of the continent, determining both its internal and external perception.

When Africans try to vocalize the histories of injuries perpetrated against them, an exercise in healing, *anamnesis*, they are often advised that these are yesterday's battles and there is no need to fight them today. Africans should rather get on with the business of development that the modern world expects of them. However, in actual fact, these are not things of the past. With globalization, they are current struggles, clearly forming part of Africa's socioeconomic and political experience, with the subject of this study being a prime example. Among the many elements tarnished with the coming of European civilization was African cultural identity. Symbolically and often literally, the tombs of Africa's ancestors, their customs and traditions, were desecrated, including by the Christian religion whose very mandate, it was later to be admitted, should have been to preserve whatever is good and noble in any and all cultures (*Nostra Aetate*, no. 2). Creation by a loving and caring God informs Christian believers that no culture is without the imprint of the divine.

Two centuries of modern Christian activity in Sub-Saharan Africa demonstrate that the evangelizing method should have been different; it ought to have been one of inculturation. Inculturation, the process of inserting the message of Jesus Christ in a particular cultural context so that it not only takes up the façade, but, more importantly, "becomes a principle that animates, directs and unifies the culture, transforming and remaking it so as to bring about a 'new creation,'" was always part and parcel of the Christian movement since apostolic times (Dhavamony 1997, 92). In the writings of the New Testament, it was championed most forcefully by Paul. Therefore, it is not inculturation that needs justification, but rather its absence.

The resistance of many Africans against "conversion" to Christianity is one of the most enduring legacies of the lack of inculturation. Framed in various ways, the issue in the mind-set of almost all Africans, to different degrees, is still why the Christian outlook toward God should completely supersede theirs. Missionary Christianity insisted it should because, sociologically, nineteenth-century European missionaries to Africa were very much children of their time. They were influenced by contemporary European philosophies, which placed everyone else in the world in an inferior position vis-à-vis Europe. Unfortunately, this encouraged the absurdity of colonialism, just as it previously allowed for the atrocities of the slave trade and chattel slavery.

Nevertheless, there has been a change in attitude since the last half of the twentieth century. Assisted by new, less prejudiced findings in the social sciences, articulate arguments to show the "translatability" of the Christian faith have been advanced. African and Africanist philosophers, theologians, churchmen and women, and members of the general population have taken up the task of recapturing the African memory, of "re-membering" Africa (Thiong'o 2009). The most striking development that goes beyond mere ideas in this matter has been the emergence of thousands of African Initiated Churches (AICs) across the continent. Their stress is on recapturing and representing the God-given values and structures within African tradition (Barrett 1968; 1971).

Calling upon African historical and spiritual memory, what we might describe as ancestral *anamnesis*, is not a lame attempt at self-pity with no hope for success. Rather, it should help the continent to avoid being misrepresented and repeatedly falling victim to previous cruelties. Africa's "repatriation" of her history, the recovery and renewal of memory, is necessary for the success of the search for a positive outlook of her own specific identity in order to put it at the positive service of the world. If some choose to reject and ridicule the contribution, pointing to the many shortcomings of the African tradition, Africans themselves cannot afford to do so. Apart from the cultural ugliness that must be corrected, there is much beauty and meaning to be proud of.

It is essential never to lose sight of the fact that without a past a people can have no future: the past influences the present, while both give direction to the future. How can one go forward without a place to stand? Core values of a people preserved in its tradition provide such a standpoint. Awareness of African spiritual values assures that ignorance should not be an excuse for failure to take notice of the blessings Africa can offer to avoid the path of destruction of humanity and nature. What we now need in the world is what Lee Irwin describes as "the negotiation of cultural understanding among responsible members of alternative communities whose concerns overlap to a degree that evokes insights and mutual learning." This process calls for an attitude of "listening and speaking respectfully" (Irwin 2000b, 2).

The language applied to the continent is often disrespectful. Certain notions, "innocently" and "scientifically" used to describe Africa, are anything but scientific or innocent in their implications—terms such as "paganism" or "nature worship," which endure in some people's minds. But, as Kofi Asare Opoku notes, if the practitioner of African Religion "pouring libation at the foot of a tree were asked to explain what he was doing, he would not say that he was practicing 'paganism' or 'worshiping nature'" (Opoku 1993, 69). If one can, one must abandon these terms, or at least make one's meaning clear from the start.

A notion that I have struggled with and sought counsel on with regard to this book is the notion of "indigenous." I present the first part of this book as a description of African *indigenous* spirituality so as to distinguish it from the Christian or Muslim variations. By "indigenous," I mean a worldview born in Africa, conditioned by the material and social environment there, and lived by the people of the continent even as they embrace and practice new faiths and religions. It provides their fundamental structure against which all other approaches are measured and understood. To make this meaning even clearer, let me borrow the explanation of the term provided by Frans Wijsen and Sylvia Marcos, who understand it as the "*pre-missionary*" or "*pre-colonial*" perceptions of life and the world lived by, in this instance, African peoples. It exists not only "as distinct from" but also "within" the missionary and colonial religions or spiritualities (Wijsen and Marcos 2010, 13).

Many people tried to dissuade me from using this term on account of the negative implications historically attached to it, usually to signify superstition, irrationality, and underdevelopment. I recognize its ambiguity. I have nevertheless decided to retain it, and I use it in the sense I have just explained. It is an assertion of justified pride that "Africa is not a dark continent" (Stenger et al. 2005). African spirituality is founded on its own values from which life yields meaning for the people. "What the label 'indigenous' . . . valuably points to is more than merely existing in a particular place." The implication of the notion is far more fundamental than that; it should recall "the celebration of the experience of continuity of peoples and places." For Africa, it "respects the almost ubiquitous centrality of elders and ancestors as holders and sharers of tradition . . . [as well as] the almost ubiquitous veneration of particular lands" as the basis of life (Harvey 2000c, 12). It emphasizes hierarchical relationships that allow community to perdure.

This is where a rationale for this study is to be found. It is motivated by sorrow for what Harvey characterizes appropriately as the "ubiquitous experience of colonial [spiritual] genocide and expulsion that has confronted and continues to confront indigenous peoples everywhere" (Harvey 2000c, 12) in the form of a certain kind of Christian evangelism, development, and globalization. Is it possible to have a "different relationship" among different peoples and between human beings and the cosmos?

We cannot completely avoid comparisons, and there will be many in the following pages. Africa is not an island; it has to and does interact and share on many levels with other perceptions of life. All the same, our primary concern is Africa.

The first part of this book is phenomenological; it describes the main structures and practices of African spirituality. The second part is an attempt to spell out some of the ways the African understanding of life might contribute generally to a more humane world order. Readers accustomed to scholarship on African Religion will find in the phenomenological account many concepts and orientations with which they are already more or less familiar. This should not be surprising, given the close relationship between spirituality and religion in many belief orientations, particularly in Africa. "While 'religion' may imply a fairly high degree of organization, with principles of faith, canonical texts, dogma and theology," as Duncan Brown explains, indigenous beliefs, where these aspects are not explicitly codified, "very often referred to as 'spirituality,' also involve specific systems of action and faith" (Brown 2009, 5). Therefore, the debate over the difference between religion and spirituality, so prominent elsewhere, will not concern us here. The holistic conceptual outlook in the African belief system, the perception of the wholeness of existence where the distinction between the two is practically nonexistent, makes that concern redundant for us. Furthermore, the notions reveal new connotations whose implications are, in the second part of the book, creatively applied to current situations.

A most significant factor in the entire project is that this investigation into the nature and structures of African spirituality comes as a result of years of personal observation and experience. It is also as a result of the literature I have read on how basic, pervasive, and "controlling" a factor African spirituality is in the continent; regardless of the denials and vilification sometimes leveled against it. The observation of researchers such as Stephen Ellis and Gerrie ter Haar confirms this. From their research, they assert that "it is largely through religious [or 'spiritual'] ideas that Africans think about the world today, and that religious ideas provide them with a means of becoming social and political actors" (Ellis and ter Haar 2004, 2). Furthermore, Ellis and ter Haar concentrate on the influence of spirituality on political behavior, demonstrating how African politicians "typically pay great regard to the spirit world as a source of power" (Ellis and ter Haar 2004, 3). This fascinating aspect notwithstanding, the goal of this study is much broader. While the spirit world is fundamental to political leadership in Africa, it is applicable to the grand story of life as a whole as much in the Sub-Saharan region (Naipul 2010) as in the world at large. The African contribution to efforts for global change is its deep spiritual or religious consciousness.

2

The Heart of the Matter

"A boat cannot go forward if each rows his own way."

Meaningful communication can take place only where there is a degree of agreement on what symbols, signs, notions, or concepts are meant to convey. Without it, there will only be confusion and a situation reminiscent of Babel. It is not possible to generate any reciprocity under such circumstances, only mistrust, confusion, conflict, and even violence. We therefore must begin with some necessary explanations.

"Spirituality" as a concept is ambiguous. There is no consensus about it among different intellectual or even faith traditions. What is spirituality? Is it *prayer* alone in the sense of devotional rites and rituals toward a numinous reality? Does spirituality have something to do with cult? Furthermore, should we understand it as an essentially out-of-this-world experience, in the sense of *mysticism*, concerned solely with extrasensory perceptions? In this sense, it would be the preserve of a few people blessed with the gift, for in common human experience true mystics are rare. Is spirituality to be associated only with people dedicated to "religious" forms of living, namely, monks, priests, and nuns? Is it therefore always to be associated with *religion*? But, then again, is the meaning of religion itself not ambiguous? And what exactly represents the supernatural? Should spirituality be conceived as the polar opposite of matter, the "natural," or the other way around?

In general, many of the definitions fall within the philosophical distinction between spirituality or religion and "ordinary" life. They seem to suggest, with only different degrees of emphasis, that spirituality and religion are in a separate sphere of human life. They understand spirituality almost exclusively in terms of specific ritual language and acts (the "devout life" of the mystic or monk), or extraordinary inspiration (the "enlightenment" of the guru or sage). Moreover, there is the understanding of spirituality that separates it from the concrete, material reality experienced in human existence, a vision by which spirituality implies "the need to distance oneself from the material or corporeal dimension" of existence (see Hathaway and Boff 2009, 311).

When spirituality is related exclusively to certain cultic practices, its main concentration is the individual person's relationship with the supernatural. In this sense, it appears to emphasize the individual's personal, often called "inner," dimension of life. It seems to lack explicit reference to the communal, everyday cosmic facets of existence. The individual's relationship to other creatures in the world is not immediately evident. In concentrating on one dimension of human existence, this understanding of spirituality paradoxically divides it into two domains, as the French sociologist Emile Durkheim saw it: "the one containing all that is sacred, the other all that is profane." For Durkheim, this division constitutes "the distinctive trait of religious thought" (see Winzeler 2008, 10).

However, a different way of understanding spirituality and religion is provided by African experience (evident also in the original Christian experience of St. Paul: see Sheldrake 2007, 2-4). It is based on interactive relationships among human beings and between humans and the entire order of existence. It understands this relationship to be the essence of religion, the sacred. In spite of his original conceptual division of life, Durkheim nevertheless came close to the African understanding of religion when he observed that "by sacred things one must not understand simply those personal beings which are called gods or spirits; a rock, a tree, a spring, a piece of wood, in a word, anything can be sacred" (Winzeler 2008, 10; Cox 2000). This perception of life is at the very heart of African spirituality; it is an approach that is absolutely relational and completely unitary. It perceives all reality, whether seen or unseen, as composed of sacral mystery and destiny. The implications of this perspective extend far beyond what is merely or immediately personal.

In Africa, there is an essentially "transcendental" perception of all life because all reality is situated in the sacred realm, which is a spiritual sphere. A people's life is their religion, so that "religion," or "spirituality" for that matter, "is not identifiable as a separate institution but permeates the whole society" (Booth 1977a, 1). The spiritual is not opposed to the physical or material, as Ben Knighton shows with the Karamojong of Uganda, but both are intricately merged. "The sacred dominates and infuses the life-world," although, as we shall see in regard to worship, there are "dense moments in the life of the people . . . [where] the spiritual is maximally present. Such power must be regulated by custom, both to bring it out and channel it for the common good" (Knighton 2005, 30; Gyekye 1998, 59-66).

Lacking the intellectual-analytical categories to name it properly, early European observers of African spirituality dismissed it as "animism," worship of spirits in matter, and subsequently as unworthy of rational religion.

Regardless of the fact that they ascribed to the term the negative sense of irrationality (Nida and Smalley 1959, 3), they had a valid insight. Although we must now avoid the term, we must not reject the insight, which is that from the African point of view, all reality is *spiritual* because it is linked together by spiritual power and is connected to mystery. Life is, in essence, a mystery. As the principle of life, mystery constitutes spiritual power that is not of human origin but is at the foundation of everything that exists. This makes all reality spiritual and of religious concern.

As Nida and Smalley explain, this principle of mystery is more or less present, though not always acknowledged, in other religious traditions as well: "you are an animist if you are a Christian, Muslim, Jew, Buddhist Hindu, or an adherent of any religion that believes in spirit, spirits, angels, demons, ghosts, or souls" (Nida and Smalley 1959, 3). In Africa, however, this belief is much more explicit and comprehensive. Once again, "spirit" constitutes not only divergent aspects of existence but encompasses all of it. It explains the fact and possibility of life, the essential and intrinsic mutual influence of all beings, making existence viable. The mystery of spirit power represents the entire philosophy and behavior of the African people and enjoys, at a depth few other perceptions do, the full support and encouragement of their societies (Nida and Smalley 1959, 3).

"Perception" is another concept whose use in our context needs clarification. With reference to African spirituality, perception must not be understood as merely a "point of view," a "way of looking at things." Perception connotes the entire orientation of the life of the community. It does not belong to the individual or group of individuals alone; it belongs to them only as part of the larger community. It is not extrinsic to the culture and people's existence in general, as merely a personal dimension of these realities. Rather, it is inherent in and constitutes all of these features. The African perception toward life as spiritual forms the basis of the individual's as well as the community's "self-definition." It delineates the "horizons, values, and purposes" of their entire being in the world (Meyer 2008, 25).

The spiritual perception of existence marks Africa's "historical consciousness" and rationality, "the process by which [the African, as an individual or society] . . . is actively engaged in the shaping of himself and his world." African thought and action, both of which structure culture, are rooted in spirituality. This is the culture by and through which Africans as agents identify themselves. The process is the same in every society and among human groups with a purpose: actions form the actor and lead the actor to certain goals; they are "subject-orienting as well as object-oriented." Any "action tends toward habit and so disposes the agent to a given line of development; moreover, action, once objectified and interpreted by interaction with others, is retracted or modified or affirmed and so enters the arena where, positively or negatively, selfhood is engaged and affected. Regardless of its object, action shapes its subject" (Meyer 2008, 25).

The source of the self-definition of the peoples of Africa, their culture, arises from and tends toward a holistic perception of the universe, which, as we have seen, is spiritual. Thus, what is not spiritual? What is not sacred?! This, for an African, is both a rhetorical and an astonishing question, for there is nothing that is not spiritual or sacred. The idea that there is a "spiritual life" distinct from any other kind of existence is foreign to the African mind and spirit. All reality is spiritual and has ethical implications. Whatever sensory, physical existence reveals is the outer dimension of life, the fulfillment of which is made possible through its intrinsic spiritual or sacred essence. In the structure of existence, life is experienced in both dimensions. No conceptual or practical separation between them is morally permissible or ethically possible.

In the African worldview, spirituality is more of an activity than a passive quality. Rather than a "state of being," it is a way of behaving or, rather, relating. It involves dynamic relationships between visible and invisible powers. Better yet, it entails the mutual exchanges of energies among all beings. Diarmuid O'Murchu's understanding of spirituality can be applied to Africa. "Spirituality is essentially a co-creative gift," O'Murchu writes, "we are partially, but not wholly, responsible for its development. As in the exchange of all gifts, there is the giver and the receiver but unlike the normal process, the gift in this case is forever being offered and received, in large or small measure" (O'Murchu 1997, 37). This happens through relationships; thus spirituality can be described as a "verb." It is an activity that is proactive. It involves the aspiration to achieve a certain degree of harmony in the universe, without which the universe in general and human life in particular would not only collapse but might indeed never have existed in the first place.

As we move forward, references to life as an interactive "power," or "energy" or "vital force," also need clarification. The notion is of central importance to this work but is easily liable to misinterpretation in many discussions on the African philosophy of life. Many scholars attest that the notion was first academically employed with reference to Africa by the Belgian Catholic Franciscan priest Placide Tempels (d. 1977). Tempels worked in the Congo for twenty-nine years, between 1933 and 1962. In his book *Bantu Philosophy* (English trans. 1959), he used the notion to explain the African understanding of and approach to life. But in acknowledging that Africans had a philosophy of life to rival any other, Tempels came under censure from many quarters, including the Catholic authorities, the Protestant missions, and the colonial government. There are, indeed, areas in the book where it is evident that he yielded to this pressure on some points, and he is rightly criticized for these errors today by some African philosophers. Yet overall, Tempels "can be cited, in many respects, as being 'above' the accepted colonialist policies and missionary methods" (Deacon 2002, 103).

One indication of this, according to Deacon, was Tempels's involvement in the *Jamaa* movement. This was a movement that formed communities that retained as much as possible the cultural perceptions and values of African converts to Christianity in the Congo, something akin to contemporary Small Christian Communities. "Through this the African 'convert' was not ripped from the frame of reference that renders his or her world meaningful." As a pastoral approach, the movement "sought to augment the worldview of Africans, rather than to subtract the very concepts that have rendered, throughout time, the existence of the African meaningful. Through the creative fusion of tradition and Western religion, Tempels achieved his goal of conversion" (Deacon 2002, 103-4). For Tempels, this was not a "one-way street"; through his empathetic, respectful collaboration with the BaLuba people, "he became changed, his religious experience being touched and amplified by the common ground of humanity shared by him and the BaLuba with whom he lived" (Deacon 2002, 104).

Since Tempels used the concept of vital power from an ontological-philosophical perspective, the notion is sometimes taken to refer to a kind of abstract, essentialist, static principle; a theoretical concept or idea without much practical consequence. However, this is far from the case in Africa, and it seems the latter does not form part of Tempels's observation of the African mind-set. At any rate, vital force is not a hypothetical, speculative idea for Africans; although mysterious, it is nevertheless a *bona fide* "fact," the invisible but actual thread that holds existence together. It is conspicuous in created beings; for existence, it is inevitable.

Vital power requires and demands the active "skill" inherent in created order so as to negotiate relationships between the visible and invisible elements of the universe. Vital power implies that nothing is what it seems to be on the surface. To realize this is to begin to know the meaning of life and start living it well and fully. One must always be watchful in relating with anybody or anything because one is never completely sure what one is really confronting. There is inner invisible power in anything at any given moment. In every activity, every thought, every word, every attitude, it is important to make sure that there is "friendship" or unity between what you see and what you do not see but is still part of the reality. This is the harmony that must be sought in life; it must be cultivated and carefully respected if life is not to be harmed. Vital energy serves life and is understood "in all those dimensions that can be explored and developed throughout an entire lifetime, lived creatively and meaningfully in mutual relation with planet Earth and the cosmos" (O'Murchu 1997, 37).

From this perspective, vital power is shorthand for the whole of life, or more specifically, the sum total of the individual or community's approach to the totality of life. Vital power, energy, or force pertains to life as defined by the beliefs, customs, and relationships among the human community, the community of spirits, and the community of goods. All of this engages the person in his or her thoughts and actions. Spirituality can be described as the process of interaction between thought and behavior and the visible and invisible existences surrounding humanity. Inevitably, all aspects of this process combine to make sense of the world and render life livable in a comprehensive manner. It constitutes the direction persons take to give meaning to their existence as persons. Accordingly, "meaningful spiritual life is inconceivable without . . . meaningful planetary and cosmic existence" (O'Murchu 1997, 37). Vital power is therefore, in essence, the foundation of life, the capacity to resist death and the agents of death.

The exchange of energy between the visible and the invisible reality that constitutes African spirituality is primordial and is generally understood to be positive, helping human life to develop and grow, and helping the universe to exist harmoniously in and with all its constituent components. But the process can also be distorted and, as a consequence, impact negatively on life, causing friction in the physical and moral fiber of the individual, society, or the universe at large. It all depends on how the exchange of energy is negotiated by humanity. The question is: has the individual or the community acted "morally" or "immorally," according to or contrary to what the order of the universe demands? Previously, we gave some examples from a sample of interviews in relation to illness. In this context, we offer a few illustrations relative to God and the ancestors, the guardians of vital power to whom we shall refer to now and then throughout our discussion.

For the Agikuyu or Kikuyu people of Kenya, right or wrong behavior consists in proper or improper handling of the order God has established to sustain life. They view God as "father and provider" and the source of everything they have (Kirwen 2005, 9). God is for the Agikuyu the origin of all life and reality, and so to deny God's existence is to put oneself in an "untenable position." "Anyone taking an atheistic position is seen to be not only immature but spiritually without wisdom" (Kirwen 2005, 4). The ancestors see to it that the divine order of existence is observed. Thus, they are a fundamental link in the force of life. For the Aembu people of Kenya, "ancestors are the dispensers of morality and venerated patriarchs of the community. They influence the behavior of the living because they are custodians of our culture" (Kirwen 2005, 24). Research shows that this is true for the Akan of

Ghana, the Tutsi of Rwanda/Burundi, as well as for other peoples from various parts of Sub-Saharan Africa.

The improper handling of the inherent power of life results in destructive consequences. Whenever this happens, willfully or accidentally, the situation must be corrected at once. If not repaired, it inevitably leads to more and more disorder in society, malfunctioning of the universe, and suffering of individuals. Often, the latter situation affects people intensely by disturbing the normal rhythm of life; it intensifies, rather than diminishes, the desire for life. In other words, suffering does not annihilate the spiritual dimension of existence; it is the other side of spirituality.

In the worldview of practically all African cultures the exchange of energies as a necessary condition for the possibility of all existence involves, most importantly, the well-being of the human vital energy and is necessary for the well-being of the rest of the created order. In a sense, the welfare of the universe depends on the health of human beings. The behavior of the human community is the foundation of the status of all existence. It bears reiterating that life's positive growth and development, or, conversely, its disintegration and death, depend on how the human vital force communicates with other vital forces. Consequently, human beings bear ultimate responsibility for universal harmony because they represent creation as conscious of itself, its most manifest spirit. By disturbing the equilibrium of the universe, humanity eventually destroys itself, meaning that the fate of humanity and the rest of the universe are inseparable. Thus, "the idea and structure of human society . . . are essentially part of a world-view that is fundamentally holistic, sacred and highly integrated. Human community . . . has its full meaning and significance within the transcendental centre of ultimate meaning" of the universe (http://afrikaworld.net/afrel/index.html). Conversely, the universe's transcendence finds visible expression in the person and his or her community.

In this structure, the task of the village diviner and all other community leaders, known collectively as elders, is to make sure that the requirement of proper existential exchange of vital forces in the universe is maintained. The balance of energies between humans, the spirits, and other creatures must not be upset. The list of experts charged with this responsibility, in formal or informal ways, is large. It includes all those with political power and social authority, as well as people endowed by nature or training with more than what is considered "ordinary" insight into things. All of them are spiritual masters at one level or another, and often there is a clear hierarchical structure to this. According to a Dinka (South Sudan) respondent, "Father, elder brother and my mother exercised authority in the family. My father would deal with issues arising within and without the family. My mother mostly deals with home issues. The punishment would be according to the gravity of the offense. . . . The spirits and ancestors are the final authority" (Kirwen 2010, 72).

Part of African spiritual experience is that the energy of life may be controlled, mainly through the skills and dispositions of specific elders. But this is only partial; everyone admits that there cannot be total or absolute control over life's predisposition. An elder may be endowed with special power to predict events, or may have medicines and amulets to deflect evil, or may even offer sacrifices and offerings to propitiate the ancestors and other spirits. Negatively, a person may be afflicted by witchcraft, or the evil eye, which can harm at a glance. The discharge and effects of all of these may be controlled by experts, but only to a certain degree. Whatever means of control an elder may have, it is merely an aid toward building proper relationships.

Relationships among all beings are basically and equitably founded on divine power. This is the inner power of existence that informs the outward forms of each and every creature, enabling them to relate. Nothing exists as mere matter; everything "lives" fundamentally as spirit-force within matter. Animals and plants are innately manifestations of spiritual forces within, an extension of human and cosmic life and order, and they must be treated as such. Every creature is important at its own level in the hierarchical range of vital energies. Whatever exists does so because of and for the benefit of the energy connecting it to other existences, therefore satisfying the need for universal harmony. The energy of a creature is its spiritual force. When the human life force is expressed in relational action, it constitutes *spirituality*, whose *telos* or ultimate goal is communion of all creation into Supreme Goodness or God, the author of harmony.

From this discussion, it is not difficult to see that the identity of the individual and his or her community and the identity of the entire universal existence, though distinct, are inextricably intertwined. This perception has several important implications.

To begin, all creatures deserve a degree of reverence. Humans may treat no creature with impunity, particularly (yet not exclusively) those creatures that enjoy sentient existence. They may be harmed, as in the case of dangerous animals or rodents destroying crops, if and when they clearly constitute a threat to human life. In addition, they may also be killed when they are needed for life's sustenance, as seen by the relationship between the hunter and the animal he hunts in the forest, the fisherman and the fish he catches from the river or lake, or that between the herbalist and the herbs he or she uses for treatment.

One hunts and kills game or catches fish in order to survive, never simply for sport or recreation. The animal- and fish-spirits must "know" and be convinced of this need for the hunting or fishing expedition to succeed or for people to avoid danger in the process. If killing game or catching fish is done for the sake of wasteful intentions, a seriously distorted relationship between humans and the other universal energies occurs. In this case, the spirits of the forest, lake, or river are offended, and eventually human life suffers because fish or game disappears or destructive flooding or forest fires happen. This is the basic ethic the International Union for Conservation of Nature (IUCN) endeavors to inculcate.

In the case of the herbalist, the power to heal is more in the herbs than in one's hands by virtue of their medicinal capacities. The herbalist does not bring them into being; he or she merely discovers them, often guided by other powers such as that of the ancestors through dreams of possession. This fact almost always is acknowledged by any authentic healer as a necessary aspect of the healing practice. As in the other cases, the point is that if nature is treated without the reverence it deserves, similarly will human and universal life diminish. Again, the philosophy of modern organizations such as the Convention on International Trade in Endangered Species of Wild Fauna and Flora (CITES) of 1973 reflects this awareness.

The power of universal life is integrated in time, space, and history. In spite of decline and death, or, indeed, because of them, life continues. As far as it involves the handing over of vital power to the succeeding generation, a "normal" death is actually an act of giving birth. Reproduction in living things expresses the desire of the species to endure in their offspring. The skies above, in the form of clouds, the sun, the moon, the stars and the earth below, in the form of the soil and the soil's products, are the dwelling places of all energies; and they enjoy an enduring relationship. The sky and the earth are the "father" and "mother" of all life, and from them comes sustenance through water, air, fire, crops, trees, and stones for various human uses. The sky and the earth make the enduring cycle of life possible.

The relationship between the sky and the earth symbolizes other relational realities. On the one hand, the sky represents the dwelling place of the primal Life Force, the Great Spirit; and it is unfathomable in its influence. The soil, on the other hand, is the mother of all living beings and as such is equally mysterious and deep in its powers over life. Life as a whole exists as a result of the "marriage" between the sky and the earth; all life must return to the earth in death. This fact adds to the soil's spiritual significance. Consequently, the earth, or the home soil in its more tangible form, is to be venerated without question. For this reason, ancestral land is especially venerable not just for social and economic reasons as the source of sustenance for a specific people. It is to be honored on account of its unseen value as the indicator of the life force of the ancestors in its strongest form, life-in-death, because this is where the ancestors lie. And is it not around ancestral life, fused completely in death with ancestral land, that all life, tradition, and the morality of the family, clan, and group revolve?

As an ongoing encounter with life, African spirituality is not a matter of mere belief or assent to doctrines and dogmas. It is "a pervasive quality of life that develops out of an authentic participation in values and real-life practices meant to connect members of a community with the deepest foundations of personal affirmation and identity" (Irwin 2000b, 3). Spirituality requires a continuous process of self-mastery in action (Zahan 1979, 110). It does not primarily answer the question of what we should believe; it responds, rather, to the question of *how we should live.* "In this sense spirituality is inseparable from any sphere of activity as long as it really connects with deeply held . . . values and sources of authentic commitment, empowerment, and genuineness of shared concern" (Irwin 2000b, 3).

African spirituality does not hold as its primary objective the achievement of a specific goal among other goals, such as piety, meekness, or fear of God. If there is a goal in the perception of African spirituality, it is to totally experience the "good life" and to completely avoid the "bad life." Indeed, formal associations, societies, or sodalities similar to spiritual groups in other religious traditions can be found, but the purpose of each is to integrate the life forces for greater, better, and more abundant life in this world achieved through the constant interaction between faith, environment, and society. Consequently, there are no movements in the indigenous traditions of black Africa that distinguish the "sacred" from the "profane" or "secular." For, indeed, just what is not sacred?

3

Spiritual Direction

"Sometimes the spirits speak for you and
sometimes the spirits make you speak."

L et us recapitulate briefly what we have established in the previous pages. We have argued that if spirituality from the African viewpoint is coterminous with the experience of life itself in all of its dimensions, then there are three essential characteristics that make up this view.

First, all existence consists of energy or power; in other words, it consists of active, existential forces that continually and consistently interact with and influence one another (for good or for evil). Through these relationships, all existence (and specifically human life) becomes possible. Described by some early European observers of African life as animism, that is, the conviction that everything has a spiritual component, this view does not divide creation into the sacred and the profane. All created order is sacred.

Second, all creatures participate in the comprehensive power of life, each to a different degree, at their own level within the whole. While each creature enjoys a measure of autonomy for this reason, that is, by virtue of its own independent life force, each exists for the sake of the other. In the structure of existence, all elements of existence are therefore complementary. They are all connected in the great circle of life. It is therefore legitimate to say that in a sense all existence is spirit.

Third, all vital energies existing in the universe, that is, the spirit of existence, coalesce to serve human life. They influence individual persons and societies according to their level of potency in the hierarchical order of existence, in which God, ancestors, and other spirits enjoy precedence. Accordingly, if one (and of course society) wants to live well, one must be familiar with this order and give due recognition to each element in existence according to its spiritual power and influence. This is the sum total of spiritual life, which in fact means one's entire manner of living.

Although the spiritual power of the universe is always greater than any of its constituent parts, and although each part only makes complete sense in the context of the greater universal whole, the principle that makes life, indeed, all creation, possible is "interdependence," "mutuality," and complementarity. Nothing can live or even exist on its own. The universe exists on account of its component parts and vice versa, and each creature needs the rest in the delicate balance of existence. Life is not possible on the basis of strict autonomy, but no creature is completely subservient to any other. There is ontological equity if not inequality in actual effect. We may apply the expression of George Orwell in *Animal Farm*, the parody of the philosophy and application of communism, and say that although all powers "are equal" (as powers), some are "more equal than others" (in terms of concrete influence on life). But in Africa, to speak of one is to speak of all the others.

As a general rule, elements of the invisible world exercise more influence than visible creatures. In fact, visible creatures possess only as much power as they are endowed with by the invisible spirits that are part of them. Therefore, we can speak of the spirit of a stone, tree, bird, animal, or anything else in existence. The difference in the impact of the various vital powers on life is the subject of discussion in this chapter.

The ideal for any human being and society is always to forge stronger relationships with the strongest vital forces, in the sense of rendering to each according to its ability to deliver life's benefits. This stimulates the relevant powers to act as guardians of life in the face of human error, as well as against various capricious and malicious energies that can cause havoc in the universal order. But how do we know what these powers are and what level and type of energy they are capable of exercising? The answer can be found only in the traditions of the people. Each identifies this gradation of forces in its structure of community. What forms community, and how are the different aspects of community related to one another in terms of the principle of life? To know the meaning and the demands of community is to understand the foundation of one's existence and, therefore, the implications of spirituality in Africa.

"Community" in the African milieu means "much more than simply a social grouping of people bound together by reasons of natural origin and/ or deep common interests and values" (http://afrikaworld.net/afrel/index. html). The African understands community as "both a society as well as a unity of the visible and invisible worlds; the world of the physically living on the one hand, and the world of the ancestors, divinities and souls of children yet to be born to individual kin-groups." Thus "community comprehends the totality of the world of African experience including the physical environment, as well as all spirit beings acknowledged by a given group" (http:// afrikaworld.net/afrel/index.html). It is understood as inclusive of three constitutive dimensions together: namely, community of place or geographical location; community of collective memory or shared history; and psychological community of personal interaction. This interpretation of community is at the root of and governs the structure of relationships. Reverence, adulation, or fear is accorded to a given force by individuals and societies depending on the rank it occupies in this community of life. The attitudes each rank of power evokes from individuals and groups form the practice of spirituality in Africa.

Allegiance and obeisance are above all accorded to the invisible components of the community, that is, God, the ancestors, and the spirits. Their claim to all forms of human piety is taken for granted and never questioned; there is no need to explain it. Whatever may be the description offered of God, no exact face is given to God. God's presence and power are ubiquitous, so ubiquitous that there is no need to point it out, even to the young, as aptly summed up in the proverb: "No one points out the Great One to a child." God's presence and power are palpable throughout the universe, by the fact of creation itself. So how can one deny or doubt the reality of creation? In other words, God is recognized by daily human consciousness, save in exceptional circumstances that may dictate special tribute through specific prayers and sacrifices. This is all that life, morality, or spirituality requires.

However, the spirits are in a different category. Ancestral spirits, who are at the center of the dynamics of human life, attract immense attention because they have more immediate control over it. Their relationship to the living is biological and therefore very direct. If obeisance to a living elder, say a parent, is a spiritual act because it fosters the strength of the elder's life in the younger person, so much more does the respect of an ancestor. By virtue of his or her higher position in the hierarchy of powers, an ancestor possesses more influence than the elder. Spirits, including ancestral spirits, are believed to enjoy bilocation. They dwell freely in the sky but can also possess any creature for a certain purpose. They can be induced by a specialist to seize things or people. Among the Akan people of Ghana, for example, a priest possessed by the spirit is able to provoke the same condition within others and thus reveal to them the real meaning of their lives.

Before the gods and the spirits, the priest possessed by the spirit represents everybody under his influence regardless of their physical condition or social status. His ritual activity does not discriminate. "He will pour libation for the possessed to help them maintain a proper connection with their dead ancestors. They will have to return later with food, goats, and other tokens of respect and hospitality and then perform the proper rituals as mandated by the Holy Priest who in his possession by the spirits has seen the destiny of the possessed who were overcome by the spirit" (Addo, http://

info.med.yale.edu/intmed/hummed/yjhm/essays/paddo1.html). In this priest's activity, everything is included; nothing is left out if it has anything at all to do with life. The more significant something is for the fulfillment of life, the more attention it deserves. The possessed priest's condition is, therefore, in this sense, "the ultimate spirituality," one that the priest cannot let go. Through this condition of ritual "spiritualization," "the gods are able to transfer a sacred consciousness to the High Priest who can then share it with the people. Hence the priest in his state of spirituality is able to help to ensure that the people are in balance with the gods, the ancestors, and other living persons, families, and nature" (Addo, http://info.med.yale.edu/intmed/hummed/yjhm/essays/paddo1.html).

The ancestors are capable of speaking in two languages; the language of God and the spirits and human language (Mbiti 1969, 108), making them uniquely equipped to unite the two worlds together. They control the secret of universal harmony and life and, through tradition, offer it to the elders. In spite of many ambiguities and paradoxes in relationships with them, often characterized by fear and anxiety (or welcome and comfort) in their presence, connection with the ancestors is the preferred spiritual direction. Accordingly, of all practical spiritual activities of consequence, ancestral cult in its various ritual forms is the most prevalent and structured all across black Africa.

The ancestors are "alive" and communicate with their kin in many and varied ways. The ancestors of the family or community are present within and around it. It is not an exaggeration to say that for an adult African person, especially if he or she is the head of a household, ancestral cult forms the center of all waking hours. Hardly a day passes by without remembering and honoring the spirits of the ancestors in thought, words, or numerous other activities and gestures. The presence of shrines around some household compounds serves as a visible reminder of ancestral presence and influence. Physical remains such as skulls may be kept in conspicuous spaces for the same reason. "The ancestors are integrated into the solidarity of their offspring because identity can only be found by not forgetting one's forefathers" (Bujo 2009a, 118). Not only identity but the good life that emanates from tradition can be assured only through ancestral *anamnesis* or remembrance and moral solidarity. In some Bantu ethnic groups, for instance, to assert the veracity of a statement put in question by one's audience, one appeals to, or swears by, the authority of one's family or lineage: "I am a son or daughter of so-and-so," or "I belong to such-and-such a clan." The inference is that if what I am saying is not true, may they disown me, which is tantamount to my annihilation.

There are only a few alleged exceptions to this spiritual experience toward "ancestors." Some ethnic groups seem not to venerate them as openly and as intensely as others. But even among these, such as (it is claimed) among the Maasai of Kenya and Tanzania, the Khoi-San of southern Africa, and other pastoral peoples of the continent, the dead, whether ancestors or not, play a big role in the spiritual orientation of the people. They are feared, at the very least. In these communities, once a corpse has been disposed of, people abandon the place.

All spirits demand a sense of awe from human beings because they are so proximate to or are part of the substances that humans need and use to live. In material-physical form, they influence life to the degree that the particular creature of which they are now an inner part would otherwise not be able to exist. Consequently, a person, animal, plant, or stone thus inhabited merits more reverence and respect than usual on account of the spirit dwelling there. If, then, certain people avoid killing certain animals, or felling certain trees, or breaking certain stones as a special expression of the spiritual outlook, the reason is not hard to find. It appears in the spirituality of totems, nonhuman objects inhabited by ancestral spirits, and the taboos associated with them.

The intensity of the spirituality of totems differs slightly from one ethnic group to the other. In some groups, though totems may identify a clan, they are seen to be distinct from it. They merely act as its symbols. However, in the more radical perception and use, totems are identified completely with the clan, so that they are seen to embody not only the spirits but the Founder-Spirit of the clan. In this case, the connection between the clan and the totem is total; the life experience of the clan is the same as that of the totem and vice versa. Love, kindness, and respect are emotions expected of the clan toward the totem, as they are in equal measure required of the totem toward the clan and any member of the clan. Both sides are expected and bound to protect and provide for the other. A lone individual walking in the darkness of the night can expect protection from a leopard if that is his or her totem. All members of his or her clan cannot therefore harm leopards.

It should not be surprising, then, to find people or communities showing various degrees of reverence or fear toward certain fauna or flora, depending on what animal or plant they are dealing with. Attitudes will depend on what type of spirit-power the animal or plant, or, indeed, any other article is perceived to incarnate. Above all, the spirit of the earth, often simply called Mother Earth, is to be especially revered for its power to bring forth and sustain life. When Thomas Berry speaks of "the natural world . . . [as] the maternal source of our being . . . , the larger sacred community to which we belong," he touches on a basic point of African spirituality; "to be alienated from this community is to become destitute in all that makes us human"

(O'Murchu 1997, 35). Alienation from Mother Earth would translate into complete absence of life as she gives life and nurtures every living thing.

Taboos find their rationale in the benevolent power with which the totem is endowed and bear that positive implication in the first place. It is from this that the meaning of "taboo" in the negative sense of precluding from harm an object connected with the clan is derived. In this latter sense, taboos that are radically associated with a given clan and its traditions and values are stricter in their demands for respect, and the punishment accompanying any violation of them is swifter and harsher. If the internal connection between the spirit-powers of the universe is to be found anywhere, it is quite prevalent here in the African spirituality of totems and taboos.

African moral pedagogy intends to ensure ethical life and thus maintain the original goodness of the world through this institution. To observe taboos not only wards off divine and ancestral wrath, it also brings the human community closer to the correct rhythm of existence. It guarantees universal order to some extent, and thereby immobilizes misfortune that would inevitably destroy life. To violate a taboo in any way is to incur the displeasure of powers that are ultimately higher than the human being. Impending misfortune remains real unless and until the anger of the spirits is appeased. Violation of a taboo automatically incurs contamination on the transgressor for which personal cleansing is necessary. To observe taboos is perhaps the nearest equivalent of ascetic behavior in other spiritual traditions.

The consequence of breaking a taboo may often be imprecise and ambiguous, to the extent of requiring confirmation by divination. However, the exact content of the prohibitions (the taboos) is explicitly spelled out in tradition in the formula: "You shall not. . . . " Individuals and groups in society must observe the taboos of the society meticulously as an act of gratitude for the goodness and concern of the ancestors. Often, unless a breach and consequent misfortune occur, not much time is spent thinking about taboos after pubescent initiation rites are over. Still, a major aspect of the adult person's spiritual life is instinctively to try to observe taboos. African spirituality is closely tied to this process.

The invisible structures of social relationships determine the visible and give meaning to people's encounter with other people and with all subjects in creation. The invisible is primordial; it establishes the order of existence and thus determines the nature and course of African spirituality in terms of the underlying reasons for human attitudes and behavior in the world. Within this structure the various forces of life make their demands known to human beings, that is, they literally "speak for you." Their requirements call for a response. In this way, by various subtle or obvious ways, they force humans to obey them, and so they "make you speak."

With reference to some spirits a negative aspect must be noted; there is a type that is innately capricious. Those of this type are likely to act in unpredictable ways against the totality and wholeness of life. Their fickleness shows itself in phenomena inimical to human and other forms of life in general. They are the root causes of epidemics, droughts, floods, infertility, impotence, disease in livestock, and so on. Human interest in them takes the form of different kinds of preventive action: people are well advised to take precautions against their unpredictability by using different kinds of charms and amulets, elements of nature that have inherent power to anticipate and counteract the spirits' evil intentions. A piece of wood from a totemic tree worn around the wrist, waist, or neck could act as protection. Some of these articles of nature are understood to be inherently repugnant to the spirits, so that they cannot be in close contact with them.

As Bénézet Bujo explains, "these natural elements, although they are apparently impersonal and inanimate, are paradoxically full of life and communicate the abundance of this life. The fact of touching a natural element or of smelling the scent of a plant creates harmony with the entire cosmos and re-establishes health in the holistic sense" (Bujo 2011, 150). For example, due to Islamic influence fitting in very well with African rationality, any part of a pig can act as an effective deterrent against possession by genies because of its intrinsic power. When prayers and sacrifices or other formal rituals are deemed necessary also as preventive strategies in cases of spiritual intrusion, it is not so much in order to appease the spirits, as would be the case with ancestral and other benevolent spirits. It is rather to get rid of them because they are not welcome. Unpredictable spirits, among whom must be counted all the dead without ancestral status for various established reasons, are unwanted intruders. They are resentful and bring about nothing but trouble. In the course of life, however, they are a real presence to confront. They command attention, if only from a negative standpoint.

Some African thinkers have identified three, rather than two, spheres of spiritual existence. Archbishop Emmanuel Milingo (Milingo 1984b; see also Ter Haar 1992) posits a "world-in-between" the visible physical order of the Earth and the sphere of God, the sky. Some spirits apart from God, according to Milingo, be they human or nonhuman, occupy a separate realm from the divine sphere. This claim flows from the perception that the divine vital power is much too grand to dwell in the same sphere of existence as other spirits.

It appears, nevertheless, that Milingo's structuring of the spiritual universe with a "world-in-between," is probably strongly influenced by Roman Catholic theological perceptions and does not contribute to an understanding of the African imagination. To say that African cosmology perceives a shared existential ambiance of all spirits is closer to the truth, given the interpenetration among the orders of existence. Lesser spirits, though not God's equal, live in the general "space" or ambiance with God, the Supreme Energy-for-Life in the material or non-material worlds. How that happens is not a question that occupies African curiosity. Some things are just the way they are; this is only logical. The important thing for the good life involves asking not *why* the spirits dwell where they dwell, but *how* to connect with them in the proper, most beneficial way to existence.

In summary, spirituality in Africa is not extraneous to the totality of the life of the individual or the community and the universe. It cannot be conceived of as having an existence detached from total involvement in the created order. Rather, spirituality in Africa is seen as human participation in the total, universal existence, the whole of human existential experience in the world. It is embedded in the entire being of people and things. The consciousness and activities this insertion implies constitute spirituality itself, that is, the spirit that dictates life's orientation. Humanity must constantly interact intelligently and compassionately with all spiritual powers for its own good and that of the entire universe.

Edward Bruce Bynum and Michael C. Kirwen argue correctly that the African approach to existence is personalist, in distinction from materialist. For African personalist spirituality, the energy of life (or anti-life, as with witchcraft), though invisible, is always embodied, personalized, or personified in some form or manner. Spiritual agency is always integrated in and with elements of the universe, and human existence and agency are interconnected with transcendent and immanent reality. The spiritual is not outside the agent, as in spiritualism; rather, the person is "part and parcel of . . . [the] dynamic, transforming flow of energy and life" (Kirwen 2006, 18, no. 2, 2). The person does not exist outside of this process but right within, or even at the center of it. This is what makes every disposition, every word, every act, good or bad, of spiritual consequence.

Though the spiritual is personified in this way, it is not objectified as in materialism, the conception that the only reality is physical and that matter comprises the explanation of everything or that matter is the highest value and source of the highest good. Personalization of the spirit does not, therefore, imply total materialization in the sense of turning the spiritual into an object to be manipulated and used. As personified, the spiritual power can, indeed, sometimes be identified and named, but this is only for the purpose of facilitating the process of bringing it into proper relationship with persons or the community. The African psyche sees "The world process . . . [as] literally one of personalized spiritual forces interacting and interconnected with each other within a nonlinear causal matrix of space, matter, intentionality, and time" (Bynum 1999, 86).

Spirituality in Africa is perhaps the one thing that is *really real*, not merely a conceptual idea. On the contrary, it is the most experiential reality in the totality of being. Stephen Ellis and Gerrie ter Haar underline this point when they point out that "in the light of . . . [the] widespread tendency to consider spirits as individual beings with a personal identity, [African] spirituality . . . becomes a power within the reach of all" (Ellis and ter Haar 2004, 52). It manifests itself in everyday life as morality or ethics, the appropriate manner of human existence.

4

You Are Your Shadow

"A snake gives birth to a snake."

One element of African perception of moral life that is unshakeable is that good actions are a sign of good intentions. The converse is equally true: evil deeds indicate an impure mind-set. Like breeds like; a snake will always give birth to a snake. Does a mango tree produce papayas? This, in African thought, is the norm on which moral judgment is made. The procedure is based on the individual's or society's dominant spiritual orientation, their practical life. You are your shadow, your personality; your behavior shows your inner identity, which is, in turn, shaped by your relationship with others (Ruel 1997, 108-33). In Africa, the specific ways of life, the customs, and observable behavior show the kind of person or society one is dealing with. And this has everything to do with spirituality.

When forming an opinion of others, as many distinguishing particularities as possible are taken into consideration. What do they eat? How do they dress? What kind of houses do they build and live in? What is their main economic activity? The questions are endless, depending on what one seeks to understand about the other or others. All of these are moral considerations, but they are also spiritual issues. The spiritual and the moral form one category of thought in African spirituality.

It is necessary to note that knowledge arising from the above questions often needs to be tested for its moral-spiritual wisdom. "African ethics does not hold that the validity of ethical norms and their application are a responsibility that lies upon the 'atomized' individual alone," Bujo explains (Bujo 2011, 154). Every adult person, and sometimes even the stranger who happens by, is invited to guard the integrity of the word. "It is possible that an isolated individual has badly chewed and badly digested the word that he or she has received. This makes the palaver [or *Indaba*, the judicious communal conversation] the ideal place for testing the effectiveness of the word and ensuring that it contributes not to the destruction but to the building up of the community" (Bujo 2011, 154). Consequently, procedure in the *Indaba* or palaver is of the essence in determining moral norms at all levels of life. The conversation must be exhaustive enough, "without maneuvering, trickery or force," to obtain a consensus. It must take into account the good life of the entire community, the living, the living dead and the communal property. This is the principle that determines change when moral custom is challenged and change is deemed necessary (Bujo 2009a, 122-23).

Morality and spirituality are indivisible and inseparable. "African ethics arises from the understanding of the world as an interconnected whole whereby what it means to be ethical is inseparable from all spheres of existence" (Murove 2009b, 28). Arguments that seek to separate *essence* and *substance* in the human person are foreign to the African perception of the person. Therefore, claims that a person "in him- or herself" is different from what behavior projects are tenuous. How can people be known by their "inner" being alone? Rather, their humanity or *Ubuntu* is manifested by their attitudes and actions, through their observance of customs and traditions. Everything one does contributes to who one is, to one's identity. One's status here and hereafter depends on how one lives one's life in relation to oneself and to the community (Munyaka and Motlhabi 2009, 71).

Thus, the position that "my humanity does not depend on my behavior" is seen from the point of view of African spirituality to be unconvincing; it cannot be used effectively to augment human dignity and rights thinking in the African context as these are not guaranteed *states of existence,* dependent merely on the fact that one is born human. In the African perception, being born a man or a woman is, indeed, of primary importance, since this is what gives the human species significantly more vital power than many other elements of creation. It does not, however, automatically accord anyone the essential, inalienable human qualities and entitlements required by *Ubuntu.* Fundamentally, *Ubuntu* and practical behavior are inextricably linked, the former giving direction to the other (how to behave) and the latter indicating the quality of the former (the attribute or "degree" of humanity achieved). *Ubuntu* cannot, therefore, be conceived of in essentialist, static terms; it is dependent on other practical and discernible conditions being met. Because chief among these demands is actual correct moral behavior, *Ubuntu* is something that must be earned.

Charles Nyamiti provides the most fundamental requirements of the African understanding of personhood or "personality" in a useful succinct summary as follows:

According to this [African] conception a person is *an ego* enjoying fullness of life or *adulthood* implying procreative and non-procreative *fecundity, ancestral wisdom, social responsibilities* and *rights, mystical vital power, fulfilled openness* (communality, relationality) to the outer world (i.e. the cosmos, living and dead human beings and the other Supernaturals with whom the ego is vitally and mystically united), *sacredness, liberty understood as emancipation from socio-economic oppression and natural evils, or as consciousness of self-giving to others and of being accepted by them* (Nyamiti 1990, 11).

Full personhood or humanity is made possible first and foremost by intersubjectivity, meaning *insertion* into, connectivity to, and interaction within a community. Physical puberty alone does not identify a boy as a man or a girl as a woman, for example. A young pubescent person, boasting before the elders that he or she was now a man or woman, would be asked "Who told you that you are a man/woman?" The emphasis is on "*who* told you," signifying approval by the community. Adulthood is a social quality in this perspective, not merely a biological or a chronological one. Thus, a person may be seventy years of age and still be considered "a child" if he or she has not fulfilled the social conditions required of his or her age, for instance, getting married. Being man or woman in the African sense follows social recognition after undergoing certain rites of passage. Adulthood "is a socially conferred role that carries with it specific expectations and responsibilities, often associated with marriage and the management of a family," the ultimate moral and spiritual vocation (Richardson 2009, 132-33).

Intersubjectivity determines the entitlements of dignity and rights. Rights from the African perspective "arise from a person's destiny of living in a relationship with family, friends, ethno-linguistic group, and nation," as E. J. M. Zvogbo explains (see Ramose 2009, 421). Generally, Africans perceive rights less as necessary attributes of human physical nature but as related to the totality of a person's moral accomplishment. The extent of conscious and well-adjusted integration shows the degree of engagement in life and the level of ethical orientation. To be ethical, personal autonomy must be balanced by social considerations. It is circumscribed by the actual encounter of one person with another. The autonomy of one person in moral action is conditional upon the nature of the encounter and its consequences. The issue is always whether or not it brings favorable results, such as fostering prosperity primarily for those within the circle whose power enables the agent and his/her surroundings "to be more."

In accordance with the hierarchy of energies we have discussed, the autonomy of a younger person vis-à-vis an older person is regarded on a different level than that between age mates. A minor gesture though it may seem, a younger person's effort to avoid deliberate eye contact with an older person is symbolically important in this respect: it indicates submission to the higher force of life in the older person. But even in the case of age mates, one has to determine the role each one plays in society, for it indicates the limits of personal autonomy in action. All of these considerations influence the relationship and the autonomy of each actor. In almost all cases, the boundaries are clearly defined by custom and are designed to preserve the proper interaction of universal forces.

The principle of individualism and self-interest as the sole criteria of autonomy fails to satisfy the African communitarian psyche as the standard for moral or ethical judgment. Self-interest apart from community interest diminishes one's full humanity. Private actions that would otherwise pass unnoticed gain importance because of their effects on community life. A small theft may not cause too much concern until sickness strikes the thief or other things start going wrong in his family or community. The issue then becomes of the utmost consequence and can no longer be ignored.

Nevertheless, a warning is frequently sounded not to "romanticize" the African communitarian mind-set by ignoring the individualistic, selfish inclination inherent in all human beings. Writers such as Placide Tempels, Alexis Kagame, and later, of course, John S. Mbiti are criticized on this account. Other thinkers subject to the same criticism include African political philosopher-politicians such as Kwame Nkrumah (Ghana), Leopold Sedar Senghor (Senegal), Felix Hophouet-Boigny (Cote d'Ivoire), Julius K. Nyerere (Tanzania), and Kenneth Kaunda (Zambia) (for their contribution, see Rwiza 2010, 93-168). Under contemporary systemic social-economic globalization, their ideas on African communalism are dismissed as completely unrealistic. According to the critics, these scholars and political leaders have created an imaginary "Africa" in their academic discussion of the notion of African communalism. They have, the critics argue, constructed an artificial "unicity" in African communities whereas, in actual fact, there is as much fluidity between individual and communal interests in African societies as one finds anywhere else in the world. One such critic, the philosopher Didier N. Kaphagawani, notes that the proponents of African communalism as a unique life-orientation fail to acknowledge "the rift between theory and lived experience, the distance between the products of intellectual abstraction and . . . 'the manifold and ambiguous character of the immediacy of a *lebenswelt*'" (Kaphagawani 2000, 77). The abstract world of the intellectual theorists and the real world of ordinary people, Africans included, according to the critics, are largely incompatible.

Though not totally unfounded, the criticism seems to be overdone. While the warnings against romanticization of African communalism and criticism of its practical application in African societies are both in order, the distinct emphasis on communal association and the social basis of moral interpretation and judgment in the African understanding of personhood cannot be in doubt. According to their ethical reasoning, you are, of course, a human being by birth, but this is not enough. Being born human only "describes" the person, as Kwasi Wiredu points out; it does not "define" him or her. What defines the person, the normative aspect of *Ubuntu*, is the individual's behavior in two closely connected dimensions: in relationship to oneself and in relationship to others. Indeed, "personhood is not something you are born with but something you . . . achieve, and it is subject to degrees, so that some are more than others, depending on the degree of fulfillment of one's obligations to self, household, and community" (Wiredu 2002, 315; also Shutte 2009b, 98). The rights conceded to you as a child (the descriptive sense of humanity) depend on biology; they do not define you as a human being in the normative or ethical sense, which entails obligations in society. "Humans . . . undergo a process of social transformation until they attain full status as persons, and during this process of attainment the community plays the vital role of catalyst—of the prescriber of ends. Achieving the status of personhood is conditional on social [and moral] achievements that contribute to the common good" (Coetzee and Roux 2002, 277; Bujo 2009a, 115-16).

On the condition, therefore, that you are fully rational and conscious of your behavior, you are what you do in and for society. Your actions, like your shadow, accompany you wherever you go; you cannot escape from them. They reveal your character and the predominant qualities that define you as a person in the eyes of others for you can only be known through their eyes. Personal rights and dignity accrue from the impact of an action upon the overall vital power of the community. A person is entitled to and may justifiably claim dignity on the basis of good, life-giving behavior. To be denied of dignity when a person has behaved ethically constitutes an injustice for which anyone, including God, may be taken to task.

Morality is intimately related to African spirituality just as two sides of a coin; both revolve around the need for the good life, and both can be understood only in the context of the community. "The good life for an individual is conceived of as coinciding with the good life of the community, and a person's choice is highly or lowly ranked [that is, is seen as moral or immoral] as it contributes to or detracts from the common good" (Coetzee and Roux 2002, 276). We might say more accurately that morality is the concrete expression of spirituality. Spirituality as the search for the good, moral, or ethical life, which means being in harmony with the universe, is the motivation for moral action as well as its consequence. There can be no conception of spirituality without morality, and just as equally, of morality without spirituality. The physical reality of an action demonstrates the interior disposition of an agent, and the disposition is known through the forms of action it embodies. Thus, although human behavior is what we see, there is always a motivating factor behind it, an instrumental power that essentially makes the behavior spiritual.

This can be elaborated as follows: right living, in the sense of doing whatever leads to a fulfilling life, is the kind of behavior that is desirable, and it is what immediately comes to mind when the word morality is mentioned. But there is a flip side to this that we must not lose sight of. Human beings, both as individuals and communities, sometimes fail to act in the interests of the good life; in short, they act immorally. This kind of behavior, the refusal to live according to established custom, affects human existence and universal harmony. Discord in society, all kinds of suffering and wants, are as a result of this. It then becomes obvious how this is fundamentally a spiritual orientation, if only in a negative way; vital forces are equally involved here just as they are in positive situations.

When good moral behavior prevails, the spirit world produces positive power, bringing forth abundance into the visible world. There are uncomplicated births, for example, or plenty of rain, good crops, numerous herds of cattle, and so on. In such times, everybody knows everything is normal. However, when immorality dominates, the spirit world releases negative forces, the consequences of which contradict the positive expectations of good life. Lack of food, disharmony in families and clans, and general disorder in creation experienced as droughts or floods, death by lightning or plagues, and so on are some indicators of moral evil; the spirit world shows its displeasure through such events.

This perspective may not stand up to social-ethical analysis, for even good people experience bad things and suffer. Nevertheless, the basic point here is that behavior is intrinsically and necessarily connected with all the spiritual elements of existence. Another way of putting this is that to guard against immorality presupposes the immortality of values. But the immortality of values presupposes the immortality and power of the ancestors. It is this connection that raises morality from the level of mere human relationships, the temporal dimension, to the level of relationships with the ancestral world, the spiritual dimension. Morality leads to spirituality and vice versa. When, therefore, we witness a certain act, we assume a spiritual basis for it. Several aspects of African life illustrate this bond, namely, the nature of tradition, the significance of rites of passage practiced in many African societies, and the role of leadership in the spiritual orientation of the community.

No African community identifies itself apart from its tradition. It is important to point out that tradition here must not be mistaken for "a system of habits and routines" to be blindly followed, seen as backwardness. Tradition

in the context of African spiritual perception should not be contrasted with
modernity; tradition and modernity in African spirituality are not necessarily opposed but complementary. As Phyllis M. Martin and Patrick O'Meara
explain, "the tendency to see a sharp dichotomy between the traditional and
the modern, to perceive them as closed systems irreconcilably separated
from each other," though a popular and persistent view in reference to Africa,
must be resisted. Beyond being simplistic and misleading, it is false. In its
true sense, "tradition implies time-depth, the continuity of ideals, values and
institutions transmitted over generations; but the process also involves continuous borrowing, invention, rejection, and adaptation on all levels, individual, local, and regional" (Martin and O'Meara 1977b, 7). Again, tradition
involves the retrieval of memory to serve an inventive and creative now.

In its deepest meaning, tradition, as used in reference to African spirituality, implies the wisdom of the community, the ability to handle the affairs of
life in the "proper" manner, in accordance with the ways of the ancestors as
indicated by the elders. Tradition "represents the 'word' of the ancestors," the
founding "story," the "good news," as it were, of the right order of creation
applied today. It is fundamental not only for identity, who we are, but also
for life, because it incorporates the "means of communication" among the
powers of existence (Zahan 2000, 47-48). To know this "skill" makes life possible, and to use it profitably in a given context is one of the most important
goals of life, if not the most important. Everyone, even the young, desires to
participate in it. Subsequently, anyone who enjoys this knowledge is held in
high esteem. This is why reverence and deference toward elders is generally
expected, because in the community structure, they are entrusted with its
interpretation for contemporary living and are charged to guard it and pass it
on, in its entirety, to succeeding generations.

What tradition says or questions about this or that issue or situation is
not simply for the answer it seeks but specifically for the ways, methods, or
techniques behind the search. How do we approach and deal with a given
problem? Herein lies the moral-spiritual aspect of the issue, and this is what
tradition unravels. In areas such as worship, and in the face of certain illnesses
and calamities, tradition can read like a catechism, a question-and-answer
manual, where procedures are provided for every problem in the minutest
detail. For instance, in the case of sacrifice, tradition specifies not only what
kind of animal to offer, but its color, the position it should be made to face
while being sacrificed, and how it should be divided up. Furthermore, whatever kind of movement or noise it makes is significant, as well as any "imperfections" that might be found on or in it.

Appropriating tradition is the purpose of the rites of passage for those
African societies that practice them (for a brief description, see Nyamiti

1987, 66). These rites are a sequence of ceremonies a person undergoes in various stages from birth to death; they are symbols of deeper incorporation into the sacred world. This incorporation is what is celebrated in the initiation and marriage rites and in elderhood, death, and funeral rituals. At death, the process of integration is complete, either positively with the person attaining full communion with the ancestors and deserving nominal reincarnation, or negatively, by falling short and remaining an unrecognized, vengeful spirit. With these rites of passage, it is not only the individual who changes but the community is also transformed with the individual. It is as if, by celebrating the particular ritual for one or several of its members, the community undergoes the same transition in its corporate life. The rites of passage demonstrate the interpenetration between the individual and the community as the essence of spirituality.

Through the rites of passage, an individual is deemed to advance in the art of spiritual communication. The pedagogical tools in this process are themselves communication devices: the myths, folktales, didactic songs, proverbs, and riddles of the clan or ethnic group designed to share the syntax of the language of the ancestors with their descendants. For the living, this is the most important gift because it enables the community to communicate with the invisible world. The motor that drives the desire for communication with this world of powers consists in a series of aspirations and practical attainments, which may be summed up as the longing to belong to the highest degree of existence, at one with divinity, with one's people, and with the universe. "Those who have passed through all the stages," writes Evan M. Zuesse with reference to the initiation rites of the Bambara people of Mali, "are 'new' beings, . . . spiritually enlightened and endowed with the 'Word,' that is, possessing an immortal soul that bears the form of the universe and God himself" (Zuesse 1979, 152).

Every rite or ritual confers both privileges and responsibilities. It moves one into closer integration in the tradition and with ancestral life and, therefore, grants one special insight into the mysteries of life. If a person lives according to the demands that each ritual expresses and expects, that person earns dignity and is accorded certain rights that non-initiates cannot claim. Consequently, as Robert B. Fisher points out, every individual "wishes very much to live well and in the end to die well in order to qualify for membership among the ancestors." However, this desire demands right conduct, the requirement to live ethically and to be an example of maturity and moral integrity to others: "one must live a life worthy of emulation; one must live normally to a ripe old age and have . . . children and grandchildren" (Fisher 1998, 97). This is the meaning of being in tune with the "Ways of Tradition."

Complying with tradition denotes surrender, not in the passive sense of the word where the main action lies outside of the agent, but rather in the sense of willfully appropriating wisdom and becoming one with it as an actor in the process. One surrenders to tradition by living like the ancestors, by following ancestral life as indicated by the elders so as to harness more human qualities and grow deeper into *Ubuntu*. Surrender is an a priori requirement for spirituality because tradition precedes the individual and the current community's existence, whereas moral demands are already contained within the community's way of life. The journey toward ancestorship demands that the individual must not only personally appropriate the tradition but must also be *seen* to live it.

Also of concern in the process of celebrating the rites of passage is the need for leadership, which is a necessary tool for guiding a wayward society back to the path of tradition. For although active surrender or docility to ancestral tradition is what people are expected to strive for, this is understood to be the ideal. In practice, human beings are not consistent in this struggle; not infrequently, they do not observe the ways of the ancestors and they act unethically. Whether deliberate or not, such behavior weakens the vital force of the universe, the community, as well as that of the transgressor. Leadership in society, whose structure is assured by the rites of passage, acts as a watchdog against any breach of tradition to avoid any threats to life. The leaders' responsibility is to keep life "holy," to interpret, for the rest of the community, the transcendent in the seemingly ordinary.

The leaders in a community are the elders, and some of their responsibilities include performance of ritual, the use of elements of creation as means of transforming human experience, and redirecting that experience toward the demands of tradition and the ancestors. No ritual is ever intended as an escape from life. It is not spoken of in illusory terms. Rather, by employing natural symbols, ritual has as its goal a deeper integration into the totality of existence in a way that is orderly and harmonious as revealed through the foundational stories of the community, such as its myths. The ultimate intention of ritual is to transform human experience, not to escape from it. It is to bring out the transcendental significance of the everyday, which humans tend to forget precisely because of its (transcendental) nature. The process of ritual is aimed at giving back, of returning reality to where it originally and ultimately belongs, in the hands of God through the ancestors.

As a rule, ritual is repetitive. This aspect of ritual as repetition is important, for if the goal of ritual is to return reality to the divine sphere, it needs to be performed again and again. This is for two reasons: first, because of the reality of change in human life, and, second, because of the reality of human forgetfulness. Any change is accompanied by certain strains that can damage universal harmony. Repetitive ritual action recalls the attention of human beings to the need to strengthen unity by correcting the inconsistencies inherent in the process of living. When there is discord serious enough to be noticed by its negative effects on life, special rites proportionate to the situation are called for, and these are the formal rituals performed by public leaders as need arises. Informal rituals are carried out on a routine basis by individuals in less formal leadership positions but with special responsibilities over families or other small entities. The routine rituals that they carry out help to forestall human forgetfulness. One of the major ancestral concerns is to be remembered through frequent offerings and sacrifices; therefore, the informal leaders, as guardians of families, will do this almost automatically in recognition of ancestral presence and assistance.

Ritual action holds an indispensable place in African prayer and liturgical activity because communion with the ancestors brings blessings, protection, and other favors in life. The ancestors expect ethical behavior from their descendants as a condition for bestowing their blessings. Although the expectation is mutual, a kind of *quid pro quo* arrangement between the living and the living-dead, the greater onus is on the living. As we have already mentioned, this is because human beings owe the ancestors all "their knowledge and wisdom as well as the guarantee of authenticity with respect to tradition." Second, humans are indebted to the ancestors "for their intervention and mediation on the level of spiritual life strictly speaking" (Zahan 1979, 51). This succinctly explains why ancestor veneration is such a central aspect of African spirituality.

5

Time, Space, History, and Human Fulfillment

"There is no difference between growing old and living."

What we have said in the preceding chapters implicitly shows that graceful old age is, in general, seen as a blessing among African societies. People desire it; and as one progresses in years, one is honored when this fact is publicly recognized and acknowledged in greetings and other acts of open social deference. Being referred to as an elder (literally "old man or woman") is not offensive, but is welcome for the deeper significance it carries: that the person thus addressed holds a special position in society. Grey hair implies wisdom. For an individual to dishonor his or her grey hair by saying or doing anything inappropriate is to disgrace not only himself or herself, but it is to shame all those in the community who have been marked by nature with this blessed distinction. This is a serious moral offense for which reparation to the group, through rituals, is usually required to placate the ancestral spirits.

In African spiritual perception, living long and growing old is the essence of living well, such that there is no difference between them. Death in ripe old age is usually not mourned as a tragedy, only as a loss to the pool of wisdom and visible spiritual energy of the community. Celebration at an elder's passing is palpable, and the more important and successful he or she was in life, the grander the feasting at death. Young generations in the family or clan of the deceased elder celebrate such passing in order to possess the spirit of the elder and move up in the hierarchy of spirit power to benefit themselves and the community. The place where the elder is interred, in many cases within or around the homestead, becomes *ipso facto* hallowed ground. Time, space, and history all combine (in life) to bring about human fulfillment.

For a good number of years, there has been an interesting scholarly debate about the African understanding of time. Two positions have dominated the discussion. On one side, there is the position advocated by John S. Mbiti in his pioneering work *African Religions and Philosophy*, in which he argues that Africans perceive time essentially in a two-dimensional approach, "with a long *past*, a *present* and virtually *no future*." According to Mbiti, "The linear concept of time in western thought, with an indefinite past, present and infinite future, is practically foreign to African thinking" (Mbiti 1969, 16-17).

To illustrate his point, Mbiti employed the Swahili concepts of *sasa* (present) and *zamani* (past) to describe these dimensions, and contended that they control the life of the African person from birth to death. For Mbiti, Africans traditionally live facing not the future, which he argued does not exist beyond virtually the next season; they live facing the past, which is long, spanning ancestral memory. "As the individual gets older," claims Mbiti, "he is in effect moving gradually from the Sasa [present] to the Zamani [past]." Thus, for the African, "death is a process which removes a person gradually from the Sasa period to the Zamani" (Mbiti 1969, 24), a kind of retrospective rather than future-oriented spiritual perception (Zahan 1979, 45). On account of this outlook, Mbiti argues further that Africans find it difficult to appreciate the Christian doctrine of eschatology, based on the linear understanding of time, when God will bring everything to a final end at some indefinite future date, because they lack the conception of a distant future (Mbiti 1969, 23).

Several African philosophers have written along the same lines as Mbiti. Newell S. Booth, for example, quotes Elizabeth Isichei, the Nigerian Igbo historian, as saying that among the Igbo, the idea of the "recurrence" of events, not their difference, uniqueness, and succession, dominates the people's perception of time. "It reflects a community closely linked with the land and nature . . . its attitudes molded by the shorter cycle of the lunar month, the longer cycle of the seasons and the farmer's year. . . . The ancestors are 'the returners', and by returning they incarnate the past among the living" (Booth 1993, 89). Some authors draw the conclusion that this outlook toward time in African societies is retrogressive for being retrospective; it inhibits economic development.

Since life in this view is anchored in a "secure" past that can only repeat itself, there can be no "dynamic perception of the future." Consequently, "There is no planning, no foresight, no scenario building; in other words, no policy to affect the course of events." What remains is that people have a fatalistic attitude toward events and a childish resigned recourse to God or the spirits when problems befall them. Given such a scenario in Africa, "There can be no singing of tomorrows so long as our culture does not teach us to question the future, to repeat it mentally, and to bend it to our will. In modern society, everyone must prepare and plan the future" (Tarimo 2005, 20).

Tarimo, however, rejects the notion advanced by critics that African culture and religion cannot conceive a dynamic future. He contends, on the contrary, that a careful examination of different African forms of speech, symbols, and rituals easily belies this assertion. "My contention," he writes, "is that the attitude of portraying African traditional religions as lacking the transcendental dimension, inferior, and incomplete has ended up weakening African value systems." It has thus acted as a self-fulfilling prophecy: "It has robbed them of their inner dynamism and thus stunted their vision of self-transcendence with regard to the future" (Tarimo 2005, 21).

Ernest K. Beyaraza, studying the Bakiga people of Uganda, arrives at a similar conclusion. Noting that the Bakiga understanding of time is "rooted in reality" and that as a rule no effort is made "to isolate and examine time as such vis-a-vis the rest of reality" (Beyaraza 2000, 133), he offers several linguistic, sociological, and theological examples to show how the Bakiga do conceive of future events, but do not let the future overtake them in a fatalist manner. An analysis of their language and customs, says Beyaraza, indicates that they "thought of," "worried about," and "planned for" the future (Beyaraza 2000, 145). Marriage customs and rituals, which generally underlined the importance of children and grandchildren, indicate this. So do many of the Bakiga names. For example, the female name Byareireeta, explains Beyaraza, implies that the newborn baby girl will bring bridewealth to the family in the distant future (Beyaraza 2000, 143).

This broad view is shared by John A. A. Ayoade in his discussion about the Yoruba people and their understanding of time. According to Ayoade, "the Yoruba do not see themselves as completely ignorant of the future." For them, "the future co-exists with the present without being coextensive with it." The future may be hidden, and nothing absolutely certain can be affirmed about it; but it is not completely inaccessible in certain of its dimensions, as the art of divination shows. Time for the Yoruba is "a locus of history" (Ayoade 1979, 83-84). As Ayoade puts it, the Yoruba "do not see themselves as of necessity, helpless victims of time but as potential conquerors of time through a careful reflection on time past, and a discreet scheduling of time-present as well as time-future" (Ayoade 1979, 85).

This debate is important, but should not detain us for too long, only as far as it clearly exposes two important points for our attention: first, that a people's notion of time has significant consequences in their religious and spiritual behavior and influences it directly. On this point there is practically no dissent. The effects of the current future-driven global culture, for example, are clear to see; "quality time" in the present seems to be nonexistent. It is often subordinated to or sacrificed for future (material) gain. The second point of the debate, whether and how African peoples conceive of the future, is much more complex and nuanced than the simple dichotomy presented by the two philosophical positions, particularly as it relates to the African people's spiritual orientation. Indeed, the complexity of the question is indicated by the inconclusiveness of the debate about it.

The African conception of time cannot be understood accurately when separated from space, history, or tradition, and the (complete) fulfillment of the individual as an ancestor. All of these elements form an integrated movement in the rhythm of life, with human existence as the focus. There can be neither time without space nor space without time. Time and space together, as an inseparable unit, constitute history, where history is understood not as merely a series of events happening "out there" but as the cumulative result of a person's or community's behavior in the universe leading to the true self, *Ubuntu*. Accordingly, in African spirituality, time "is determined by human action and organized according to the spatial, visible course of natural events, the rising and setting of the sun. Temporal distance is given as the distance between spaces. The crossing of spatial distance allows time to happen." Actions also determine time. "In their acts, people create time. Whether there is passage of time without human activity is an unimportant question. It is the human being who gives everything 'weight', and therefore 'being'" (Sundermeier 1998, 24).

It is true that Africans tend to conceive of time in a cyclic and phenomenal way. As with everything else, time is sacred because it is inserted into the cycle of life and serves it. Time is not an abstract idea moving toward an imagined "future" existence. The future is tied up with the human reality. Time, in the African perception, corresponds with the life-giving events of birthing, undergoing certain rites, marriage, worship, and death. It has meaning in connection with actions related to planting, harvesting, hunting, fishing, constructing a house, and so on. When do the cows come home? When did the cock crow? When is the market day? When do the women go to the river to fetch water? Today they would be phrased differently: when do we go to church? Or to a political meeting? Or to a dance? But in substance, all of these are the indicators of time.

Rain, floods, drought, famine, or epidemics are natural phenomena; they do not carry much significance apart from how they affect existence. They become a matter of serious and public social, moral, and spiritual consideration when they upset the expected order of things, when the rhythm of seasons changes, causing floods and drought that claim the lives of humans, plants, and livestock. Then the interplay of the life forces and human responsibility must be gauged, and appropriate (moral) behavior to restore needed balance determined. Communal ritual activity toward God and the ancestral spirits proliferates during these periods for the specific purpose of human flourishing. Negatively, but also linked with life, major incidents associated with human behavior concerning interethnic hostilities and war act in the same way. They are linked with in-depth time-space conceptions and constitute history, not in themselves as events but in the impact they had on life at the time, as well as their lessons for the business of integrating life forces for the present-day community and the community of the unborn.

A frequent way of naming children is after historical and historic events, important personalities (living or deceased), battles or wars, or natural happenings such as we have just mentioned. Children are also named after animals and other creatures with certain significance to the family or clan as totems, or for certain permanent ritual purposes to ward off misfortune. After a serial death of infants, a child may be named *Ondiek* ([hyena], Luo, Kenya/Tanzania), for example, to scare away the malicious, vengeful spirits that caused the previous deaths so that it may survive. Similarly with *Mbiti* ([hyena] among the Kamba, Kenya); the naming of a child "hyena" is accompanied by the silent prayer: "We vow away this child to God. He does not belong to us, but to God. Let it be an animal, a kind of offering to God" (Kalu 2000, xvi). Other names used for totemic purposes as a perpetual remembrance include *Nguruwe* (pig) and *Ngonyani* (ape).

Many children in Africa bear the names of significant events, such as *Madaraka* (internal self-government), *Uhuru* (independence), or important personalities such as Mandela, Kennedy, Nyerere, and so on. Some people born after the Second World War were named after Hitler in various parts of Africa. There are also credible reports that after the bloodshed that accompanied the elections in Kenya in 2007–2008, some children, born during this time, bear the name of "Post-Election Violence"! This may sound amusing and exaggerated, but the spiritual significance of this or similar names lies in the fusion the name brings about with visible or invisible reality. Involved in this is the belief that the naming act and the name itself will bring about blessings or ward off misfortune, as the case may be. A name may also recall in some permanent way the influence of a person or effects of an event on society and the cosmos. The name thus becomes an enduring lesson as well as an indicator of time. But since names are usually derived from the past for the benefit of the present, does it indicate an exclusive concern with the past and present, at the expense of the future? Does it justify the assessment that Africans lack the notion of an indefinite future?

A closer analysis of the practice of naming, among others, will show that this is not the case. The naming system may indicate a concern with cyclic and phenomenological time. However, there is always a trajectory implied to the circle or consideration of the event. Although the cycle of events or phenomena repeats itself and is not broken off completely at any point, it runs along a route toward a goal, a future greatness. The greatness is already present in the experience of the good life made possible by faithfulness to ancestral tradition, yet it is not complete, because occasional imbalances happen. The "future" consists of the human attempt to adhere completely to the tradition and eventually make the whole community ancestral.

To employ an analogy, time in African perception can be compared to a wheel running along a road. The wheel revolves around itself but also runs forward along the road. The road, on the other hand, is a constituent component of the wheel's capacity to perform, for it enables the wheel to advance; without the road, the wheel would not progress as well as it should, and perhaps not at all. So the wheel and the road feed into each other to make perfect motion possible. Perhaps this is what R. Lawlor, borrowing from the Greek notion of *gnomon*, or sundial, calls the "gnomonic" perception of time, involving the effect of the sun rays against a physical object. It pertains to a sort of "gnomonic expansion," in which the dial does not obliterate the shadow but defines it. In the African conception of time, the present does not obliterate the past but incorporates it and moves it forward. "This is time as an expanding growth upon growth, an evolution, one might say, belonging to the conscious energies which transcend their transitory forms and substances" (see Taiwo 2000, 178). It means, as Ali Mazrui notes, that no absolute division is established between past, present, and future: the past and present indicate what is possible for the future (Murove 2009b, 27, 28).

In terms of African spirituality, the practice of naming assures the stability of ancestral, community, and cosmic life through mutual nourishment of these elements. In short, a name may be given in view of ensuring that the ancestral past nourishes present and future existence. The past is amalgamated into the present, with one trajectory: "to behave like the ancestors so as to be . . . worthy continuation of them" (Mulago 1991, 122). In this way, time can be calculated only with reference to the stability and survival of the individual, family, and clan in the cosmos, not only up to a certain foreseeable future but in the context of an unceasing present: the good life.

Perfecting the human community is, therefore, an essential aspect of the African conception of time. Again, time is conceived of in terms of behavior that inspires better and higher experiences of existence. To stop an "important" activity one may be currently engaged in to exchange a long greeting with a neighbor or to share a meal with an unexpected guest is not to be considered a "waste of time" with regard to the previous activity. In the hierarchy of values, because it helps to perfect society and life in general, human communication takes precedence over all other concerns. This means that behavior related to human communication, hospitality, and friendship actually creates time, inasmuch as it is the foundation of universal stability.

History in the African perception is in the now: it appears in the present, in the cycle of phenomena, to lead people inexorably to the "future," that is, to a fuller experience of the good life. History rallies people to attend to the business of assuring stability for themselves and their descendants *in this world* of experience. This constitutes the future, which cannot be evident except in benevolent human and cosmic experiences. A cyclic and phenomenal conception of time shows that time is at the service of the human person, who draws sustenance from every happening. The future is integrated in the desire to maintain, prolong, and perpetuate life.

The sanctity of time on account of its link with life in the context of ancestral tradition is also connected to and dependent on a conception of sanctified space for the same reason. All space is sacred because its physical, material appearance contains the invisible powers that make life possible: the world of the spirits is integrated into that of space. In space as well as time, sacrifices and offerings are made to strengthen the community's soul. For this reason, some spaces carry more significance than others, with places of worship requiring the greatest respect. Trespassing in places of worship is generally taboo; usually, only a few selected elders are allowed to enter the sacred groves or climb the sacred hills when special prayers are needed. To locations where everyone can go during worship, access may be interdicted outside these times at the risk of great negative consequences. Moral or physical purity may be required to be present at these locations. Evil people may have their secret, anti-life intentions involuntarily exposed if they go to such places.

Communal spaces and places of worship often inspire awe by their locations, sizes, or shapes. In this respect they are out of the ordinary, and mystical powers are associated with them. Rocks or trees, for example, may be reputed to possess the ability of movement or speech. Legends tell of strange creatures being associated with them, reputed to be apparitions of appropriate ancestor spirits. These may be huge snakes or other animals such as birds (a reminder of the previous discussion on the spirituality of totems), or actual ghosts. Sighting them may cause an unforgettable fright or worse. It is for this reason also that these locations are best left alone, except when absolutely necessary.

The significance of ancestral burial grounds in African spirituality has already been noted, but it warrants mention again in the specific context of time, space, history, and human fulfillment. Ancestral land, which means the space or location where the ancestors lie in death, is *home*. It represents the fulfillment of time, of human life, of history. Wherever a person may actually reside, he or she is not complete without ancestral identity, symbolized by ancestral land. You may have a house in the city far away from your ancestral burial grounds, but that is just a house. You may even spend most of your life there, but it is not home. "Home" remains the ancestral space. This is where one desires to be buried in death, together with "one's own people." The ground connected to the ancestral resting place is where parents bury the umbilical cords of their children, to link them concretely and unambiguously with their ancestry. Sometimes, when any difficulty arises in naming a child, the correct name is affirmed by a ceremony performed there.

The importance of ancestral space such as burial grounds best represents the spiritual connection between the past, present, and future. Here, the presence of the ancestors and other spirits is pervasive, thoroughly influencing every thought and behavior. Here, the ancestors lived as elders and now live as supreme powers. Here, through the ancestors, we encounter the most palpable representation of the divine. Here, therefore, the living go to learn the tradition to enhance the life of the universe for the coming generations who will themselves find sustenance to a more complete degree. Hence "to remove Africans by force from their land is an act . . . of great injustice. . . . Even when people voluntarily leave their homes . . . there is a fundamental severing of ties which cannot be repaired and which often creates psychological problems" (Mbiti 1969, 26-27). The good life can be realized only in communion with ancestral land in which the living dead reside, in the concrete phenomena found there. This communion must never be broken, for "The dead are not dead"; they are all around us "in the thickening shadow . . . in the tree that rustles . . . in the wood that groans . . . in the breast of the woman . . . in the child who is wailing . . . in the firebrand that flames . . . in the forest . . . in the house" (Kalu 2000, 54).

A word on the sacredness of persons as the foundational element of time, space, and history is necessary at the conclusion of this chapter. What the foregoing discussion has attempted to show is that, for the African, these are not independent entities but are constituted in the human person and the community's behavior. Therefore, the rhythm of time, space, and history is inherently bound together with human life; ideally, they form a natural harmony. When people sanctify the land, the land blesses them in equal measure. On the other hand, unbecoming behavior toward Mother Earth eventually spells disaster.

Time and history should come to a glorious end with the blissful passing of one generation of people to be taken up and amplified by the next in the cyclical-forward manner that we have just discussed. When disaster strikes in an epidemic, flood, or famine, the ethical and spiritual lessons of human failure are not forgotten but become part of tradition and history: We suffered such and such a disaster because we failed to act according to the demands of tradition, and this is what happened (for example, for the Karamojong, see Knighton 2005, 58-61). In today's globalized world, which has in many respects become a village, the "sin" of the human community in one part can affect everyone in every place. Global warming and acid rain are contemporary examples. In many African communities, the message of particular historical events may be preserved in songs and dances, but most indelibly in naming individuals or in designating age-groups after them.

The gradual integration of time and history takes place in the natural development of human life. The sacral nature of age can be explained in this context: "As infallible individuals who have mastered the act of existence, elders await their finitude on earth . . . assured in their posterity . . . that they have succeeded in bequeathing to future generations names that would be recalled eternally" (Ephirim-Donkor 2011, 8). Old age normally implies greater self-integration within the *be-ing* of the individual, leading ultimately to the complete fusion of time and space in death and burial on ancestral land. This can also happen with people who possess special abilities if they conform to the moral expectations associated with their status in life. Failing to do so, the individual in question is ignored as a "useless person" or "a fool" (Ephirim-Donkor 2011, 6). To arrive at the point of final union, to reach human fulfillment, is a prerogative of those who exhibit complete *Ubuntu* in life.

6

Piety, Worship, and Health

"If you want to speak to God, tell it to the wind."

It must have been a fine, bright morning on that day of November 22, 1957, when one Mr. Gosiani oMwita, a Kuria man from the southwestern part of the eastern African country of Kenya, just across the border from northwestern Tanzania (which his ethnic group straddles), got up and, facing the sun, prayed aloud to the sun "for things . . . many things": healthy children of both sexes for himself and his sons, healthy and productive livestock, so that his name might be revered. "Sun, it is you I am asking for all these things, you who can give them to me, you who are the force in all things" (Ruel 1997, x).

For Gosiani oMwita, the sun could see, the sun could hear, the sun could convey his wishes and desires to whatsoever power could grant them. In the radiating sun, he perceived the sacral and creative power of life concretely in terms of health, children, and material wealth (Ruel 1997, 18-19). For him, these were signs of life's presence, order, and blessing. This assumption is basic to African spirituality, as becomes clear when we examine the African experience of piety, worship, and health. The vital force that is understood to surround and guide all human activity is made most conspicuous in the activity of communal worship, where it is perceived literally to be like the sun or the wind, invisible but palpably present and all-encompassing, seeing and listening to everything that goes on.

Humans can know God only through history or through human experience, which implies human interpretation and understanding of divine activity in the universe. This is what in many religious traditions is called revelation. The direction ordinary African piety and the African approach to worship takes is based on the same conviction. Neither separate nor distinct from creation, God is encountered in the practical details that surround everyday human life and make it possible, from the smallest detail of life to the most complex of events. If we want to make distinctions between personal and communitarian spirituality, we might say that while piety is more personal and concerns itself with the quotidian, worship is public and takes account of the extraordinary. Nevertheless, the distinction is fundamentally academic, because both piety in the individual and worship in the community take the same basic orientation and aim at the same goal.

It is understood that the purpose of both is to seek the good life, which only God can give. Piety and worship arise out of the realization of human dependence on this supreme power, as human beings experience fulfillment or lack of it. Piety is the instinctive awareness of divine and ancestral presence in the world; worship acknowledges and dramatizes it in a formal and concentrated way. As the Karamojong people of Uganda see it, worship seeks to achieve special intensity, or creates "dense moments" of communion with the ancestral and divine presence, so that it becomes more tangible and fuller than what is experienced in the habitual order of existence (Knighton 2005, 30).

All negative spiritual elements in human life, the immoral behavior that brings disorder in the community and the world, is evidence of lack of piety. In practice, it involves violation of interpersonal, family, and social relationships. Respect for elders, observance of taboos and tradition in general, daily veneration of ancestors through prayer, or frequent pouring of libations to them are all acts of piety and are necessary for the good ordering of the life of the community. Proper male and female social roles, sexual relations in marriage, providing for the needs of the family, and protecting the homestead against any evil intruders are equally issues of piety, graded only according to the degree of their influence on life in the order of things. To weigh the gravity of an offense, the question always is: Has a wrong been committed against an ordinary individual (and therefore the consequences are limited), or is it against the community or personified community, the effects of which are much broader and more grave and therefore must be counted as criminal?

Some examples can illustrate this distinction. Adultery is a serious offense against piety in any circumstance because it disrupts social order and community life. But adultery with an elder's wife, or especially the chief's wife, becomes behavior in a different category altogether, on account of the position that the elder or chief holds. If adultery with a commoner's wife disrupts social order, adultery with a chief's wife does so even more. It has therefore more disruptive potential on account of the chief's integrating power in the community. It should be obvious that, because of the damage it does to the honor of the ancestors, its spiritual consequences are more grave. This equally applies with regard to rape or acts of incest. Whereas rape violates the feminine spirit of consent and tears apart the harmonious communion that should exist in sexual relations between the sexes intended by the ancestors, incest, whether consensual or not, is a form of "rape" of an even more serious order, because it radically tears apart the communion of the family by flouting a taboo.

Similarly, assault on an elder constitutes a crime against piety. To raise one's hand against an older person is not only to act against the individual concerned but against his or her whole age group. Ultimately, it is an aggression against the land, since the elders are the representatives of the land. It becomes extremely grave if the person assaulted is one's mother, a practically inexcusable act that often calls for immediate excommunication from society, the moral equivalent of capital punishment. To abuse your mother physically or verbally means, once again, to dishonor yourself, all your age mates, and their mothers and fathers who *are* equally *your* mothers and fathers. Less severe forms of punishment for these offenses may include social ostracism and non-cooperation with the perpetrator, inability for him to get a marriage partner in the village or even elsewhere if his story becomes known, verbal reprimand from the elders or physical punishment from age mates, or a fine involving reparation in kind. Depending on the gravity of the offence, the punishment may be spontaneous or it may be decided on in a tribunal or palaver.

African piety is based on the conviction that human beings are "stitched into the natural world so closely as to share in the actual 'livingness' of animals, trees, rocks, and rivers" (Thorpe 1991, 120). It is connected with and bears ramifications for all reality, which, in turn, dictates the rules of piety. This follows from the fact that for the people, "everything that surrounds them exhibits a sort of transparency that allows them to communicate directly with heaven. Things and beings are not obstacles to the knowledge of God; rather they constitute signifiers and indices that reveal the divine being" (Zahan 2000, 5). Everything is connected to humanity and deserves respect. Thus, piety is like "talking to the wind" or "bathing in the sun," in the sense that as the wind and sunlight surround human beings, they are totally dependent on God, the ancestral spirits, and all other vital powers for their existence.

Certain conceptions and understandings arise from this awareness of human reliance on spiritual power, which leads to attitudinal requirements from human beings toward spiritual power. One important understanding is that because it is ever-present, spiritual power cannot be permanently flouted; it always asserts its authority on life. As no one can defy the wind and the sun and remain whole, any attempt to do without the vital forces demonstrates human folly and wickedness, and invariably boomerangs unfavorably on humanity. Surrender to the discretion of the powers of life, or swimming with their current, is the only wise path that provides insight into the mystery of the good life. If one would live well, one must be pious; that is, one must acknowledge and pay obeisance to the powers of life. In this matter, the personal piety of each member of the community translates into and augments social piety to assure communal happiness. Piety in this sense is compliance with the innermost pull to goodness that is the essence of *Ubuntu*. As I mentioned, it is most intensively expressed in acts of worship or cult.

Organized piety as public worship or cult represents in the most visible form some of the significant aspects of quotidian spirituality. Cultic worship enacts those moments in life when the community senses that it needs special bonding with and therefore special assistance from the spiritual powers. As is the case also among other indigenous peoples (Native Americans, for instance), "Human and other-than-human mutuality . . . [is] understood as both the social and cosmic ideal, and the goal of ritual action" (Morrison 2000, 36). In public prayer, as Mbiti asserts, "people are addressing themselves to the invisible world" (Mbiti 1975b, 56) to strengthen ties between the spirits, the living, the living-dead, the yet-to-be-born, and the cosmos. "Communal prayers . . . help to cement together the members of the group in one intention, for one purpose, and in one act of worship" (Mbiti 1975b, 57). Cult is thus a deepening of everyday piety and not a disconnection from it. Its goal is to confirm existing harmony in thanksgiving or to remedy transgression in petitionary prayer in the sincerest manner human beings can muster.

The word and the power it bears play an important role in the integration or breakup of relationships in African societies, but in every utterance, and especially in prayer, the emphasis is placed not on the words as such but on the *unity* or *union* words bring about between the ritual word-action and the intended result. Prayer "is the soul of the act that it accompanies" (Zahan 2000, 20). What is more fundamental in prayer is, therefore, what the words are meant to produce; again, the connection between the words and the goal (Hamminga 2005, 92-93). Are the words used in this particular prayer ritual able to depict the aim well enough so that the two are, as it were, fused into one? A community requires a good prayer leader to achieve this.

The African accords "eminent value . . . to the efficacy of his word accompanied by gestures directed toward the Invisible" (Zahan 2000, 20). If then, for example, prayers are said for rain, or fertility, or victory in battle, the words must be formulated in such a way as to be capable of bringing the answers to those needs into effect. Similarly for prayers said to end negative, anti-life situations such as illness, conflict, injustice, and more (Mbiti 1970, 194-212, 235-43; 1975a, 27-163; Shorter 1975, 29-143). The words are understood and believed to be efficacious and are chosen for that purpose. A Luhya (Kenya) prayer addressed to God (*Wele*) to ward off the spirit of illness asks him to "drive away black god" from the sick person and from all the surroundings, because God, who is all powerful and cares for his people, can do so (Shorter 1975, 84).

This, therefore, is the deeper intentionality at work in every prayer. Because words by themselves tend to reduce reality to finite human imagination, ritual prayer struggles to insert words into the reality or goal prayed for so that the two become one thing without distinction between them. In the Luhya prayer above, the words are part of the healing, and so the healing must be reflected in the words. Only in this way can the words of prayer become efficacious. Actually, it is more accurate to say that the intention of the prayer is that the healing (the goal) should "prevail" over the word so that it "swallows up" the word, making it redundant. The healing is the divine spiritual action overpowering the human word and making it effective. In being conquered, the word accomplishes what it asks for from the abundance and generosity of the more powerful invisible world.

Apart from certain brief responses by the assembled community designed to confirm the word of the prayer leader, there are generally no standardized forms of prayer in African rituals. But there is certainly a "style and structure" or modality to African prayer (Shorter 1975, 8-13, 19-21; Mbiti 1975a, 1, 21-22; Ephirim-Donkor 2011, 137). "Structurally," according to the analysis of Ephirim-Donkor, "a prayer first acknowledges God as sovereign and creator of everything, and then earth, major deities of the land, departed kings and ancestors, elders, and finally the reason for an invocation" (Ephirim-Donkor 2011, 137). It is part of every prayer to implore the invisible powers to be present at the worship service and to bless the elders and give protection and happiness to the community. The specific reason for the assembly is always mentioned, and in some form the whole assembly must testify to it as a real need. The prayer always ends with an attitude of trust that what is requested will be granted (Ephirim-Donkor 2011, 137).

Nevertheless, the prayer structure in African worship does not necessarily determine the language of the prayer itself. What does is the "occasion" and "purpose" of the assembly (Shorter 1975, 14-19), the circumstances necessitating the prayer gathering. The words of the prayer and the gestures are formulated spontaneously to capture the occasion and to be transformed by it into the reality desired. The words and gestures are evidence of the breath or vitality, and the reason they are uttered in prayer is to communicate or coalesce with the need for more life. Three points must therefore be kept in mind concerning prayer. First, prayer is necessarily "a growth in awareness, involving increasing commitment and even risk," because it involves openness to a different level of mystical power, which, if not properly handled, can be dangerous. Second, prayer is "a dimension of life that transcends and interprets every social relationship and social experience" because it is based on the deepest relationship of all, one with God himself. Third, prayer is "a continuous mode of living, a living communion, by no means limited to occasions of formal utterance or formal communication," because it arises out of and feeds into perpetual piety (Shorter 1975, 3-4).

The fundamental characteristic of prayer is the recognition of the power of the supernatural "perceived in experience" and confidence on the part of the worshipper that a beneficial conversation is taking place between them: the worshipper presents the need he or she has, convinced that there is compassion and empathy in the listener. "It is the certainty that the power is listening to the worshipper's story as it unfolds that encourages him to speak and to develop in a way he could not do outside this experience," on the one hand. On the other, "the one who listens has an effect upon the worshipper . . . through listening. . . . Yet, at the same time, the worshipper is also listening, becoming conscious of the change that is being worked in him" (Shorter 1975, 4).

Change that is being worked in the worshipper involves deeper purity of life, even though this is itself also a condition for acceptable prayer. Purity of heart or deep piety creates a communion of vital powers. It is life orientation that integrates a whole range of attitudes: "humility," "trust," "tranquility," and so on (Mbiti 1975a, 22-26), As much as possible, every prayer leader must possess and exhibit them in his life. At prayer, he or she must, in turn, choose his or her words carefully. The fusion between word and effect, and intention and reality, greatly depends on the disposition of the praying community as represented by the prayer leader and his or her ritual words.

Communal worship takes place in or at a sanctuary of one kind or another, a shrine, grove, hill, boulder, or tree that is set apart from ordinary use. Sitting arrangements there are usually quite well defined, indicating the hierarchy of life forces. The position of the sacrificial animal or offering is also clearly determined by tradition. African places of worship have been characterized as "channels of communication" (Ray 2000, 26-37); on account of their size or other peculiarities, they symbolize and enable intercourse among the vital powers, especially between humanity and the invisible world.

> The altar gives something to man, and a part of what he has received he passes on to others. . . . A small part of the sacrifice is for oneself, but the rest is for others. The forces released enter into the man, pass through him and out again, and so it is for all. . . . As each man gives all the rest, so he also receives from all. A perpetual exchange goes on between men, an unceasing movement of invisible currents. And this must be so if the universal order is to endure. The Word is for everyone

in this world; it must come and go and be interchanged, for it is good to give and to receive the forces of life. (Griaule 1965, 137)

We might understand the significance of African sanctuaries as places of concentration and diffusion of spiritual power in a very complex way. First, as just mentioned, the sanctuary itself symbolizes intensity of power by its nature, location, shape, or reputation. The hill or the forest or the clearing in the bush where prayers and sacrifices are made is usually seen as the dwelling place of the gods. This is common throughout the continent; shrines like these are to be found in practically every village of any consequence. In prayer at the shrine, holistic healing among humans and between them and the cosmos is brought about. It means "solidarity with creation as a whole . . . [including] people, animals, trees and herbs since all share the same cosmic origin, ultimately rooted in God" (Bujo 2009b, 284).

One of the best-known shrines in African literature, made famous by Jomo Kenyatta in his book *Facing Mount Kenya* (1953), concerns Mount Kenya or Kere-Nyaga, the "mountain of brightness" for the Kikuyu (also Gikuyu) people. Mount Kenya "is believed by the Gikuyu people to be Ngai's [God's] official resting-place," writes Kenyatta, "and in their prayers they turn towards Kere-Nyaga and, with their hands raised towards it, they offer their sacrifices, taking the mountain to be the holy earthly dwelling-place of Ngai" (Kenyatta 1978, 234). A similar example is the Muhabura volcano in Rwanda, on top of which the great spirits of the people live. "Certain women become the wives of the volcano and are in charge of a permanent cult based upon these fire shrines emanating from the bowels of the earth" (Zahan 2000, 19).

Second, the community brings with it to the sanctuary extraordinary moral power not experienced on a daily basis. The purity required of the community in every sense of the word before approaching the sanctuary anticipates and creates communion. The intention (the prayer at the shrine) and reality (the result) greatly depend on the disposition of the assembled community. It is no wonder that "The religious attributes of the agent of a cult are handed down in order of priority to the oldest member of the group who is, because of his age, at the limit of this world and of the world of the dead. He is considered, therefore, to be in a good position to assure relations with the invisible" (Zahan 2000, 20).

Finally, it is at the sanctuary where the concentration of vital power is dispersed back to the community for the sake of greater healing and health. The prayer at the shrine is a sacrament of universal reconciliation that indicates health, the first and most important quality of the community, in the absence of which there cannot be personal well-being. No one can enjoy tranquility, happiness, and, consequently, good health where there is ill will, jealousy, excessive competition, pride, anger, lust for power, or material wealth. Witch-craft, which in African spirituality is the embodiment of ill health, arises from these dispositions.

Diviners and herbalists, as well as various other professionals who are agents of personal healing, also draw nourishment from the dispersion of spirit power from the shrine. Since ritual at the shrine often reveals, in a macrocosmic outline, the causes of the disharmony in society, specialists use this map to chart out the path of healing to those who need it in society. In this way, the art of healing is seen not only in terms of the body, healing the individual body in a mechanistic way, but primarily and holistically in terms of healing the cosmos. The cosmos, the entire social and environmental body that constitutes life and health, is therefore perceived as a person. The experi-ence of personal disease and suffering is understood, as is the case with so many other things, in terms of "relatedness and interrelatedness between the individual and all those realities that constitute existence" (Murove 2009c, 168). Health and healing are not individual concerns; they are fundamen-tally communal in the broad sense of the term, which includes the surround-ing physical environment. And on account of the symbiotic relationship between the good life and the ancestors, they are fundamentally spiritual experiences. This forms part of the spirituality of aesthetics in African com-munities.

7

Performance and Aesthetics

"You don't listen to music seated."

Olaudah Equiano, an African slave captured from Igboland, Nigeria, published his autobiography in England in 1789. Titled *The Life of Olaudah Equiano, or Gustavus Vassa, the African,* Equiano described the Igbo people in the book as "almost a nation of dancers, musicians, and poets." Expanding on that notion, he wrote: "Thus every great event, such as a triumphant return from battle, or other cause of public rejoicing is celebrated in public dances, which are accompanied with song and music suited to the occasion" (Equiano 1999, 12). Equiano's observation is an accurate perception of African life and how it should be lived as a celebration.

Life is not a "spectator sport" or something to be experienced by proxy. What is expected for one to grow into *Ubuntu* in Africa and become fully human is to participate in the dance of life, one's own dance within that of the community. One executes one's dance steps of life by personal involvement, and one is assessed on the basis of performance. The dance of life includes everything that is connected with nurturing life in the world, that is, social institutions, economics and politics, cookery, painting, sculpture, architecture, the art of speech, music, gestures, and sense of beauty among others. All of these are dynamic activities, and depending on the extent to which they affect human life and signify the presence of the spiritual energies in the world, they are communication systems between human beings and spiritual powers. They may be rightly referred to as symbols or "sacraments," concrete manifestations of spiritual presence in the world.

Because participation is action, the conception of "dancing life" in Africa may be described in terms of "performance," an artistic feat toward the discovery of beauty, which involves the process of both learning and producing meaning and constructing cultural norms and social identities. It includes the entire mental route of perception, understanding, and appropriation of values. Aesthetics, as the term should be applied in the African context,

69

concerns the ongoing attempt by a people to structure the ordinariness of its experiential reality by calling forth into the present moment the memory of all that is good and noble (or, as sometimes necessarily happens, the dreadful and unwanted), and making it conspicuous and tangible so that humans can relate to it appropriately. In other words, aesthetics in its deepest sense in Africa is the result of perceiving and constructing meaning-toward-life, the activity of recognizing and confirming the necessities of desirable human existence. It refers to "the expression of creativity, autonomy, agency and relationships in objects that people make, wear, display, inhabit, exchange, view, and . . . venerate or honour" (Harvey 2000b, 158).

Among African peoples, aesthetics is based on the idea of health, which to the African is the most "beautiful" thing imaginable. Aesthetics is, ultimately, a question of life-building dispositions, so that, as among the Yoruba people of Nigeria, "someone who *embodies* command, coolness, and character is someone extremely beautiful and like unto a god" (Hallen 2006, 242). As such, aesthetics forms an essential aspect of being human and living as a human being, *Umuntu.* The endeavor makes not only the past but the future present, thus integrating faith in what has been and hope in what will be into the experience of living in the here and now. The social, religious, and aesthetic levels are unified when one approaches life, as Africans do, from the point of view of construction of meaning and perception of values.

It is argued that performance in this sense characterizes spiritual systems that see the sacred in the immanent and the immanent in the sacred. Scholars have distinguished between religions or spiritual systems of "salvation" and those of "structure." Evan Zuesse, for example, argues that spiritual systems of salvation "have a low estimation of all that is relative, due to their longing [for] what is absolute, immutable, finally real." Spiritual systems of structure, however, in which he places the spirituality of African religion, are in a different category; they find "fulfillment . . . in the norms and eternal relationships which structure all process and change in this world." While the spiritual orientation of salvation "revels in abnormal, anomalous and extreme states because they betoken the exceptional breakthrough into unworldly eternity," Zuesse explains further, the spirituality of structure "rejoices in the sanctification of everyday life, and finds eternity in the midst of change" (Zuesse 1979, 7). The ultimate desire for the latter is not abnormality and unworldly immutability, but rather the ordinariness, orderliness, or harmony of life here and now. When the abnormal is desired and happens, it is for the ultimate purpose of serving normality, the good life as the community conceives it.

Therefore, when people live together in peace as families and communities, when there is no hostility between ethnic groups, when there is no drought or flood, there is cause for celebration because this is how life is expected to be. At times like these, life is marked by attitudes of thanksgiving to the spiritual powers. Only when strife reigns and there is lack of life's essential necessities does the outlook become one of sadness and sorrowful repentance. Still, trust that things will be righted dominates even at these times, and because of this the spirit of hopeful anticipation is not completely absent when ritual prayer is called for in order to return the structure of life to its state of normalcy; people may still dance as a sign that life has not been totally obliterated and that it will finally triumph.

The dynamics of aesthetic performance involves integrating the past and the future into the present, and in the process producing knowledge in terms of perceptible symbols or symbolic actions that speak about the good life. These symbols and actions become, in turn, part of aesthetic performance. To this end, significant aesthetic performances are usually public affairs requiring as much social participation as possible. By its very nature, then, aesthetics is intended to serve community as an endless pilgrimage into the possibility or horizon of life's meaning, ideally "to fit one's own personal rhythm seamlessly into the flow of the whole" (see Taiwo 2000, 173). The view of the individual toward society and the world at large and how to act in these two interconnected realms must continually be shaped by this pilgrimage and must constantly be impressed on the minds and hearts of people by various rites, and thereby be simultaneously confirmed and improved. Aesthetics is a form of ongoing initiation; it incorporates and constitutes all forms of initiation.

The process begins with conception, continues with marriage and the implied desire and intention of conception and childbearing, and is intensified at all stages of the life process: at naming, young adulthood, and induction into elderhood. For the individual, it is completed at his or her death and mourning rituals. In these events the life-energy of the spirit world is transferred to the initiates at every stage. Conception and birth show that the spiritual relationships sustaining universal harmony among all beings are in order. Birth is, consequently, a spiritual event of the utmost significance and is surrounded by celebratory acts of thanksgiving whose purpose is to strengthen the communion among all members of the family and clan.

Elements of decorum in the process of initiation demonstrate aesthetic values. Take, for example, the strict prohibition of physical or intimate social contact between a son-in-law and mother-in-law or daughter-in-law and father-in-law. The intention of this requirement is to preserve the moral structure of the community by preempting any risk of incest, something that would endanger the configuration of the entire clan by confusing the order of relationships and, therefore, the representation (and performance) of the hierarchy of vital powers. The requirement stipulates that if contact should take place in any way, even accidentally, a cleansing ritual must be performed, a form of aesthetic performance.

Intergender or sexual performance plays a central role in African aesthetic values because it constitutes the fundamental energy that makes the life-giving relationships in the universe possible. In the experience of the African community, nothing unites one person to another, to the ancestral and divine spirits, and to the universe as a whole as much as the conjugal bond; this is where the energy that activates life in the form of conception and birth is most present. Understandably, celibacy is almost always disapproved of, even abhorred. "The single person is disobedient to the ancestors, even to God, since he or she destroys the stream of life" (Sundermeier 1998, 187). Permanent homosexuality, infertility, and sterility are, from this perspective, equally abhorrent as spiritual failings because "they plunge the person concerned into misery, they sever him from personal immortality, and threaten the perpetuation of the lineage" (Kisembo et al. 1977, 105). Any degree of physical attractiveness notwithstanding, a barren woman generally possesses no beauty where it counts most; similarly, regardless of any other physical attribute, a man without children is "worthless," of no use to himself or the community (Fortes 1987, 193-94). In very few and carefully acknowledged cases, however, celibacy is allowable, and impotence or barrenness are qualities for prophets/prophetesses and diviners for the sake of the "greater" fecundity of the community. This may be understood as "spiritual fecundity."

On account of the power of marriage to produce and continue human life, it is a reality to be reverently celebrated. Courtship, the art of preparation for marriage, is "no mere recitation of love songs"; beyond sentiments between two individuals, it involves courting people "in the background," people yet unseen and unknown but who will certainly be needed later in the course of the marriage (Maillu 1988, 164). If the marriage is polygamous, the second wife soon realizes that "she married not only the first wife, but the children of the first marriage, the man's relatives, and also the relatives of the first wife!" A woman "marries an institution, not a single person. . . . As the proverb goes, he who buys a cow buys its cow dung too" (Maillu, 1988, 164). In fact, the more extensive the connections become, the greater the abundance of spiritual energies.

In a similar way, the husband bears responsibilities not limited to his wife and their children alone, but to the whole of his wife's clan. This is already made clear during the courtship period and bride-wealth transactions, where both the living members and ancestors of the lineage are implicated in the process. Beyond the human community and that of the living dead, the physical environment is included; the local fields where food is grown, the woods where game is found and vegetables and firewood gathered, and the rivers and lakes where water is drawn and fish are caught constitute elements of the marriage union, because they are filled with ancestral spirits who act as referents and guides in the new relationship. Wherever the marital residence happens to be set up, whether patrilocal or matrilocal, the bride or groom must be in touch with the new surroundings. It takes time and care for the newly married, often accompanied by several rituals, to be inducted into the new environment so as behave properly and avoid the risk of dishonoring the local spiritual forces.

This can be quite an educational process, perhaps lasting a lifetime, given the number of spiritual forces an individual can potentially have to deal with in a new place. Among the Igbo of Nigeria, as we have seen, Kitikpa is the deity of smallpox. When this and other diseases strike, it is important to know how to appease the spirit. But there are many other spiritual forces, pertinent to each and every activity. Among the Yoruba, also in Nigeria, the same deity is known as Sonpono. There is also in Yorubaland the spirit or deity of iron, who protects hunters (Ogun); of farming (Orisha-Oko); and of thunder (Shango). These are important activities that closely impinge on human life, so the forces behind them cannot be ignored. In short, it is important to be familiar with them and their local aesthetic representations so as to develop the devotional emotions proper to each.

The nature of aesthetic performance embedded in African spirituality can also be seen in the powerful intercessory role of the mother. The mother is universally recognized as mediator, even if often inconspicuously. Peace and tranquility in the family depends largely upon her skill in handling the members of her family. Tacitly, she is accredited with the know-how and know-why in family management and gets silent credit for it. Women play the role of conciliators in the wider community as well, and failure to heed their advice often brings unfavorable consequences. Women as mothers intercede constantly for the fertility of the clan so that it may avoid the curse of childlessness.

Reverence for Mother Earth is identified with the mystical power of the woman in her ability to bear and nurture life. Consequently, many significant taboos surround the woman in association with the rhythm of the natural seasons. The woman is regarded with awe as the symbol of divine life itself. As we have mentioned previously, ideally the mother is untouchable for that reason. Her displeasure can be seen as the displeasure of the land, and so it is feared. Just as a mother's curse is dangerously effective, her favor is courted. To honor one's mother is to honor the life of the community and the land, and consequently to please the ancestors.

Queen Mothers (or queen sisters) played a central role in the governance of many African societies. In the Ashanti Kingdom in Ghana, West Africa, she was known as *Nana Ohenmaa*; in the Buganda Kingdom in Uganda, East Africa, as *Nnamasole* (and the queen sister as *Lubuga*); in the Swazi Kingdom in Swaziland, southern Africa, as *Ndlovukati;* and among the Yoruba people of Nigeria, West Africa, as *Iya Oba.* (Among the latter, the *Iya Oba* did not even have to be related to the king by blood or advanced in age. Her power was invested ritually.) In all these cases, the Queen Mother wielded considerable political influence, and often nothing of profound significance to the community happened without her knowledge and approval.

The ultimate goal of performance as aesthetics is to distinguish right from wrong and thereby manifest right directions for the community to follow or avoid for the purpose of obtaining the good life founded on the memory of the tradition of the ancestors. Aesthetic imagination therefore implies maintaining "the continuity of life and human relationships beyond death, the unbroken bond of obligations and the seamless web of community" (Kalu 2000, 55). Consciousness of this link acts as a powerful vehicle of regulating behavior and social conduct by "affirm[ing] the values upon which society is based," as Kofi Asare Opoku argues (see Opoku 1993, 75). "The constant reminder of the good deeds of the ancestors acts as a spur to good conduct on the part of the living; and the belief that the dead can punish those who violate traditionally sanctioned mores acts as a deterrent" (Kalu 2000, 55). The consequence of pollution by violating ancestral tradition has a ripple effect beyond the transgressor.

There are various peak moments of aesthetic performance in African spirituality. Among them are spirit possession, song and dance, and art.

Occasionally, for various reasons, a spirit may "enter into" a human being and transform or "take over" the individual and act visibly through him or her (Larsen 2008). The usual indigenous terms for this are more accurately rendered as "to be visited" by a spirit (Perman 2011). The individual in question then becomes controlled by or turns into the "property" of the spirit for as long as the spirit may wish to stay. This may be for a short or long duration or even, in cases of possession indicating a call to certain vocations, such as some forms of divination, healing, or petitions for rain, it may last for a lifetime. During this period, the possessed individual acts at the whim of the possessing spirit, often in an altered state of consciousness in the form of trance or ecstasy, or simply through abnormal behavior, something readily recognized by onlookers (Lovell 2002, 80-82). Possession allows the spirits "to express their wishes" through the individual they inhabit "and to receive, in exchange, a direct act of devotion" (Lovell 2002, 80). As a rule, "a certain receptivity is needed on the human side that is expressed through having an open mind" to receive the possessing spirit (Plancke 2011, 389).

Broadly speaking, spirit possession can be benevolent or malevolent, depending on whether the possessing spirit fulfills positive or negative expectations. In possession, the presence of the spirit is always something to be reckoned with whether it is desired and sought after or, conversely, feared and resisted. The point to note in all cases of possession is that although the devotion the spirit seeks is manifested by the individual, the lessons imparted are intended for a larger audience of the family or community. The public dimension of possession for divination is usually easy to know, but in familial situations the message may be subtle. Why does a woman or a girl sulk and show signs of spirit possession? In the first case it may be on account of domestic violence; in the second, because the girl is prevented from marrying the man she loves. These possible causes for possession must be investigated. Once ascertained, the pedagogical value for the larger society to reform unjust systems is recognized. Because it is not possible to integrate immediately or completely the "new" values in gender relations into the regular social lifestyle, possession of this nature is recurrent.

"Through spirit possession the new and the unusual breaks into a society" (Sundermeier 1998, 142), but since new things can be threatening, ways must be found to "domesticate" them in order that they can be handled without upsetting excessively the normal rhythm of life. For this purpose, it is important that the possessing spirit power be manifested as much as possible so that its intentions are known; only then can they be internalized by the community. "Possession activates people to accept something new. They enter into dialogue with it. The phenomenon is personalized, becomes negotiable and assumes a social form" (Sundermeier 1998, 142). Jan G. Platvoet gives an illustration of this among the Akan of Ghana, where "the gods in nature must be 'tamed'" and turned into "house gods" by giving them forms that make them visible and "part of human society . . . easily addressable and even consumable. . . . Only as part of the networks that constitute society are the gods manageable and trustworthy, to a degree" (Platvoet 2000, 92).

Accordingly, among the Akan, a god is identified with a medium-priest (in Akan, *okomfo*) for purposes of meeting with people; a shrine (*yawa*) and shrine room (*bosomdan*) or temple (*bosombuw*) for receiving prayers or gifts of libations, food, or sacrifices; and also its means of divination (*nsuo Yaa*) and "medicines" (*nnuru*) (Platvoet 2000, 92). Among the Kel Ewey Tuareg of northeastern Niger, rituals of domestication of the spirits that surround spirit possession also serve this purpose. Since spirit possession "illuminates the inherently contrary and conflictual aspects of experience and action," its implications must be interpreted to be useful to society. This happens partly through the ritual activity itself, through the "interaction among patients, musicians, and audience, and the reactions to the dance motions of trance and its accompanying music." But the "multiple meanings the event has for participants and non-participants" in new contexts are made clear also by the commentaries that accompany the ritual acts (Rasmussen 1995, 109).

Witchcraft, as the ultimate expressions of possession by evil spirits (or, more precisely, spirits of evil), is approached in the same way. As a witch, a person is so possessed by the power of evil that, in fact, he or she becomes the human incarnation of evil and so causes evil despite him or herself. The Zulu people of South Africa see the sole goal of the witch as "the destruction of what is good, especially those processes that create and enhance life" (Lawson 1985, 23), and as such it is the ultimate sin against the ancestors:"The *abathakari* (witch) is the specialist in evil, the one who twists the system with its centers of power for destructive purposes" (Lawson 1985, 23; see also Awolalu 1979, 84-86). The witch is the "astral cannibal who feeds on the life force of the living. . . . Whereas people eat animals and seek companionship from their own kind, witches eat people and prefer the companionship of a familiar," becoming shape-shifters (Isichei 2004, 309). No ingenuity or energy in Africa is spared in trying to combat witchcraft.

Many rituals revolve around the effort to fight against witchcraft; most persons in the social hierarchy responsible for the welfare of life at any level are actors in this struggle. They use either the energy of benevolent spiritual powers from the invisible realm or the energy inherent in plants and animals that is revealed to them from generation to generation. But there is neither ritual nor medicine that can remove the power of witchcraft from an individual; the only and final act necessary is to eliminate the witch from society. This perception appears cruel; cannot the witch as a person or witchcraft as a condition change? Yet underlying it is the understanding that hardcore evil cannot successfully be negotiated with. Fortunately, however, even in the negative situation of witchcraft, the powers of life are interwoven. Through the power of the "word" (incantation, song, and dance), witchcraft can be known with relative certainty: "Festivals, feasts, dances, artistic expression, and the recitation of myths celebrate the communal existence and at the same time strengthen the community against evil influences" (Booth 1977b, 8). Seasons of the year and gatherings of any significance to the community (new moon, harvest, initiation, funerals, conciliation, whether joyful or sad occasions) take place with some form of singing and dancing that "not only affirms wholeness and healing; it contributes to them" (Booth 1977b, 8).

The word in any of its forms is the most potent vehicle of communication; it becomes even more evocative of communion when it is combined with bodily movement in song and dance, which is not merely a form of entertainment but a healing performance (Gore 2007, 134; Merriam 1977, 247), expressing the will for endurance and survival. This is common all over the continent, but can be exemplified by the activity of the Punu people of Congo-Brazzaville. Among the Punu, dance, especially the trance-dance of possession, is evocative of life in its source, a symbol of birth and vitality. The dance that induces possession "opens one to energetic, vital resources beyond the individual level. In trance the possessed . . . is in immediate contact with the source of life embodied by the *bayisi* [water spirits]." Thus among the Punu, certain "dance celebrations, by stimulating possession trances . . . aim at realizing the maternal regenerative capacity in its cosmic dimension. . . . Hence trance dancing . . . can clearly be interpreted as a manifestation of a woman's maternal receptive power" (Plancke 2011, 383).

Singing and dancing transform the personality; the singer or dancer becomes "something more" than him- or herself (Booth 1977c, 56-57). Significantly and tellingly, many songs and dances mimic animal, occupational, symbolic, or mechanical movements and sounds, combining the spiritual, verbal, and visual in one performance so that, in a sense, the performer becomes the expression of the energy of the object that he or she impersonates (Sundermeier 1998, 141-42).

Music and dance are associated with and dictated by the occasion. If we take the Tuareg again as an example, "the role of music and song in possession suggests . . . creative ability . . . to comment on the human condition in ways consistent with socially structured beliefs about personal identity" (Rasmussen 1995, 154). As such, as Alan P. Merriam observes, "African songs often have no titles at all" (Merriam 1977, 247). There are social songs for the various periods of the rites of passage, for example, or songs to point out errant ways in society, or political songs to praise or mock a leader. "The connections between religion and music are especially strong, for songs and instrumental forms are used to celebrate . . . [human] relationship to the cosmos and its beings" (Merriam 1977, 247).

In the stratified social-spiritual systems of African societies, talent in using the word in this way, or through oratory ("some songs are shouted, spoken, or whispered" [Merriam 1977, 257]), is revered for the goal it achieves, the unification of life. It is little wonder that this performance not only leads to possession, but it can also identify a situation of possession and help to remove it. The identity of spirits can be discovered through singing and dancing. Some undesirable spirits can also be cast away only through ritual dancing. The spirits of the dead are sent on "home" (or in case of bad deaths, sent away) through the word in the form of wailing and singing of dirges, appealing to the power of the ancestors to settle them where they belong (Gill 1982, 54-57; Obiego 1984, 172-94).

Death is one of the most intense experiences of integration, first of all as a profound incentive toward *anamnesis* as the deceased passes freshly from the world of the living to the ancestral world. "The occasion of death is one on which the remembrance and communication with the ancestors is particularly appropriate and immanently possible," writes Gill "for upon death the dead connect the world of the living to the world of the ancestral spirits in the funeral rite of passage." It is the responsibility of the living to introduce the deceased into this new state by proper rites (of passage), for "not only may the ancestors be remembered and honored, but also the one newly dead who is to become an ancestor must be associated with them. This function gives structure to the dirge" (Gill 1982, 56). The dirge is in actual fact a three-way conversation, between the living, the newly deceased, and the ancestors, with the mourners as the visible actors. But the deceased and the ancestors are very much present in the situation and are often addressed by name and asked to grant the petitions in the dirges or to accept praise expressed there.

The spiritual imagination that leads many African communities to create dirges as aesthetic expression is the same genius that leads African sculptors and painters to execute their works of art. The unification of all creation in the spiritual realm is at the center of African art, even understood in this narrow sense. Elias K. Bongmba is probably right when he argues that it may be overemphasizing the point to assert, as Chukwulozie K. Anyanwu does, that "what is significant about African art is not style but the meaning and the religious ideas that have influenced the production of art" (Bongmba 2009, 188). Still, we must not lose the point that Anyanwu and similar other observers remind us of, that the religious/spiritual and emotional *meaning* takes precedence over mere abstract *beauty* or the visual appearance of the object of art, both for the artist and the African patron. Seldom is art in Africa "for art's sake" (Sieber 1977b, 221). The reluctance to claim ownership of works of art in Africa is significant in this respect; it shows that as a spiritual article, a work of art in sculpture, mask, or painting is public property.

The performative dimension of African art indicates primarily that it is created "for more than decorative purposes—to serve instrumental ends—to worship, to perpetuate the memory of an ancestor, to serve as one component of a masquerade" (Hallen 2006, 237-38), to protect the user or the community from harm, to promote fertility, as a sign of authority and governance, and so on. "Masks may honor the dead, implore rain, cleanse the village of disease or witchcraft, or celebrate a deity. Other carvings may depict ancestors or symbolize nature spirits, aid a diviner or protect a shrine or household from evil forces" (Sieber 1977b, 238-39). Arts touch upon all aspects of life, from infancy through initiation (where masks were especially useful as pedagogical instruments), to symbols of secret societies, to old age and death. They also concern all activities, from sex to farming to eating. Throughout the wide "range and variations" of functions of art, "ultimately each seeks in a specific fashion to make more secure the way of life of its users," as Roy Sieber notes. Thus, "art becomes more than the symbol of a better life, it serves as an active agent in the attainment of that goal" (Sieber 1977b, 240).

According to Olu Taiwo, it is accurate to see "artistic expression [in Africa] as utility, which as a process, falls under 'design' rather than 'Art for Art's sake'" (Taiwo 2000, 179).

> In design there is always a tension between form and function. What is produced is a result of this tension. The design process is closely linked to, and encoded by the prevailing culture and its tacit or silent knowledge. The stratagems adopted in these design processes emerge from this tacit, presumed knowledge. These design processes are then maintained by and interpreted by each generation. This is the wisdom of our ancestors, which motivates our elders to encourage the present generation to embody the design processes within culture, our ancestral inheritance, and reinterpret these tendencies in the world of the living. So it is not the mask as object divorced from anything that has major significance, but the mask as subject connected to a ritual life that has social value. (Taiwo 2000, 179-80)

Ultimately, the goal gives the piece of art aesthetic character; a particular mask transforms the one who dons it into a particular spirit. As such, once again, as Barry Hallen argues, African art is "utilitarian," and is intended as a means of human communication with the vital forces of the invisible world for the purpose of securing life (Sieber 1977a, 141-57). It is only when African sculptures, masks, figurines, and paintings are removed from this "African background and context and hung on a museum or gallery wall that an attempt is being made to transform them into exclusively artistic works for Western(ized) eyes" (Hallen 2006, 238).

What has also been westernized is African indigenous architecture, which now (particularly in towns and cities) is used in the construction of places of recreation for tourist purposes. Even in villages, "box-style" housing is quickly replacing indigenous round, cone-shaped structures, known by different names in different places of the continent. But the African "rondavel," both in terms of individual structure or compound, it has been suggested, was not without deep spiritual significance. In the opinion of some, it implied the human embrace for the community of persons and existence as a whole, a notion deeply seated in the African psyche.

The fixed plan of the compound, with exact locations for the house of the head of the family and for each of his wives, sons, and so on, suggests as well that there was a spiritual meaning to the layout, implying both the hierarchy of vital force and the oneness of the family. Among the Dogon people of the West African state of Mali, for example, every aspect of the house has spiritual symbolism. The floor and roof symbolize earth and the heavens, respectively. The entrance represents the man as the head of the home, and the central part of the house represents the woman, with food stores at both sides as her arms and hearth as her head. The posts represent the intimate union between man and woman. "So the family house represents the unity of man and woman and God and the Earth," completing the unity of all existence (Parrinder 1967, 69). The building materials are, of course, dictated by what is available, but whatever is used for this purpose also in turn calls for respect and responsible custody. The stones, soil, cow dung, tree limbs, and grass used for building must not be needlessly wasted.

All of this careful arrangement in physical aesthetics cannot, as is obvious in the Dogon example of residential construction, be separated from spiritual aesthetics. For the African spiritual imagination, the "symphony" of life is one integrated whole; with its foundation in the invisible universe, the orchestra is organized and perceptibly performed in the visible, with the propriety of the arrangement taken into consideration. But the music is heard in both universes, and in different rhythms; it is danced in both. For the very possibility of existence, it *must* be danced harmoniously in both and with both. Much of the responsibility in the dance of life and existence, for good or ill, falls on humanity either as individual persons or communities. No one listens to the symphony of the music of life seated.

8

Death: Final Exit
or Deeper Reunion?

"The dead are not dead."

Although it is obvious that in every living creature there is a strong, instinctive dread of and flight from death, human beings must confront it consciously as they travel through life. It is not absolute, but contemplation of death distinguishes humanity from the rest of sentient existence.

For humans, death is an intensely personal but also immensely communal and communitarian concern. Although everyone experiences death in the same way in terms of loss of mental and physical faculties, each individual must do so by him- or herself; thus the saying that "we are all in this together, alone." No one, either as an individual or as a community, can cast away the shadow of death. From time immemorial and to different degrees in different societies, the consciousness of death has informed and shaped the way humans live, love, eat, construct dwellings, pray, play, and generally behave. It has influenced their economic planning, political organization, and cultural outlook—their worldview and aesthetics. Some theorists have even surmised that death, or the fear of it, is the origin of religion and morality (Tylor 1958).

In the African experience, the reality of death functions to connect personal and social imagination with the invisible powers we have been discussing in the foregoing pages. If there is anything in human existence that evokes the necessity for relationship between human beings and the invisible world (God, the ancestors, and the spirits), emphasizes its central role within the human community itself (the living and the yet-to-be-born), and highlights human dependence on the land and the rest of creation (the material community), it is the awareness and experience of death. Death, therefore, constitutes a fundamental dimension of African spirituality, without which no discussion on the subject can be complete.

Death in Africa is perceived as mysterious and ambiguous. Though known as inevitable, its exact origins and reasons are at the same time unknown; though accepted, it is feared; though constituting the path to ancestorship, something that is desired and sought after, it is assiduously avoided because it is "dangerous." There is no African community where this ambiguity about death and dying is not experienced in one form or another (Kirwen 2005, 248-53; 2008, 223-35). In speech it is described as "natural," "a journey to the forefathers," a mere "rite of passage" into another stage of life, or something to be "celebrated" if the dead is an elder; but it is also spoken of as being "a very bad thing," "an evil," a "sorrowful" event, or something to be "cast away." The following response concerning the Luo (Kenya) perspective on death and dying illustrates the equivocation inherent in the experience. It is not particular to one African ethnic group but can be observed in practically all African ethnic groups in their attitude to death.

Among the Luo people, death "is viewed as a rite of passage from physical life to the ancestral world." Various linguistic images are used to explain this. Among them, people say that the dead person "has gone on a long journey to another country." In addition to rituals of purification of the entire homestead and "chasing away of evil spirits," there are rituals related to cleansing of persons at time of death: for example, a widow must be cleansed if she is to enter into another marital or sexual relationship. While a married man was accorded honor at burial, such as being smeared with oil, an unmarried man was covered with ash, symbolizing shame. An honorable death is the way that God provides for the living "more ancestors who become intermediaries between God and the living members of the lineage. Death, though not welcome, is [therefore] not a loss." The living, therefore, have reason to celebrate (Kirwen 2008, 230-31).

It is probably because of the mystery that death presents that African spirituality surrounds it with the most elaborate and extensive rituals that the people's imagination has been able to muster. This is so as to make the uncertain in death somewhat certain, the ambiguous a bit more clear, the feared to some extent acceptable, the impenetrable fairly graspable, and the evil somehow understandable. It may also be the reason why in many African communities mortuary rituals have stubbornly endured through the generations. Of all the rites of passage, rituals of death and dying have proved quite resilient to change or adaptation, both in terms of the beliefs and meanings they encapsulate and convey as well as in their practical forms of execution. Whereas, for instance, naming ceremonies and initiation rites have undergone some visible modifications under the influence of Christianity and other forms of westernization, the same cannot be said for death rituals.

For example, for many African Christians, indigenous naming rituals have not been abandoned, but they do take place before the Christian rite of baptism. But most people attend the Christian ritual of baptism gladly because it provides the opportunity to get a "Christian name," which means added vital force from the particular Christian saint. There appears to be nothing of the sort for African peoples with regard to burial rituals. In fact, since many of the indigenous rituals surrounding burial and mourning are proscribed in the mainline Christian churches, the Christian ritual is seen by African Christian communities as taking away fundamental dimensions from the meaning and implications of death. In my pastoral-ministerial experience (spanning forty years) as a Catholic priest, I have observed that African Christian faithful have consistently performed the indigenous funerary rituals after the "Christian" ones that I or my assistants have conducted. When, in one instance, a priest in a neighboring parish explicitly forbade their performance at the risk of excommunication from the parish fellowship, a good number of the older members of the parish voluntarily left to join another parish where this was not turned into an issue of faith. But even those who stayed continued to perform the rituals in question clandestinely.

The preceding example concerning the Luo people indicated that death, burial, and mourning rituals in Africa contain and express a double message, that the death of some is simultaneously a loss *and* a gain (if the dead person is perceived as an ancestor, "living-dead") or, tragically, for others, a *complete* loss (if one is not considered as an ancestor, thereby becoming "dead-dead"). All mortuary rituals are formed around, shaped, and controlled by either of these perceptions. The nature and significance of the rites and rituals change according to how the death of an individual and the perceived consequences of it for the life of the living are interpreted and understood. If a person is considered to be dead-dead, not much ritual is performed or, if it takes place, its purpose is to send the deceased's spirit far away from the family, the community, and the village. The ultimate aim in this case is to forget the individual as quickly and as completely as possible and to assure that the individual's spirit does not "hover around" to harm the community in any way. Curiously, there seems to be no rite of reconciling the spirits of the dead-dead to the community other than to cast them away.

The disposal of the remains of those who die "a bad death" is unceremonious for this reason; it shows the general repugnance toward death without a future. Suicide is an example. If an individual hangs him- or herself, a hole is dug underneath the corpse and the rope is cut to let the corpse drop into the hole, which is quickly filled. More significantly, the location of suicide is not marked, a sign of total disappearance of the individual concerned. Still, suicide is feared for its contaminating capacity and, therefore, should be avoided. So too is a childless death. The ambiguity here is that though suicide or death without offspring in a sense renders one completely dead, it still has the power to cause pollution for the living. Consequently, while social-religious consciousness considers suicides and the dead without children as being dead-dead, it still regards them as powerful evil forces. Their presence and influence, often quite palpable, are universally resented.

Some dead people, however, simply transform into benevolent vital energies. These are the ancestors, individuals who live a good life and die a good death. Because growth as a person is the point of living, what is generally expected is that as individuals advance in age toward the maturity of death, they become better persons ultimately as ancestors. Ancestors form the axis of African spiritual orientation. Human attention is concentrated on them as bringers of fulfillment in life, and elaborate rituals are performed at their death, befitting their rank, since ancestral status is generally already determined before death. Mortuary rituals for this category of people emphasize their continued existence in a different, nonphysical form and their continued concern for the living. Their presence is desired and welcomed, and their involvement at death rituals is taken for granted. Everyone's participation in the rituals as a form of communication and communion with them is expected. Two examples illustrate the seriousness of this perception and expectation.

After losing his father in 1986, a Roman Catholic priest from one of the staunchest Christian regions of Tanzania had to go through the rituals of purification and inheritance of his father's property and life as required by the ethnic group's indigenous customs. Unfortunately, he had to do this secretly, since his Catholic diocese officially frowns upon it. But Michael (not his real name) assured me that his was not an exceptional case in which diocesan policy was ignored. Only very few priests and religious in the diocese refused to perform the traditional funerary rituals for close relations, he said. As the oldest son in the family, it was necessary for him to "acquire" the vital force of his father through these rituals so as to transmit it to the family; to do otherwise would imply or actually spell the eventual death of the clan.

I come from a different ethnic group from Michael; our villages are separated by hundreds of miles. Yet I went through a similar experience when my own father passed away in 1989. I was eventually exempted from participating in the cleansing ritual symbolizing "sending away death" from the family and "welcoming new life" because I am a priest. But this was allowed only after a long and heated discussion among the elders of the clan. The ritual was simple; it involved having my hair completely shaved off and bathing with all the other male members of the family in the nearby lake early in the morning of the last day of the mourning period, the day of "distributing the clothes." (The female members also did so at the same time in a different location at the lake.)

The expectation of most of the elders was that I, though a Roman Catholic priest, should participate along with the others in the ritual because it was important for the life of the entire family, Catholic teaching notwithstanding. This was opposed by a few but vocal and influential Catholic elders, not in fundamental objection to the rite as such, but because they were concerned that it would cause "our son" (myself) and themselves trouble with the diocese if word went out that I had done so with their approval. However, the factor that finally contributed to my exemption was the consensus among the elders that because I had an older brother, his participation in the ritual sufficed to represent all of us and to protect the life of the family. Had I been the oldest surviving son, there would have been no choice except to participate in the ritual lest we displease the ancestors and endanger the life of the family and clan.

Burial and funeral rites and rituals are potent symbols for managing the sting of death socially and imparting spiritual hope. As is the case with other rites of passage throughout a person's life, mortuary rituals consist variously of sacrifices, offerings, and libations as tradition indicates in each case. Furthermore, there is always singing, dancing, all kinds of gesticulations, and jovial speech (Blakely and Blakely, 1994). The latter are forms of prayer and are intended to indicate and invoke continued good life for all concerned. Through these expressions, people envision personal and social survival, which constitutes the norm that controls and directs the most important dimensions of their life in terms of social, economic, and political activity. Underpinning these practices is the conviction that the terror of death must not be hidden, not from children or the weak or the feeble, but must be confronted and overcome by symbols showing the primacy of life.

The rites and rituals that follow death and burial focus "on the boundary" between the visible and invisible domains of life," with an emphasis on the visible "as a matter of practical urgency rather than speculative curiosity" (MacGaffey 1986, 63). Rituals are designed and intended to emphasize the continuation and endurance of the community. They are meant to put an end to or "finish" death as such as well as each particular occasion of it. What is celebrated in situations of death and mourning is "health, long life, children, and prosperity in this life" (Fisher 1998, 100). While the reality of the afterlife is not denied, on the contrary, significant aspects of death and funeral rituals for elders prominently depict it, the immediate concern of the rituals is about the welfare of the visible domain. Thus, on the practical level, although funeral rites intend to assure "the correct passage of the deceased to the abode of the ancestors" (Fisher 1998, 95), they also provide "occasions for family reunion, therapeutic expression of anger and grief, mutual consolation, healing of strained relationships, courtship, socio-political succession, transmission and creation of knowledge, historical commentary, and performance of verbal and gestural art, music, and dance" (Blakely and Blakely 1994, 399). All of this is supremely a spiritual performance.

"Through mourning rites, the living are assisted to come to terms with . . . death and at the same time are helped to re-integrate themselves with the community in the absence of the deceased member" (Kirwen 2008, 144). It is expected that the entire community be present at funerary rituals as an expression of last respects to the deceased, but also, and perhaps more significantly, as a sign of solidarity with the family, something that must continue beyond the death of one person, as the essence of life. It is a very serious thing for a member of the community to be absent from a funeral without sufficient reason. Such a person risks being considered the cause of the death, a witch. Among the Nubians (South Sudan) and many other ethnic groups, "everyone who joins the mourning crowd is expected to wail loudly. Many will speak of the good that the dead used to do. Others will talk of how they will miss the deceased even when he did not matter to them when he was alive" (Kirwen 2008, 153).

The rite of publication or announcement of the deceased's last wishes is significant, especially when the deceased is an elder. This is the occasion when major rearrangements of the life of the family (and the community) are recognized, essentially a transfer of spiritual (and thereby social) and even economic and political power onto the survivors. It matters very much who among the deceased's children, for example, gets what piece of land, or who gets what cow, or how many cows, or who is entrusted with the care of the household. These allocations, because they represent and contain the vital force of the deceased, give the receiver certain spiritual and social standing. As a rule, these arrangements are predetermined by the rules of primogeniture in the family or lineage, but an elder before death, or the clan after death, always has the prerogative to adjust them to prevent life's energy falling into unworthy hands. As a respondent reports about the Banyankole of Uganda, "The senior son becomes the heir or the father may choose any other son to become the heir if the firstborn son is hopeless" (Kirwen 2008, 176). In exceptional circumstances, the clan may also determine the heir.

The rite of distribution usually comes at the end of the mourning period, the period of "sleeping outside" (or even after the "second burial," which is described below). The distribution of property is important also as an exercise in communal reconciliation and unity. During the period of mourning after the burial, which may take up to three days for a woman, or as many as five for a man (but custom varies), the male members of the clan spend nights outside and sleep in the open air, around a fire, watching and communing with the spirits of the lineage. In conversations during this time, wide-ranging issues about the health of the clan, whether pleasant and unpleasant, are brought up and discussed. The aim is to pinpoint, acknowledge, and heal existing or potential animosities and divisions, with a consciousness that it is at this time that the ancestors are keenly watching, listening, ready and able to help or punish incorrigible behavior. Similar discussions go on among the women indoors, guided by the same spiritual awareness.

The major concerns from both groups are brought together and articulated, preferably personally by the aggrieved individual, but always publicly, at the ritual of the division and distribution of the property of the deceased. All members of the clan assemble together, though in different groupings according to gender, and every adult has the full right to speak, particularly to express a grievance against any individual in the clan or even against the clan at large if one feels to have been in any way unjustly treated. The "ill-treatment" may appear in the way the distribution of the deceased's property is done, because this always indicates how the elders perceive the quality of relationship of the potential receiver to the deceased. The individual may read between the lines and has the right to bring up the matter for consideration. Once brought up, any issue must be discussed and, as far as possible, a solution found. For the dispersal of mourners to take place with signs of discord is a dishonor to the dead and the entire company of ancestors. It cannot augur well for the future of the clan.

Some ethnic groups perform the following important ritual much later, up to a year or more after the mourning, and call it the "second burial" or "welcoming the spirit back home." The ritual may involve the actual exhumation and cleaning of the remains of the deceased and placing the skeleton (usually the skull) on a permanent basis in a place of honor in the main house at home or in a grove or thicket (Harris 1978, 83-84). It may also involve more elaborate festivity than was the case during the first burial. In the second burial, the dead person is present with the family physically, not merely theoretically in the imagination. Libations are poured near the remains, and major disagreements may be settled there by appealing to the ancestor's "physical" presence in the homestead.

In a not uncommon ritual (and one with only minor variations among ethnic groups in Africa), the Budja-Shona people of Mudzi, Zimbabwe, share in what is known as *Kurova Guva* (literally "to beat the grave"). It is worth recounting in some detail the main features of the ritual because it illustrates the desire for communion with universal vital powers as a way of galvanizing the inclusiveness of the African community.

Elderly, post-menopausal women brew beer over a period of seven days prior to the actual day that the ritual is to be performed. During the night preceding the celebration, the assembled community sings and dances around a black goat tied in the compound. Sometime during this performance the goat is expected to kneel as a sign that the deceased's spirit is ready to be brought back home. At dawn on the following morning the oldest son-in-law (*mukwasha*) of the deceased must cut with a single blow a branch from a certain tree (perhaps symbolizing the energy of the deceased), wrap the cut end of the branch in a white cloth, and bring it back to the homestead. (If the first son-in-law fails to fell the branch with one blow, he must pay a fine of one goat, and the second son-in-law attempts the same activity, and so on until successful.) At this time, some elders will have gone to visit the grave to invite the deceased's spirit back home. They return at dawn, at the same time as the branch bearer, to be received by wailing, singing, and dancing relatives, and even to the spectacle of trading of jokes by friends (*sahwira*).

The branch is unwrapped on arrival, planted at a visible spot in the homestead, and "watered" with the ritual beer from a clay pot (*hari*), while the older members of the family of the deceased drink some of it as they "speak" to the spirit. The goat is then killed by drowning it in the pot of beer. It is skinned, roasted, and shared among the closest family members and joking or mocking friends. One of the *sahwira* then sprinkles the property of the deceased with sap from the branch before distributing it among the family members. If the deceased was male, a (black) bull is sprinkled with some of the beer and given the name of the deceased. From then on, the bull is "respected" as the leader of the herd owned by the deceased because it is believed to be his reincarnation. At the conclusion of this ritual, the spirit of the dead is now "alive" in the family, and, in fact, enters into one of the family members, the heir, who is from now on expected to guide and protect the family.

This ritual, like so many others, is full of complex symbolism, but though rather involved in conceptualization and signification, the general intention of the symbols is straightforward. It is a representation of connectedness and the sharing of a lifeline with the deceased and with nature. For anyone who dies, "The highest form of reward is to return to this life. . . . Once the rituals are carried out, the living can live in peace and the dead are assured that one day they may return to this world" (Fisher 1998, 105). The community is again the central concern outside of which neither the living nor the dead has any meaningful existence. To be dead-dead means that you are outside the circle of life; you do not belong anywhere; you do not have a place you can call home. More often than not you go about causing suffering and misery. Even in life, one of the severest penalties is to be cast out of the family or community: in Zulu, "*ukuhlamba* (to wash one's hands of a person)." This is done only for the gravest of reasons and after the members of the community have attested to the incorrigibility of the person in question. When these conditions are fulfilled, the loss is not felt; otherwise, there would be a void in the community and the action would haunt it (Dandala 2009, 276).

9

Cosmology and Community

"The dead . . . are in the tree that rustles . . .
in the wood that groans."

Once again, death signifies deeper communion not only in terms of human and spiritual relationships but also with regard to the material community. "When one dies one does not leave the earth but moves deeper towards the centre," where, indeed, if people cared to speak about it, which they do not, even God is to be found. From birth, and ultimately and supremely in death, the earth becomes one's "eternal home." It is therefore "the common property of all people," not to be owned by any one individual (Shutte 2009b, 96). And if humans stake a claim on the material community, the latter likewise has a claim on the human community on the basis of reciprocal relationships.

Thus the Shona people (Zimbabwe) experience the presence of spirits as *shave,* "the spirits of animals and strangers, who never speak; *midzimu,* family ancestors; and *mhondoro,* royal ancestors." For instance, every royal ancestor "has a precise territory, often called a spirit province." Royal ancestors "are called *mhondoro,* 'lions,' because this is the form they take when not speaking through a human medium" (Isichei 2004, 248). The connection between the dead and the elements of creation is therefore deep and intimate. The Dogon in Mali, usually apprehensive about displaying family wealth to common gaze because it is, for the particular family, a symbol of "cosmic knowledge," have no hesitation to do so at the death of the head of the family, since now in his death "the whole universe" has been " 'gathered up' . . . under the form of the symbols which also constitute wealth" (Griaule and Dieterlen 1954 [1999], 107).

In death, one's existence is joined to and becomes part of the earth, the vegetation, the animals, the stars, and indeed, the cosmos. Consequently, it is not surprising that any of these creatures may sometimes openly and directly manifest a dead person on earth as his or her personification, because the spirits of the dead often choose to inhabit them. Thus human interaction with any other being also means possible, or even probable, contact with the spirits of the dead.

In a village, every element of significance to the life of the community is associated with a spirit, often ancestral but also "natural," or spirits created as such. A well, a lake, a river, a hill, or a forest could be such a place. Significant spiritual legends for each community lie behind this association and enforce judicious use of these resources.

When I was growing up, it was against custom for anyone in my village of Mabuimerafuru to go alone to the communal well, early in the morning or late in the evening, and if one did, it was believed that one would encounter and perhaps be harmed by a large snake that lived there to guard the water. The legend was that the snake was actually the ancestor who located the well and had it developed. In actual fact, his family, whose head at that time was Mugonya, still had special responsibility for seeing to it that the well, which was seasonal (filling up with the rains and almost running dry in the dry season), was well kept and not misused in any way. It was believed that people could go there safely only in groups of two or more and in broad daylight, probably to assure the safety of the water from ill wishers. There was another smaller well not very far from there that never ran dry because it was fed by a spring and its water was purer, but its guardian was a family thought to practice witchcraft. The well had an aura of mystery around it, and one needed the explicit permission of this family to draw water from there. Not many people had the courage to do so or go there!

Across the continent, there are countless examples of similar locations, sacred hills, forests, animals, and so on, where access or use of anything found there is normally prohibited because the primary owners are the spirits. While the pattern of belief is the same everywhere, namely, that the location or creature is either sacred to the ancestors or haunted by spirits of the dead, approaches to deal with the presence of the spirits vary and can be very complex. The communal funeral mask-dance, called *Sakon Kwyie*, of the Bobo people of Bobo-Dioulasso in southwestern Burkina Faso, may be taken as an example that illustrates similar practices elsewhere among other African ethnic groups.

The purpose of the *Sakon Kwyie* dance is to escort the ancestors from Bobo-Dioulasso to the ancestral world by first uniting them very closely with the major dimensions of the life activities of the community. This is achieved through the mask-dance, whose preparation must involve as much as possible the close cooperation of all artisans in the community: "potters, weavers, dyers, makers of masks, dancers, and the best available musicians," in simulation of the original order of the universe that Wuro, the creator god, has established, but which through their daily activities humans are likely to and often do upset. For the ancestors to accept the invitation to "depart" from Bobo-Dioulasso, they must be content that this effort of integration is satisfactory. This means that although they are expected to "leave" as the dance suggests, they actually do not depart but transform themselves into the order that is the lifeblood of the community (visibly represented by the masks of the god Dwo). Thus, the ancestral masks used in the *Sakon Kwyie* dance represent creatures that are a constant physical reminder of ancestral presence; they represent birds, animals, wood, and so on, all things useful for human survival (Bravmann 1977, 152-55).

The practice of medicine, augury, and witchcraft detection provide further illustration of the African perception of the connectedness among the dead, the community of the living, and the cosmic order. As a rule, the medicine professional or herbalist gets his or her knowledge in one of (or a combination of) three ways: by inheritance from a parent or an elder, by direct revelation from a spirit, or by a long period of apprenticeship and induction with an established practitioner. In all three, a transference of knowledge takes place, from the senior to the junior, from the guide to the apprentice. But it is not only technical knowledge that is transmitted; more importantly, the power inherent in the medicinal plant, which is above all a divine, ancestral, or spiritual power, is what is communicated. This is the power that activates the healing process, without which medicine cannot fight the illness. Since illness is a manifestation of a strong, evil spiritual power (depending on the nature and gravity of the disease), it can be confronted successfully only by equally powerful ancestral energy inherent in the herbs.

A characteristic of the genuine African healer is, therefore, the state in the healing process of becoming "possessed" by a spiritual power to different degrees. As we have seen, sometimes this is a condition for the calling itself. In the moment of ecstasy during the exercise of healing, the individuality of the healer may cease to exist, as it were, so that the possessing power truly encompasses and acts through him or her. The healer becomes an instrument of the healing power, or communicates personally and closely with it through the medicine. Among the Yoruba people of Nigeria, it is the deity (*orisha*) Orunmila who plays this role. Healing comes about through a power distinct from, even though embedded *within*, the healer. An authentic healer anywhere in Africa will disclaim personal agency in the act or result of the healing process and attribute it to God: it is God alone who heals, not the healer or the herbs, which are only the instruments of the spirits.

Here, then, is the reason why knowledge of medicinal herbs and trees cannot be divulged carelessly or indiscriminately to unworthy recipients or sold for profit, both of which are considered causes of desecration. Because healing knowledge primarily belongs to the ancestors, its transference and use must be judicious at the risk of angering them and rendering the medicine's healing power ineffective. This is why many persons would rather die with

the knowledge than hand it over to unworthy heirs. The healer is at the service of God and the ancestors, and ideally should not charge for services rendered. Ethically, the medicine practitioner may receive a "thank you" offering
only of the patient's own determination and only after the patient is healed.

But even when payment is determined and expected, as surely happens
with some healers, the genuine healer makes the effort to disclaim the payment as his or her own; rather, it belongs to the healing power behind him
or her. Thus, the payment when given is not personally handled immediately
by the healer but is laid on the ground or, if it is an animal or fowl, is tethered
somewhere by someone else other than the healer. The ethical and spiritual
inference is that the herbalist or healer is merely an agent of a greater power
and acts as mediator of this power so that, in strict justice, the gift belongs and
should go to the latter. Conversely, the healed person who refuses to return
thanks or pay for his or her experience of health slights the power behind the
healing. Ultimately, such people put their own and their family's well-being in
jeopardy; the healing power may not be inclined to assist them in the future.

The situation is similar with diviners. Divination or augury in Africa is
a method of spiritual diagnosis for illness or other kinds of spiritual affliction, or a type of prophecy, a way of foretelling the future. The diviner "gives
his treatment soberly and sympathetically, according to the knowledge and
skill handed down to him during his apprenticeship," with regard to the
health and well-being of the individual or community (see Dube 2009, 205).
Essentially and ultimately, divination is a barometer of the state of social harmony. Often, the process involves an examination of the state of relationship
between the patient and his family and neighbors, as well as with the dead,
because these are held as "integral" to one's health. To obtain good health
again, it is not unusual that reconciliation rituals are prescribed (Dube 2009,
203). This mentality is transferred to the practice of modern medicine. Diagnosis and treatment are seen as a communal concern.

On one occasion when I had to go to the hospital for a minor surgical
procedure, I had not informed my oldest surviving sister of the matter. She
was so upset she refused to come and see me at home after the surgery. A
few years later (in August 2011), I needed to go to the hospital again for
another surgery. This time I made sure to tell her and my younger brother of
the eventuality. I insisted to both of them, as my two older nephews did to
their mother, that it was all going to be well and that, since I was at the time
staying in another country, and considering the physical distance between
us and the cost for travel and accommodation, they should not bother about
coming. But they both insisted on being there, at enormous financial expense
for them and me, for I had to foot part of the bill for their travel and stay.
Their deep motivation for being present was that my experience of illness

concerned them as well, and that it would mean that there was disharmony in the family if they were not present during my surgery. Before their arrival, I had planned to go for tests by myself, but a friend, reflecting the same mindset, insisted on coming with me. "How can a person undergo something like this alone?" she wondered aloud when she sensed my puzzlement and resistance. All three persons typified in practice the African worldview toward illness: "Communal participation is indispensable to the quest for wholeness that is the healing process" (Murove 2009c, 170). It is a pattern of thought and behavior in search of integration and wholeness, and it is repeated every moment all across the continent.

Although there is a clear difference in people's minds between healing with herbs and divination, it is possible to say that all healers are to some degree diviners, and vice versa, because they all deal with spiritual energy. The difference is in the methods they use. In fact, both are generically referred to as "healers" (in Swahili and many Bantu languages with slight variations, *Waganga*). Some use herbs (*Waganga wa miti shamba*), others augury (*Waganga wa ramli*). The latter, in the strict sense, are the diviners.

Divination takes many forms, but common to them all is that it involves the explicit reading of the "behavior" of objects, whether they are stones, shells, or gourd shakers, but mostly animals and fowl. In the latter instances, it may be a matter of just listening to the sounds these animals make. Among many peoples, the screech of the owl or the laughter of the hyena portends bad news against which medicinal antidotes must be sought. These creatures are seen as manifestations of witches, as we have seen; they are witches shifted into animal form, called "familiars." In formal cases of augury, however, the animal or fowl representing the afflicted person must be killed and opened up. It is believed that the evil power causing the illness, the "witchcraft substance," as well as its origin, can be pinpointed in the innards of the animal in question, in its heart, liver, lungs, or intestines. These organs are symbols of life, and anything that seeks to destroy the life of an individual lodges there first. From the diagnosis, called an oracle, the proper antidote, which may include herbal medicine or ritual action, is prescribed.

In African disease etiology, disease is ultimately a moral-spiritual issue beyond what the apparent cause may seem to be. For Africans "all human problems, such as infertility, illness, and trouble in hunting, are ascribed to moral conflicts within the human community," some spiritual discordance, or lack of harmony. Consequently, "the diviner's task is to disclose acts of immorality which have provoked the vengeance of the ancestors and to reveal the destructive hand of witches and sorcerers" in the situation (Ray 1976, 104). Invariably, witchcraft as the source of evil is diagnosed by augury as the cause of illness. Again, what is significant is that not only can the offending witchcraft-substance in a living creature be found there, but so can the indications as to who the culprit might be. The point is that evil as a spiritual substance, including its manifestation as evil spirits of the dead, is not simply ethereal but makes of certain creatures its abode, necessitating care in handling or associating with all phenomena of creation.

The unity of the human being with all creatures in death is connected to notions of the original cosmological state, when the power of life was one and there was no illness or death. Various myths explaining the origin of various peoples and the separation between God and humanity address this point (Belcher 2005). Originally, God was at one with creation, living in intimate unity with it. On account of some folly on the part of humans or one or another of the creatures, God's close identification with the world, symbolized by the image of his residence and social intercourse with humanity, was negatively affected. The picture painted in some of these myths is that of divine physical separation from the visible world, so that God's world, though powerfully present, is now generally unseen. Humanity must now seek clearer self-manifestations of God through petitions, supplications, and sacrifices, and often by means of intermediaries, the ancestors. At all times, however, divine power continues to sustain the world and to animate every creature in the universe. Even though an individual continues to exist in death as spirit with the ability to inhabit or possess physical objects, the vital power of the dead dissolves into universal energy that exists in all creation and effectively becomes indistinguishable from it. The universally recognized strength of their influence over other beings, for good or ill, derives from there.

Since a mistaken conception persists in scholarship, it is important to make it unmistakably clear that African myths addressing God's self-removal from the world at the beginning of time are not meant to depict a world without God; they intend to portray, rather, the *human longing for God*. In other words, African cosmogonic and cosmological myths (like similar myths elsewhere) are an attempt to explain the human condition, particularly the reality of evil, and answer the question, as Rabbi Harold Kushner titled his book, why "bad things happen to good people" (Kushner 1997). Why is there suffering and death in the world, and, consequently, how should human beings relate to divine power to avert these evils that, in African moral perception, are caused by antisocial individuals and forces associated with them? The myths must be read within this context for their meaning to be understood correctly. They are not about a "withdrawn" (*Deus otiosus*), "hidden" (*Deus absconditus*), or "inactive/idle" God, which some observers have attributed to African spirituality. The myths principally concern themselves with laying down the structures of right relationships among the forces of life; they are primarily about the morality of relationships.

Divine transcendence exists together with immanence in the world in a "complementary" manner, as do all spiritual forces (Mbiti 1969, 32). Generally, as has been sufficiently noted in the foregoing discussion, the immanence of the spiritual powers, including God, is much stronger and more powerfully felt in African religious consciousness than their transcendence. This means that all human attitudes and behavior affect the spirits of the dead in one way or another. Sacrifices, prayers, and other forms of worship, where spiritual power and presence are assumed to be concentrated, manifest this dimension of African spirituality. But in daily human conversation, acknowledgment of spiritual agency is likewise on everyone's lips and can be heard in expressions of joy or grief, pleasure or pain, thanksgiving or complaint, or hope or despair, or even surprise. Spirits punish or vindicate and enforce or render curses harmless. As a rule, an elder curses or blesses in the name of an ancestor or some other spirit, or by the spiritual power naturally invested in the cursing elder himself or herself as a representative and representation of the power of the spirits.

The universal omnipresence of the spirits, however, may present a problem, and sometimes people wish that spirits were not so near or so immanent. Spiritual presence suggests the need for perfection on the part of human beings, but this is bound to be problematic because human beings are not perfect. Malcolm McVeigh writes with regard to the all-encompassing divine presence that people have "no problem [with it] when things go well, when there is success, health, life," for this is the order God established and which manifests divine pleasure about human morality. "But when things do not go well, when there is tragedy and failure, the tables are turned. If God is the author of this also, he may be seen as oppressive or even intolerable" (McVeigh 1974, 133). Despite this feeling, trust in and dependence on divine benevolence is ultimately not questioned, even when "natural" calamities or tragedies strike. Whatever happens in the world, God "knows" and "wills" it, even if the reasons are hidden from humanity. The spiritual conviction of Africans lies here.

When ancestors act, it is God acting through them because they share intimately God's power. God acts as a parent for humanity, although not in the familiar sense that the image of "daddy" would portray. The social implications of such designation in African family structure befit not a father or mother but a grandparent, although God cannot be characterized as such. The relationship of a person with a parent is more formal and, even if very affectionate emotionally, is somewhat distant socially. Like those between husband and wife, the duties and responsibilities of the parent-child relationship appear more in the foreground than affection. Relationships between the living and the dead are dictated by the same social structures.

The proper functioning of ancestral energies in the community and the world in general depends upon how family, clan, and other lineal ties are nurtured. It is worth recalling the conviction that because of the actual presence of the dead in society, any community is bound together not only by the traditions which they bequeathed to the descendants and continue to guard, but also by the land they lived in and were buried on, which serves as the visible symbol of their presence and unity with the living. It is for this reason that ancestral presence is considered immediate, and everything is sacred because imbued with this presence. Personal identity as a member of a given community secures the continued existence of its dead members.

While belonging to a community entitles an individual to the use of the goods there, it makes sharing an obligation and, much more, a spiritual requirement, because it is a means of bonding within the community and so with the ancestral spiritual powers. Sharing, especially among non-equals, brings about a sense of social equality and equity, and thereby deters the destructive emotions of jealousy and hatred that social inequality, oppression, and exploitation breed. Sharing is thus an act of prayer in that it implicitly acknowledges the giftedness of possessions, the primary owner of which is God. Where essential needs of food, clothing, and housing are concerned, it is immoral (or sinful) not to render a helpful hand to the needy in whatever way possible.

An example of this is the obligation of hospitality to travelers and strangers. Visitors and travelers are to be welcomed without question or reservation, and accorded the best possible treatment. "A visitor is a blessing," a popular saying goes. One never knows what kind of spirits or what sort of energy accompanies a stranger. If well intentioned, a visitor brings with him or her blessings to the home. Although unknown to the host, a visitor may have some advice, medicinal knowledge, or skill that might be beneficial to the family. More importantly, on account of the hospitality, the spiritual power a visiting stranger may transfer to the host can bring about unimagined benefits. Nevertheless, no one is unaware of the risks involved in this attitude as well, for a visitor may also harbor ill intentions toward the host or village, or may have the harmful power of contaminating witchcraft. Still, the moral consensus seems to be that whatever the potential dangers, it is better to take risks on the side of hospitality.

A leader is particularly obliged to share wealth on a wider scale than his or her subjects as a sacred duty, because in so doing the community as a whole coalesces around him or her and receives blessings. By sharing, the ruler literally passes on life, the energy of the ancestors, to the beneficiaries, all of the ruler's subjects, and confirms *Ubuntu* among them. For, although *Ubuntu* has, in the final analysis, to do with personal adult behavior, it requires demonstration, public witness, or ethical performance. This is the role played by the leader in sharing as the subjects see and learn. Sharing determines character; it therefore matters a great deal where a person belongs geographically as well as socially, what family one is born in, what clan or ethnic group one claims, and how one's people generally conduct themselves in sharing. All of this plays a role in the development of *Ubuntu*; good nurture usually produces good people, and relationships are easily formed around this principle.

From this, it should be clear that *Ubuntu* is also a quality of groups and communities, in whom certain reputations of kindness, hospitality, and sharing are perceived. Conversely, the question is: are they quarrelsome, aggressive, and inhospitable? Either way, the implications are far reaching. Again, significant associations such as inter-ethnic marriage unions and friendships among the youth will be encouraged or discouraged depending on these perceptions. Since character is the person, it is not expected that one can shed oneself of it easily, if at all. Instead, the fear is that in imprudent associations with greedy people, bad character will be communicated to and contaminate the innocent, rendering original benevolent ancestral power less effective. To avoid this risk, ambiguous associations are best avoided.

Apart from broadening the population base of the family and clan, marriage, particularly in its polygamous (or polygynous) institutional form, also serves to expand the material power of the clan, with profound spiritual implications. First of all, in those ethnic groups that practice the tradition of "bridewealth," the amount asked for involves the ancestors on both sides of the families in marriage, since they all have a share in what is given. In fact, often an animal must be slaughtered, or some other article (a blanket, a cooking pot, or an amount of beer or food, for example) must be given by the groom in the ancestors' name and honor. If this is not done, all aspects of the marriage, including its fruitfulness in terms of children, is put in jeopardy from the start. Further, in the exchange of bridewealth, the incorporation of the bride into spiritual forces of the groom's family in matrilineal and patrilocal societies, and the bride's in matrilineal and matrilocal societies, takes place. This cannot happen in the absence of bridewealth exchange, an indication of how spiritually significant the tradition is. The spiritual marital journey begins here with the exchange of material things, culminating in the incarnation of the ancestors in the family and clan through the birth and naming of offspring.

Beyond the institution of marriage, the vital energy of a family, lineage, or clan can be broadened through friendship, another much valued convention in African social-spiritual traditions. The Igbo people of Nigeria say of a friend who is visiting, "There is a brother [or sister] in town" (*nwa nne di na mba*). A friend can adopt the ancestral spirits or insignia of his or her friend's clan, depending on how deep the friendship is. Blood pacts as a method of forming deep friendships may be dying out now, but the social and spiritual meaning of friendship as a communion of trust and respect between people for mutual support is very strong in Africa. The marriage of the children of friends sometimes happens and strengthens the friendship (Kirwen 2010, 106-20). Without friends a person is very poor indeed, whatever material wealth he or she may own, but especially spiritually, because such a one lives in a very limited, constricted, and constricting world of mystical energies and influence. While a person must retain his own spiritual sources and resources, it does not hurt and is in fact helpful and wise to amplify the circle with whatever beneficial assets one is capable of acquiring.

Part II

Conversations:
The Contribution of African Spirituality

Connections and Innovations

"Ex Africa . . . aliquid novi"—"Something new out of Africa"

Sometime in the first century of the Common Era, Gaius Plinius Secundus, commonly known as Pliny the Elder (23–79 C.E.), wrote these famous words: *"Ex Africa semper aliquid novi"* ("There is always something new out of Africa," at the time referring to the part of northern Africa that is now known as Tunisia). Around the same time, according to John's account of the life of Jesus, Nathaniel was told by Philip that Andrew, Peter, and he had met the messiah, the one "spoken of by Moses in the Law and by the prophets . . . Jesus son of Joseph from Nazareth." Whereupon Nathaniel, skeptical, exclaimed equally famously: "Nazareth! . . . Can anything good come from Nazareth?" (John 1:43-46). In the following chapters I would like to affirm both that there may be something new out of Africa and that, yes, *pace* Nathaniel and similar skeptics all over the world, even something good.

The purpose of this second part of the book is to draw from the foregoing discussion on African spirituality certain directions pertinent to human perception of life in the world today, particularly in relation to being Christian in the world. Its aim is not to find strict parallels or to make biased comparisons between African and other spiritual systems and approaches, which are bound to occur if we try. Every spiritual approach has its own unique character, and to try to conflate them in the name of unity or any other name would be to do a great disservice to each and all of them. The thrill of understanding is in recognizing the differences in the process of open and respectful encounter or dialogue, where true insight might emerge. It is rare that wisdom is any one individual's prerogative alone: "One head does not [indeed cannot] contain all the wisdom," an African proverb affirms. Nor is it true that tolerance in this respect is the same as relativism. Dialogue does not necessarily involve thoughtless surrender of personal convictions in favor of anything else, which is relativism, but it is an attitude that is open to enriching one's position through deep personal sharing of the experience of another.

101

The common ground of all human beings, and certainly all believers, is the life they share, the very practical dimensions of social relations, politics, economics, religious affiliation, and the environment. If life in the world for many belief systems is the only way to God, it should form a starting point for dialogue among all believers. On these issues, then, what does African spiritual wisdom have to contribute, not as dogma, but as part of the conversation among people of different backgrounds and convictions, which is the other head of human wisdom? I propose to address this question in the context of the Christian faith.

This is by no means the first attempt to show the implications of the major dimensions of African spirituality for the Christian faith (and human life in general); it may be "new" only in the sense of systematic, written academic articulation and presentation, but not of awareness. On the practical level of intuitive application, this endeavor began with the introduction of the Christian faith in Africa. Hearing the gospel preached, Africans (like anyone else) could receive and make sense of it only from where they stood, that is, according to their cultures, all other appearances notwithstanding. Thomas Aquinas bequeathed to the world the principle that "whatever is received into something is received according to the condition of the receiver" (*"Quidquid recipitur ad modum recipientis recipitur"* [*Summa Theologiae* 1a, q. 75, a. 5; 3a, q. 5]), and that "a thing known exists in a knower according to the mode of a knower" (*"Cogitum . . . est in cognoscente secundum modum cognoscentis"* [*Summa Theologiae* 1a, q. 12, a. 4]). The principle may be understood in many different ways, but it certainly applies here.

Since the early twentieth century, in more explicit ways and with different degrees of success, the endeavor in dialogue has been carried on by the African Initiated Churches (AICs), big and small across Sub-Saharan Africa: central, eastern, southern and West Africa (Barrett 1968; Sundkler 1961, 1976; Welbourn 1961; Welbourn and Ogot 1966; Peel 1968; Isichei 2004, 157-214). Much of this effort has taken place under charismatic leadership without much attempt to articulate its theology academically. Nevertheless, most observers agree that it might be within the AICs that "the most positive and creative relationship is being established between Christianity and African culture" (Richardson 2009, 131).

The most notable AIC that has attempted to develop a systematic *written* theology is the Church of Jesus Christ on Earth by the Prophet Simon Kimbangu (*Église de Jésus Christ sur la terre par son envoyé special Simon Kimbangu,* or EJCSK). In a 1977 document, prior to admission into the World Council of Churches (WCC) and the All Africa Council of Churches (AACC), the EJCSK spelled out and clarified all the major theological topics that the church was concerned with, particularly in its practice of inculturation. The other churches, very numerous and of various sizes, still depend mostly on oral theology and charismatic leadership, with minimal rigid ecclesiastical structures.

In West Africa, the major AICs include the Harrist Church, founded by William Wade Harris of Liberia (1913); the Church of the Twelve Apostles in Ghana, founded by Harrist converts Grace Tani and Kwesi John Nackabah (1918); the Aladura (or praying) churches that originated in Yorubaland, Nigeria (c. 1918); and the Celestial Church of Christ (*Église du Christianisme Céleste*, ECC), founded in what is present-day Benin (formerly Dahomey) by Bilewu Joseph Oshoffa (1947). By 1998 the ECC had 2,316 parishes (*Cambridge Dictionary of Christianity* [hereafter, CDC] 2010, 14). As already mentioned, EJCSK (founded c. 1921) is a member of both the AACC and the WCC, and has over fifteen million believers spread across central Africa (Democratic Republic of Congo, Congo Brazzavile, and Angola) as well as other parts of Africa, Madagascar, Europe, and North America (CDC 2010, 688-89).

There are numerous AICs in East Africa as well as southern Africa. In Kenya alone, it is estimated that there are 700 denominations with more than 6 million members, comprising 20 percent of the Christian population. In Uganda they make up 3.7 percent, and in Tanzania 1.9 percent of Christians. By 1995, there were more than 3,000 AICs in South Africa with a membership of about 39 million people. The largest of these churches are spread across the region (South Africa, Zimbabwe, Mozambique, Botswana, Zambia, and Malawi) and include the Ethiopian, Zionist, and African Apostolic groups of churches by different founders. In general, AICs "are African responses to [Western] Christianity aimed at shaping Christian experience according to African cultures and under African leadership" (CDC 2010, 12). They are characterized by "a strong missionary outreach across ethnic and national boundaries, a rigorous ethical code, concern for social and individual salvation revolving around healing rituals, a quest for holiness, a great sense of community, and innovative liturgy" (CDC 2010, 13). "Mutual assistance in their group is an important element of Christian brother/sisterhood. Many of the greater churches among them also have contributed to the economic development of their people." Apart from the Kimbanguists, Baur mentions the Zionist churches in South Africa and some other smaller churches such as the Aiyitoro in Ghana: "There remain of course many groups with a purely religious, otherworldly outlook, or with utopian dreams, such as the few messianic movements" (Baur 1994, 356).

All AICs have allowed a basically African spiritual vision to guide their Christian convictions and actions, particularly in their prayer and worship services. At times, as with the EJCSK, they have tried to express their vision in theology and doctrine based on African systems of existence and thought (Spear and Kimambo 1999), namely, on the "African way of feeling the truth about things," or the African "feeling after the truth" (Taylor 1963, 12). Today, as Baur notes, "many Independent Churches are moving from the periphery to the heart of Christianity.... Their approach to practical religious inculturation reveals their point of departure: African and biblical worldviews, and the areas that concern them most: the Holy Spirit, prophecy, healing, community." But there is a negative side to them, too. "The dangers of a superficial inculturation appear in their deficiencies and limitations and they suggest one clear postulate: inculturation has not only to be an Africanization of Christianity but must also . . . imply a Christianizing transformation of the African soul and the world" (Baur 1994, 358).

The spirit of the dialogue to be pursued between Western Christian and African spiritualities aims at constructing a credible *African Christian* spiritual orientation, one that responds to the needs of African indigenous perspectives while respecting the uniqueness of the gospel message of Jesus Christ. The process is important and takes the course the AICs have seriously tried to charter.

There is the question of methodology. As an academic discipline, the attempt to comprehend the foundation stones of African Christian spirituality "is intrinsically and irreducibly interdisciplinary," as Sandra Schneiders points out with reference to the task in any context: "because the object it studies, transformative Christian experience as such is multi-faceted. Every topic of study in this field requires that several disciplines be used together in a reciprocally interactive and not merely juxtaposed way throughout the process of investigation" (Schneiders 2005b, 7). In addition to understanding biblical tradition and the wide range of schools, Christian theology in many of its branches must pay equal attention to the wisdom that anthropology, sociology, psychology, economics, and politics provide for the "art" of human existence.

Spirituality is intricately related to and intertwined with the realities to which these disciplines address themselves. It is generally accepted today that theology must be based less on some assumed fixed metaphysical principles than on these human sciences. The latter approach serves to make theology (and the church) more open and more flexible, and therefore richer. It recognizes the fundamental role time and place play in theological development. Theology must play itself out in the present, but it is influenced by the past, and always has an eye to the future, which in turn becomes a developed present. Recall here the image of the wheel revolving along the road, as Africans visualize time. The practice of mutual integration or tension and the filtering and pooling together of wisdom from the various traditions and disciplines needs to be maintained throughout.

Consideration of the contribution of the African host cultural environment, in terms of language, symbol systems and, indeed, the very physical universe, to an expanded understanding of the gospel is indispensable for contemporary African Christian theology; one that is necessary, reflective, and discriminating (Dulles 1978, 26-30) in the process of discovering and explaining metaphors, similes, symbols, and images that speak deeply to the African religious psyche, sensibility, and imagination. These must evoke and readily express the African experience of the sacred in connection with the never-ending task to understand better the meaning and implications of the Christian faith for humanity.

10

Combining Old and New Treasures

"We drink from our own wells."

If we are to understand the deep meaning of spiritual identity and to come to terms with its implications for Christians in Africa, we might want to keep in mind the wisdom of maintaining the continuity between old and new realities in human life rather than succumbing to the temptation of creating a radical break between them (cf. Matt. 13:52). It is not required of anyone to give up one's entire cultural heritage in the name of the gospel, critical though one must be of some aspects of it. On the contrary, the call for the adult, intelligent Christian is to attempt to bring out as clearly as possible the treasures from both one's old cultural heritage and one's new Christian calling, just as in the case of the New Testament the task was to bring about a fruitful encounter between the Mosaic Law and the Law of Christ.

In the New Testament, both the Law of Moses and the Law of Christ are important and necessary for the moral-spiritual imperatives of faith, hope, and love, which the early church made its practical foundation. Both Christ's message and the Mosaic Law contain values that not only reinforce one another but, as they encounter each other, become transformed in such a way as to produce a *new, better* thing, a fulfillment of the human innermost desire (Matt. 5:17-18). The encounter means a new way of living life, as shown most perfectly by Jesus' own life. Based on this precedent of primitive Christianity, the African Christian can be at ease with the practices of his or her own (cultural) religiosity when these are taken up and transformed by new Christic values accessible in the Western Christian tradition as historically received here. This, in short, is the result of the process that current African theology characterizes as inter- or cross-cultural dialogue, generally referred to as inculturation.

Referring to this process, the Second Vatican Council in its Constitution on Divine Revelation (*Dei Verbum* [DV]) affirms that "God . . . in his wisdom has so brought it about that the New should be hidden in the Old and that the Old should be made manifest in the New" *(DV 16)*. The task in this situation is one of interpretation, which leads to "accommodation." African spirituality, Western Christian spirituality, and the contemporary world in its political, economic, cultural, scientific, and other dimensions form the dialogue partners in the process. Despite, or even because of, the differences among them, each must listen to the other and others as each tells its story in honest and patient conversation.

This procedure is what has constituted the history of Christianity from the outset; it is not possible to avoid it given the confines of human existence. Christianity is based on the belief that God encountered humanity most radically as a human being in Jesus Christ and became like humanity "in everything but sin" (Heb. 2:7) so that communication between them would be possible. African spirituality similarly affirms that the most radical way that the spirit world encounters and communicates with humanity is through possession, when the spirit powers take over certain individuals and speak through them. This is the nature of divination or the charism of revealing the secrets of the spirit world. How can Jesus encounter Africans except in African form, taking on the treasures of their African religiosity? As culturally situated people, how can they obtain maximum appreciation of what is at stake in following Jesus except through their cultural universe as Africans?

The question in this process is not one of "putting new wine into old wineskins" or "sewing a new patch onto an old cloth." It is not a question of adding layers of beliefs one on top of another or any procedure of that variety, because doing so would be spiritually destructive and should be categorically rejected (Matt. 9:14-17; Mark 2:18-22; Luke 5:33-39). The question, therefore, does not involve imposing one reality forcibly over another so that one reality is completely eliminated from the picture. Rather, the issue is one of developing new (and hopefully more profound) sensitivities and horizons from the meeting of different spiritual experiences and expressions that are transformed into fundamental values of each. In concrete terms in the African context, the encounter should lead African Christians to recognize themselves much more intensely as incorporated into the reality of God. Their new realization and transformed existence through Christ's gospel should fill their hearts with wonder and joy. Further, it ought to stimulate their imagination in the knowledge and deeper understanding of Jesus' message and its implication in their lives as culturally situated people. Indeed, this is what all Christian communities from any cultural origin are called to do.

To be very specific, *Christian* spirituality in Africa is a child born of two parents, the African indigenous approaches to God and the gospel of Jesus Christ. These two parents must mate. Without this intimate union, on the marriage bed of the contemporary religious experiences of African communities and born of ecstasy, evocation, critical interpretation, evaluation, and integration, genuine African Christian spirituality is unlikely to happen; instead, a merely confusing imposition or superficial mimicry of a foreign religiosity, which inevitably ends up in messy divorce, will occur. It is not befitting of human beings sincerely questing for God, because it is unable to move the heart or inspire the mind to accept God's invitation to grow into communion with the divine reality. But if human communion with God is what holiness means, becoming "one flesh" with or being possessed by him, the procedure is voluntary and cannot be imposed. Christian spirituality is fundamentally an act of free will inspired by the desire to become like God in all things. It is a quest for perfection (cf. Matt. 5:48).

From the point of view of African spirituality, African theology (as an academic discipline) looks into the systems and structures of African experience and thought that inspire relationships between people and the spirit powers. It considers how the Bible helps to evoke these experiences in and from the various African cultural contexts, or, in other words, how it "reveals" the divine in and from the African experience, leading to a more complete and ultimate way of being human and God-like in Africa and the world. African theology investigates the ways in which Christian thought and practice might articulate a renewed Christian tradition in the African context, one that ultimately means a deeper relationship between all human beings and all creation. The trail it follows is that of the rediscovery of the power of God working in the continent—in conventional language, God's self-revelation there.

However it is expressed, spirituality is a form of travel, a sojourn, a pilgrimage. It is like the mysterious journey involved in the growth of a living organism; it is at first small but with time it grows in size and becomes more complex in activity. What is amazing is that from the very beginning, it contains all of the elements required for it to grow and mature; the organism's genetic or DNA map is inherent. This means that the process of discovering the systems and structures of authentic African Christian spirituality is similarly intrinsic; it cannot be a ready and complete blueprint brought in from outside, from other traditions, even if these are Christian traditions of other local churches. Each organism grows in its own particular way into its final particular shape.

Applied to spiritual growth, this analogy implies that other spiritual traditions can inspire but cannot replace the basic shape of African spirituality, short of grotesque transmutation. We need to start relating to African spiritual perceptions from the African situation, from where African peoples are today in their living memories. It is necessary to draw and drink from Africa's own spiritual "wells," as the Latin American liberation theologian

Gustavo Gutiérrez writes with reference to his own people's "spiritual journey" (Gutiérrez 1984). If, indeed, spirituality involves "singing songs" to the Lord in joy and thanksgiving for what the Lord has done for a people, how can they do so in cultural and linguistic captivity? One experiences a sense of deep loss and alienation at being deprived of spiritual self-identity in these matters. With reference to Israel's exile in Babylon, the psalmist laments on behalf of the people that it was impossible for them to rejoice and sing the "Lord's song" for their "captors" and "tormentors" in "a foreign land" (Ps. 137:1-4).

There are extrabiblical sources that reflect similar sentiments. For example, the nineteenth-century social philosopher and political theorist Karl Marx (1818–1883) expressed something about his socio-politico-economic program that is relevant to meditate on. Issa Shivji explains that according to Marx, personal and social change are rarely givens, but have to be struggled for continuously by looking at reality, analyzing it, and advancing solutions for the present in relation to the past and future (Shivji 1973, 304). In the process, Marx cautioned that courage is needed to accept the conclusions of the analysis, undeterred by the uncertainties and risks involved in the short or long run.

Another social theorist, Julius K. Nyerere of Tanzania (1922–1999), pressed home a similar thought about the task of nation-building. As national leader of a poor, technologically underdeveloped country, Nyerere was convinced that African tradition and modern technology must not be divorced from each other; they must instead be integrated if they are to be beneficial to the people of Africa. Apart from this horizon, he said, the process is bound to be destructive. "We have deliberately decided to grow, as a society, out of our own roots, but in a particular direction and towards a particular kind of objective," Nyerere announced as his method for his program to pursue equality and respect for human rights and dignity in the land. "We are doing this by emphasizing certain characteristics of our traditional organization, and extending them so that they can embrace the possibilities of modern technology and enable us to meet the challenge of life in the twentieth century" (Nyerere 1968a, 2).

Considered carefully, these ideas contain serious implications for Christian spirituality in Africa. When one looks at Marx's and Nyerere's arguments with Christian faith-filled eyes, it becomes clear that a new way of relating to God cannot be imported wholesale from outside; rather, it must be discovered, uncovered, and recovered or retrieved from the two basic theological sources at the African Christian's disposal: African religiosity and Scripture. Once again, this is the same thing as saying that African spirituality cannot but be distinctive; it must quench its thirst for the divine by drinking from its own wells. It must find nourishment there, and from there it must flourish. African Christians must sing their songs in their own land, in languages that make and give sense to them. To talk meaningfully about African Christian spiritual identity is to take seriously into account this principle.

Given the importance of ritual in African spirituality, one may wonder whether liturgy might be the ideal meeting place or the concrete location of convergence between Scripture and African spirituality. Can liturgy serve as the "platform" that embraces Christian tradition as interpreted across time and cultures and place it in dialogue with the African context? In liturgy the African context would explain Christian tradition at the same time as the latter would help modify and shape the African contextual understanding of the faith. The liturgy's central dual focus on divine power and human need easily opens up dialogue between and among cultures to realize this goal more than any other situation where cultural competition is all too rife. Concentration on the goal of worship should make cross-fertilization of modes a realizable endeavor.

One of the most complex realities of creation is that no two persons are the same; every individual is distinct and unique. Theology similarly affirms that every person is designed by the Creator in a special way. Scripture, underscoring the Hebrew cultural perspective, attaches great significance to the importance of singularity in the symbol of the name. Consequently, because God is one and only, without likeness or equal, the Old Testament insists that God's name is unknowable. Jehovah (Yhwh) or "I Am," as the divinity revealed itself to Moses, does not, therefore, expose completely the inner "nature" of God; by its vagueness and incompleteness it is designed to drive home the point of divine uniqueness.

In Hebrew tradition, even this partial divine identity cannot be uttered, let alone duplicated for any other person or being. To utter God's name was for the Jews the highest degree of blasphemy, and the only adequate punishment for this presumption was death by stoning. It means that the revelation of God's uniqueness through his name, even though partial, is a great privilege; it bestows on Moses the advantage of becoming a prophet like no other, or, in African terms, a diviner who knows the language of the ancestors and spirits. By this revelation, the power of God enters into Moses to heal people on God's behalf. The communion begun between God and Moses carried over in the New Testament, when St. Paul tells the Galatians that through Jesus they can call God "Father," or even affectionately as "Abba," "Daddy" (Gal. 4:6). By baptism they are incorporated into the Christian lineage and its ancestral tradition, becoming heirs and elders there (Gal. 3:28; Rom. 10:12), with the right of inheriting the land. The prayer that Jesus taught his disciples tells the same story (Matt. 6:9-13).

Jesus' identity is defined by his complete unity with God through which he assumes divine vital force and is able to dispense it to his earthly relations. Consequently, he is healer *par excellence*. Based on his pastoral ministry of special care and concern for each person, and especially for the marginalized and those who respond positively to his invitation to discipleship (Luke 4:18ff.), Jesus also merits the title of the Good Shepherd, capable of knowing and calling each of his sheep "by name" (John 10:3). Being positively identified by name by a chief is something that can lift up anyone's spirits, because it symbolizes the individual's communion with a higher power who thereby acknowledges the individual's existence, distinctiveness, character, fate, and yes, one's very being. Jesus suggests that his followers can and should aim at the same kind of union with God (John 14), a process that at the same time builds an identity of healers in the community. It is an identity that serves the community by making it strong and wise.

This new approach to spirituality is vitalistic in the sense that it requires a positive engagement with the world and creation in a friendly, noncombative and noncompetitive way to promote harmonious existence in the universe. It is a step away from the "subtle mood of isolation and withdrawal from [the] life current" (Bynum 1999, 93), which tends to remove the divine from history. The latter is sometimes promoted under the logic that science, especially physics, renders null the espousal of the mystery of God. But such logic spells alienation from human wholeness, as the Adamic myth of Judeo-Christian tradition intends to show. In the story, Adam and Eve are symbols of the human race. At first, because they are internally at peace with the mystery that is God, they are at peace with the universe. Once they reject this mystery, they recognize their "nakedness," their sin of alienation from wholeness. This leads to general disharmony in human relations and between human beings and creation (Gen. 3:19).

In African mythology the same insight is expressed in terms of God's self-removal from the world. However, in both traditions, God does not leave people without hope. He leaves them with some aspects of the divine self. The pull to recognize divine authority over humanity, through sacrifices and offerings and acts of worship, points to the human desire of communion with God in both the African and Judeo-Christian traditions. In the Christian tradition, the greatest sacrifice is the hospitality Jesus offers by making himself food for humanity so that those who partake of it in self-sacrificing love for others (following the symbol of the Eucharist) may be in full communion with him.

Individuals who achieve the deepest and highest level of love also achieve the highest level of unity with God. Those who are able to visualize this perfectly through prayer and contemplation are called mystics in the Christian spiritual tradition. They are holy men and women who "feel" the presence of the God of love suffused throughout their entire existence as persons. The mystical experience is first of all God's gratuitous gift of inspiration to the individual, something that St. Teresa of Avila insisted cannot be acquired by human industry alone. Although human cooperation is required in the experience if it is not to dissipate, mysticism involves the *before* and the *beyond*. Just like the gift of healing and divination in African spirituality, the mystical experience of God in Christian spirituality is before and beyond human ingenuity. It calls for surrender to a higher, unifying divine power as the principal element in the spiritual life on which everything else is dependent. We have seen that the healer in Africa will constantly utter the disclaimer, "It is God who heals."

Saint Paul rightly calls for discernment of spiritual powers because there are some that lead (in the African context) toward *Ubuntu* and others that lead away from it. These latter constitute witchcraft, the ultimate symbol of evil in African spirituality. The spirit of "love, joy, peace, patience, kindness, generosity, faithfulness, gentleness, self-control" is the spirit of *Ubuntu*, while the spirit of "immorality, impurity, licentiousness, idolatry, sorcery, hatred, rivalry, jealousy, outbursts of fury, acts of selfishness, dissensions, factions, occasions of envy, drinking bouts, orgies, and the like" (Gal. 5:19-24; 1 Cor. 13) is one of witchcraft. These human life-attitudes define human spiritual orientations.

How do individuals conduct their lives in communities, and how do communities of people live in relation to one another and to the rest of creation? In tandem with St. Paul's insight, spirituality refers to either of the attitudes above. Another way of putting this is to say that morality and spirituality have to do with the *quality* of people's *relational* life, as we have repeatedly insisted. How is their relationship with other people in various areas of life, such as economics, politics, and general social relations? The academic study of morality in this approach takes into account the various methods, values, and consequences of these arrangements on the well-being of individuals, societies, and the world at large. As an academic discipline it reflects on the nature of human relationship with the whole of creation.

Spirituality and morality should not be seen as separate realities in the African Christian orientation, but as parts of the same human endeavor to become fully human. If there is a distinction to be made between them, it is only that morality is the practical manifestation of spirituality; it shows concretely spirituality's basic "state" at any given point in time. Mysticism, understood as deep union of love with God, can be arrived at only through deep union of love with people, never in separation from them. This is the implication particularly of the prophetic literature in the Hebrew Scriptures, where cult is subordinated to love-justice. Whenever this is not the case, it is sharply denounced by the prophets. Perhaps more clearly than the other prophets, Amos and Hosea exemplify this theology. Through Amos, God declares to Israel that he is not interested in their worship of words, songs, material offerings, and sacrifices: "But if you would offer me holocausts, then let justice surge like water and goodness like an unfailing stream" (Amos 5:21-24).

The prophet Hosea summarizes all of this in one sentence (Hos. 6:6), one that is recalled twice by Jesus in different words: "For it is love that I desire, not sacrifice, and the knowledge of God rather than holocausts" (Hos. 6:6; Matt. 9:13; 12:7). Jesus insists that reconciliation, or communion between and among people, is a precondition for true cult. Unity with God is not possible, Jesus warns, until a person has advanced in unity with other people, for the possibility of the former depends very much on the practical evidence of the latter (Matt. 5:23).

The most dramatic and clearest statement of this spiritual vision, however, is the portrait by Matthew of "the last judgment," the final stage of human growth where a person is determined to be an ancestor or otherwise, in African symbolism, or in heaven or hell in traditional Christian imagery. At this stage, one must face one's past to give an account of one's life on earth. In a sense, therefore, you are your shadow; where you have come from determines where you are going. The past and the future are intimately linked. Jesus applies standards to this pilgrimage that are not exotic but quite ordinary requirements of *Ubuntu*: love and compassion, feeding the hungry, offering drink to the thirsty, clothing the naked, sheltering the homeless, visiting the sick and imprisoned, and burying the dead. Further, it involves instructing those who do not know the life-giving ancestral tradition, advising the doubtful, correcting those in error, cultivating patience, forgiving offenses, and comforting the afflicted (Matt. 25:31-46). Once again, the Lord's Prayer with its fourfold petition also addresses the same issues of ordinary human needs: food, forgiveness, right thinking, and right living (Matt. 6:9-13; Luke 11:1-4): in a word, *Ubuntu*. This, extended to all of humanity as the new clan, is what makes for peace and stability in the world.

11

Engaging Language

"Don't break the furniture!"

Cross-cultural or intercultural contact inevitably involves some form of "speech" or language. If it is to be fruitful or even begin at all, the integrity of the symbols of each mode of speech becomes crucial. The success of any conversation calls for a spirit of listening with deep respect to the experience of the other, which over a long period has been synthesized into symbols, whether these are verbal, artistic, ritual, putative, or virtual. When you are invited into someone's house, the simple rule of thumb, one of elementary courtesy, is "Don't break the furniture." Of course, you may bring to your hosts' attention new designs on the market, some of which you yourself may be in possession of, thus opening up new horizons for them. Perhaps then your hosts might want to change some of theirs and acquire new ones. But that would be entirely up to them, a free decision coming from within their new consciousness. At the same time, they may be in possession of better furniture than yours. If you are wise, you will allow them to let you in on where they acquired it. Perhaps you too might want to take the trouble to acquire some for your own house.

With a similar principle in mind, Father Adolfo Nicolás, the Superior General of the Society of Jesus, spells out the spirit that should be at the center of and guide all aspects of human relations, including evangelization, the conversations between Christians and non-Christians in view of making the message of Jesus Christ known. Speaking about this process, Nicolás warns against the belligerent spirit that marked former Christian missionary endeavors, which was nothing but "an 'assault' on the listener's personal religious world," his or her furniture. It amounted to demolishing "the system by which those others have lived and on which they have built their self-identity up until now." According to Nicolás, this procedure always runs "the risk of eliminating not only the negative and harmful aspects of a particular religious mentality, but also the good and the positive things that the Spirit of God has already brought to birth in the hearer's heart" (Nicolás 2010, 30-31).

The spiritual journey and mystical experience of a people fundamentally involves language that transcends ordinary, conceptual systems of thought and speech. Much of religious language forms a sort of "syntax" of its own. Although it is not realistic to claim that conceptual or rational speech is totally irrelevant in the realm of spiritual and mystical experience, it is not necessarily the dominant form of expressing the experience. Another way of explaining the matter is to point out that notional speech in the sphere of the spiritual life is often a stammering effort to appreciate the reality of often inexplicable deep union with the spiritual reality. This desire and union are first of all conveyed in symbolic, analogical, poetic expressions, some of which can appear paradoxical.

The spiritual experience of a diviner has to be interpreted by the diviner or by an adept surrogate. It is the same with the experience of possession, in which the possessing spirit takes over the individuality of the possessed. Both the diviner and the possessed often use "strange" language in comparison with ordinary language and ways of understanding. Both tend to engage in unconventional behavior, which indicates an extraordinary presence. The lay terminology for this is "babble"; but to those in the know, the prophets and mystics, it is far from meaningless. On the contrary, the depth and weight of meaning render any other form of language inadequate to express the experience satisfactorily. These experiences were common in the Hebrew as well as Christian Scriptures (for the latter, see 1 Cor. 2:10; 14:2-40; Mark 16:17; Acts 2:1-4; 10:45-46; 19:3-6).

Empirical, scientific evidence therefore constitutes only one form of speech. To account for the whole of the human experience of self-understanding and expression, the symbolic, metaphorical, affective, and emotional modes of speech must be taken into account. In no way are they necessarily evidence of immaturity, nonsensical credulity, or superstition, as is sometimes thought. Belief in super- or supranatural existences, beings by definition empirically and materially indemonstrable, is not inherently irrational; nor is religious cult and ritual, which rely heavily on and employ symbolic language. The emotional, affective aspect of the human person is a component of being human, and it is central not only to religion but to human civilization itself. To bracket it from consideration of what it means to be an adult person, a holistic human being or *Umuntu*, the actual physical individual with all the qualities of *Ubuntu*, and all in the name of rationality, is to destroy the meaning of the human reality.

The full force of the experience of love, hate, respect, or fear and their foundation at the center of human existence cannot be explained entirely by their practical outcome. Their foundation is much deeper than the consequences shown by the end result that can be captured by verbal explanations. The deepest language of love or respect, for example, is symbolic; it is a language of images and metaphors and gestures, which indicates the origins, reasons, and meaning of these feelings. It is a language of gift giving, of offerings, of touch, of looks, and "unintelligible" sounds. In the end, it is a language of awe, which often cannot be interpreted "by reason." Yet, as everyone knows, it is not unreasonable. Culturally, the images, metaphors, and gestures born of and giving birth to this language are culturally reasonable, as they represent and express deep human awareness. The African ritual dance (and, indeed, in a manner of speaking, all forms of dance), song, dirge, and curse exemplify this kind of speech.

Many studies have now brought this to light. Deep symbols are very subtle in their signification of meaning. They "speak to man existentially and find an echo in the inarticulate depths of his psyche." Symbolic "images communicate through their evocative power. They convey a latent meaning that is apprehended in a non-conceptual, even a subliminal, way." Well rooted in a particular social context, symbols "transform the horizons of man's life, integrate his perception of reality, alter his scale of values, reorient his loyalties, attachments, and aspirations in a manner far exceeding the powers of abstract conceptual thought" (Dulles 1978, 24). In other words, symbols confirm identity at the same time they entice one to go beyond oneself into a deeper reality and thus become "born again," if we may use the expression. They are "imbued with plenitude or depth of meaning that surpasses the capacities of conceptual thinking and propositional speech." In its dynamics with the human mind and spirit, a deep symbol "evokes a realization of that which surpasses ordinary objective cognition. Symbolic knowledge is self-involving, for the symbol 'speaks to us only insofar as it lures us to situate ourselves mentally within the universe of meaning and value which it opens up to us'" (Dulles 1992, 18-19).

The distinction between deep and superficial symbols is important. A deep symbol is usually relatively unintelligible; that is where it finds its "virtue." "A symbol loses its grip once its significance has been rationalized, and it has become generally understood. But so long as it remains unintelligible, it can, if it is a good symbol, exercise astonishing powers" (Bridston 1965, 82). Spittle, for example, which in a different context is the essence of "opprobrium and vilification" (e.g., Matt. 27:30) is for the Maasai people of East Africa the ultimate symbol of forgiveness, because it represents and expresses for them the "very sacred element of a living, breathing human" power. Spitting on a person in a ritual situation effected what it was meant to effect, and more: it "was not just a sign of forgiveness. It was forgiveness"

(Donovan 1982, 59-60). Offering true forgiveness in this case thus turns the forgiver him- or herself truly into the gift of forgiveness itself. As a young person going to school far away from home, I was blessed by my own father with spittle at sunrise on the day of departure as protection against evil while away, but also as a concrete expression of his paternity and the necessary protective responsibility accompanying it.

Of all the linguistic images, Dulles explains that the religious ones are the most intricate. "Religious images . . . focus our experience in a new way," he explains. "They have an aesthetic appeal, and are apprehended not simply by the mind but by the imagination, the heart, or, more properly, the whole man" (Dulles 1978, 24). To get in touch with the numinous, to become religious in any sense of the word, human beings have to resort to the use of symbols and metaphors in this way. Songs and dances and the entire range of art, sculpture, sacred spaces, worship forms, and divination "techniques" are such images in African spirituality. They are means to be in touch with supernatural power. The spoken word augments these symbols or is in turn augmented by them. It would seem that one without the other is incomplete. Initiation without masks, mourning without dirges, marriage without bride-wealth, childhood without naming, and burial without the second burial (*Kurova Guva*), the ritual of "welcoming the spirit of the deceased home," would leave out part of the human reality as Africans perceive it and would thus reduce it to certain physical dimensions only.

The dance as an expression of the conjunction of body and spirit is a particularly significant language of African spirituality. Dance and song supersede word as an expression of deep joy, health, power, anger, and even pity. They express as no other symbol can the hope of freedom and life. Song and dance were ubiquitous in the campaign for freedom by the black South Africans in the days of apartheid. The very poor all over Africa sing and dance as an expression of hope for redemption from their pitiful conditions. Moreover, nothing is as effective in coaxing the spirits to join human activity in terms of possession, divination, augury, or casting away witchcraft as song and dance. Prayer is best expressed by song and dance.

Symbols are, therefore, "tokens," according to Ashbrook and Albright. "We throw out symbols as tokens of larger ideas. They thereby point beyond themselves toward a greater structure in which they participate." The same thing applies to metaphor, which implies transference of meaning from one quite understood reality to another usually less understood and deeper one. "Metaphors are images that bridge different meanings by showing a likeness between them. . . . [They transfer] meaning from one object to another, thereby suggesting new and different understandings" (Ashbrook and Albright 1997, 168n19), More intricate than signs and analogies, which are direct pointers to what is indicated, symbols and metaphors are more evocative, thus requiring much imagination and human involvement in deciphering meaning. What places symbols, metaphors, and signs in the same category of speech, more or less, is only the fact that they all point not to themselves but to something other than and beyond them. We may also say without exaggeration that all life in Africa is symbolic in that sense; for the African, everything is sacred, because it points beyond itself to a sacred power. As we expressed in Chapter 2, this constitutes the "heart of the matter" of African spirituality. Personal life is symbolic of the life of the community and vice versa, and both are often associated together as different levels of one entity. Personal life is also symbolic of ancestral life, so that ethical living recalls and actualizes ancestral presence within the individual and through the individual, the community—and the other way round.

Hospitality and gift exchange, which characterize *Ubuntu*, take on important significance in this perception. An illustration can be seen in the engagement ritual. When a boy gives a piece of cloth, such as a handkerchief, to a loved one, he symbolizes commitment to her, so that refusal to accept it on the part of the girl or subsequently the decision to destroy it in public means the end of the relationship. This symbol speaks with greater power than any words, which may be interpreted as just a sudden outburst of anger. On the contrary, the action of destroying a symbol speaks to the people involved more radically; with its absence, the giver no longer exists.

Another category of symbols with regard to ill will and witchcraft will also help in understanding better the significance of symbolic speech. Among many African communities, human waste is associated with ill will and witchcraft. Consequently, if placed in a strategic place by an enemy in one's homestead, it points to the destruction and death of whomever it is intended to affect. If nothing is done to prevent its bad consequences, ill health or death is bound to occur in the person. Again, as in many other cases of symbolic speech, it is pointless to inquire whether the consequence is empirically demonstrable, that is, whether it *actually* occurs. What is relevant is the power of the symbol to transfer meaning, in this case from human waste to the larger idea of destruction of life. As we pointed out earlier, the power of evil may be associated and symbolized in Africa by certain animals and birds, certain plants, and even inorganic things such as shells or rocks. When strategically used by evil powers, they lead to palpable ill effects.

What is true of material symbols is equally true of gestural and psychic symbols such as looks, dreams, and so on. To look at someone with evil intentions is the equivalent of killing him or her, especially when the victim is vulnerable, that is to say, has less power than the agent. This is the perception behind the efficacy of the evil eye. What gestures or body language demonstrate joy or tranquility or peace? Which ones define defiance or hostility or rejection? It is important to emphasize that all of these symbols and their interpretation are subtle, so that the same gesture may contain two or several different meanings depending on the context (time, place, and personal relationships) in which they are performed. They may even be devoid of meaning in one situation while they may be pregnant with good or bad implications in another.

William Ian Miller provides an interesting illustration of how symbolization works in his book *The Anatomy of Disgust* (1997). Miller explains that humans often link the emotion of disgust with contamination, and, in many instances, contamination has moral and spiritual implications. An encounter of Charles Darwin with a person in Tierra del Fuego, an archipelago off the southernmost tip of the South American mainland, shows this.

When he visited Tierra del Fuego, Darwin relates that "a native touched with his finger some cold preserved meat which I was eating at our bivouac, and plainly showed utter disgust at its softness; whilst I felt utter disgust at my food being touched by a naked savage, though his hands did not appear dirty" (Miller 1997, 1). How so, these two spontaneous reactions to the same action? It is not surprising that Darwin's "naked native" judged him immoral for ingesting such "filth," on the one hand. On the other, it is not too difficult to imagine that Darwin, in his presumed mental and physical superiority, considered "the naked native" socially and morally inferior, unworthy to touch his food even if his hands were clean. With slavery, colonialism, imperialism, racism, sexism, and class differences, similar judgments repeat themselves throughout human history. All of these are not just facts of history; they are at the same time powerful symbols.

There is no need to emphasize the point that, in Christian tradition, the Bible is highly symbolic as a book. Furthermore, its language does not intend to offer direct understanding of God's will because it is often mythical in character, as Scripture scholarship has established. Bronislaw Malinowski explains myths as stories whose purpose is to legitimatize tradition. "The function of myth, briefly, is to strengthen tradition and endow it with a greater value and prestige by tracing it back to a higher, better, more supernatural reality of initial events." As such, it is "an indispensable ingredient of all culture." Like symbol, it is a result of and creates identity. Myth is "constantly regenerated; every historical change creates its mythology. . . . Myth is a constant by-product of living faith, which is in need of miracles; of sociological status, which demands precedent; of moral rule, which requires sanction" (Malinowski 1948, 146). As mythical or symbolic language, the language of basic spirituality, biblical language is deciphered through hermeneutics, or interpretation, the language structure of concepts, theology, and dogma. This is the task facing African biblical interpretation (see Mundele 2012, 16-90; Kinoti and Waliggo 1997).

Images, metaphors, parables, poetry and stories dominate religious language, and unless one is familiar with the specific language in worship and prayer, "they may look and look, yet not see; they may listen and listen, yet not understand" (Mark 4:12; Matt. 13:14; Luke 8:10). They will miss the deepest significance of the acts of prayer and worship in the search of rational intelligibility. We come to know and become united with God initially through images that transcend or may even defy logical rationality. Thus, individuals who glorify reason above all else, who scoff at or reject outright any sign of transcendent religious experiences mediated by symbolic language, do miss a comprehensive vision of reality for symbolic speech.

Dulles again explains that because religious imagery is "both functional and cognitive," that is, on the one hand religious images point to the sacred, and on the other serve to help humanity access the sacred, "In order to win acceptance, the images must resonate with the experience of the faithful" because "if they do not resonate, this is proof that there is some isomorphism between what the image depicts and the spiritual reality with which the faithful are in existential contact. Religious experience, then, provides a vital key for the evaluation and interpretation of symbols" (Dulles 1978, 25). This means that what the symbol says at any given time derives from the mystical experience of the people where it has its origin. Mystical or symbolic language is "consubstantial with human existence" (Eliade 1969, 12). Needless to say, in order to foster a deeper awareness of the holy, discursive language in Africa needs to be in touch with African symbolic language as a foundational tool for the summons toward union with ultimate power. Catechetical language must be available to the majority of the people by speaking deeply to them and expressing adequately their mystical experience.

Much symbolic language in Africa speaks of the presence of divine power through the reality of creation. Ancestral language in which much of African spiritual awareness is founded and integrated is a prime example (see Nyamiti 1984, 15-24). It is not possible to have an inner understanding of God without the ancestors. Models of divine life on earth, which everyone must imitate, are embedded in the ancestors who connect the individual and the community with the spiritual world. Ancestors play this indispensable role toward a culture that is more attuned to the concrete in order to appreciate the good life that is shaped by divine power.

The vacuum created once ancestors are conceptually removed from the spiritual picture is unbridgeable, for it completely undercuts the life of a people from their source of identity by blocking the "ongoing communication and participation of the departed with the family" (CDC 2010, 30), which for Africans is the very essence of ongoing life. Replacing known ancestors with putative others appears incredible. More seriously, it removes individuals who contributed and fashioned families, and are expected to continue doing so, from the immediate communion of the community, making the understanding of time, space, and human wholeness unachievable. The defining questions for African spirituality—where did we come from, why are we here, and where are we going—are unanswerable without the real presence of the ancestors.

The sentiment "Honor your father and your mother, that you may live long in the land," or "Remember your ancestors, those who first spoke God's message to you; and reflecting upon the outcome of their life and work, follow the example of their faith" found in the Scriptures (Exod. 20:12; Heb. 13:7) forms for Africa the foundation of ancestral cult. The specific expressions of this cult vary from one ethnic group to another and are open to development and change. But the deep intentionality of preserving communion of the vital forces of the departed for the sake of the good life of the living traverses the spirituality of all ethnic groups. The universal expression of this, which we have discussed above, is the obligation to marry and beget children. Because of the spiritual depth of its symbolism, this is not a light obligation, and therefore the inflexibility with which polygamy has been condemned in African societies and celibacy imposed as a condition for ordained ministry in Catholic Christianity indicates a lack of sensitivity to inner meanings of symbolic cultural expressions.

The efficacious power of nature spirits constitutes another of the symbols of African spirituality whose indiscriminate destruction is highly questionable. With our contemporary understanding of theology, helped by the social sciences, it has become easier for the open-minded to appreciate the impact of spiritual beings in African religiosity than was the case in the past. Perhaps this is also true in Christianity as a whole. The monotheism of Christian dogma does not obliterate the reality of spirit beings, even in Christianity itself. Although Christian dogma and theology consciously tone it down, the power of the Evil Spirit, or Satan, in popular Christian consciousness is not very far below God's. In African Christian consciousness, the power of Satan and the power of God are practically perceived to be on the same level; only the circumstances distinguish them.

Representations of spiritual beings in art depend, once again, very much on the physical and social environment of a society. These stimulate the imagination of the particular societies concerned. In the predominantly dry areas of Africa, for example, there is no cult of the water spirit or goddess of healing, fertility, and wealth, with slight variations generally referred to as *Mami Wata*. But she is extremely popular elsewhere where there is plenty of water. Her presence in art, music, literature, and film is widespread in parts of West, Central, and southern Africa and across the ocean from Africa in the Caribbean islands and parts of South America. This shows that the introduction of new images and symbols into the spiritual landscape of a people must take even their physical surroundings into account. Symbols are useful if they are capable of touching the deepest feelings of a community, what Adolfo Nicolás characterizes as "'right feeling' (*orthopathos* or *orthopatheia*) rather than 'right thinking' (*orthodoxia*)" (Nicolás 2010, 27). But *orthopathos* is conditioned by one's environment and cannot be artificially abstracted from it.

To end this chapter on a note with which it started, the importance of the guest respecting the furniture in the host's house and refraining from gratuitously breaking it cannot be emphasized enough. Religion or religious consciousness is a prerogative of every human society, and it is impractical to suppose that the old is nonexistent when offering a new consciousness through positive notions. Among human societies, new and unknown religious and spiritual perceptions become "real," so to speak, only through images of the old and familiar life experiences.

12

The Spirit of Interreligious Dialogue

"What are they really aiming at?"

In the last few years, theologians (particularly of Asian origin) have discussed the possibility of double or multiple religious belonging. This is a situation in which an individual or group perceives and accepts a sense of meaning for one's religious belief from more than one religious-spiritual orientation and tradition while strongly rooted in, firmly belonging to, and espousing only one among them. Is it possible to have a "hyphenated," non-hybrid" cultural-religious identity, whereby, for example, one is an African-Christian or a Hindu-Christian?

In order to understand the sense of hyphenated religious identity properly, it is important to distinguish it from "hybrid" identity. Though related, the two are significantly different. While hybrid identity claims to spiritually profess and socially and institutionally identify double or multiple faiths at one and the same time, hyphenated identity espouses only a single belonging. In hybrid identity, a person may claim to be both a Christian and an African religionist, for example, or a Christian and a follower of Hinduism; in hyphenated belonging, a person is Christian who may be inspired by African or Hindu religious values, as the case may be. It is, therefore, possible in hyphenated religious identity for an African Christian, for instance, to be sincerely convinced about the efficacy of and consequently participate in the rituals of *Kurova Guva* (welcoming the spirits of the deceased home), or for a Hindu-Christian to be committed to the practice of *hatha yoga* (meditation to bring about sacred energy for spiritual purification) without abandoning his or her Christian identity.

Perhaps an analogy is useful to make the distinction clearer. A Christian with a hybrid identity stands with one leg, each in multiple religious worlds, in Christianity *and* African Religion or Hinduism, for instance, practically alternating one with the other as circumstances demand. A Christian with a hyphenated identity, on the contrary, stands with both legs in a single religious world, in this case Christianity, but is willing and ready to welcome values, insights, and practices that enhance the horizons of the Christian faith and expand its understanding. Thus, Michael Amaladoss, an Indian Catholic priest and theologian, admits, "My heritage is . . . Hindu. My ancestors were Hindu." This has consequences for his Christian faith. "If God has spoken to my ancestors, and if the Spirit of God has been present and active in their religion, there is no reason why I should not reclaim my Hindu spiritual heritage and integrate it with my Christian heritage." And this without regret or apology. "I am heir to two traditions, namely Hinduism and Christianity. I feel proud of both of them and seek to integrate them in myself. This is how I become Hindu-Christian" (Amaladoss 2011, 103).

Apart from the work of Amaladoss, another important scholarly attempt to explain multiple religious belonging by a Catholic theologian is by the Vietnamese-born Peter C. Phan in his book *Being Religious Interreligiously* (2004). But there are numerous other scholars engaged in interreligious dialogue who have made similar assertions arising from the same theological belief that religious faiths other than Christianity are more or less ways of divine self-manifestation in the world. As such, they have to be respected. Practically, they need not be approached antagonistically as hindrances against Christian belief, but in many cases positively as partners or potential partners toward the quest for higher horizons into God. Is it possible for Christians to have a glimpse into what the faith of our neighbors is aiming at? How does Christian belief agree or disagree with the paths followed by other religions to attain the goal of transcendence shared by many religious faiths? How fundamentally divergent are they from the Christian fundamentals? Are there certain points where they connect with Christianity or teach it something, or, conversely, where Christianity can offer something to them?

From the Catholic point of view the question is generally now answered positively. Vatican II taught that points of contact are possible not only among Christian denominations, leading to ecumenism (*Unitatis Redintegratio*), but also, and just as importantly, with regard to non-Christian religious faiths, leading to interreligious dialogue (*Nostra Aetate, Ad Gentes, Dignitatis Humanae, Gaudium et Spes*). In a well-known paragraph, *Nostra Aetate*, for example, explicitly states that "the Catholic Church rejects nothing which is true and holy in . . . [other] religions." Instead, "she looks with sincere respect upon those ways of conduct and of life, those rules and teachings which, though differing in many particulars from what she holds and sets forth, nevertheless often reflect a ray of that Truth which enlightens all." The document not only exhorts the Catholic faithful to "dialogue" and "collaborate" with people of other religions, but, more significantly still, to "acknowledge, preserve, and promote the spiritual and moral goods found among . . . [them], as well as the values in their society and culture" (*Nostra Aetate*, no. 2).

Even from the position that explicit belief in Jesus Christ and membership in the Catholic Church are the only genuine way of being religious, it is officially unobjectionable today to affirm that non-Christian faiths may be "ways of salvation and that religious pluralism is part of God's providential plan" (Phan 2004, xxiii). Among many eminent advocates of this view toward religious pluralism, Catholic scholars such as Jacques Dupuis, Paul F. Knitter, Roger Haight, and Elizabeth Johnson consider the existence of a plurality of religions not as an aberration but a necessary expansion of horizons into the divine reality; in different ways they may all be aiming at the same thing (Dupuis 1997; Knitter 2002; Haight 1999; Johnson 2007).

Recently, serious criticisms and warnings have been raised by the Congregation for the Doctrine of the Faith (CDF) and the United States Conference of Catholic Bishops (USCCB) against the views of these and other theologians on this matter. Concerning Phan specifically, the USCCB took exception to what it called "ambiguities" in his book, mentioned above, in three areas regarding the church's teaching that "Jesus Christ . . . [is] the unique and universal Savior of all humankind"; that non-Christian religions contain only "seeds" of the gospel and therefore do not have the fullness of salvation; and that the Catholic Church is "the unique and universal instrument of salvation" (see http://www.zenit.org/rssenglish-21240). The theologians in question claim not to reject these teachings, but point out that the affirmations are *statements of belief* that should be open to dialogue with other assertions of belief from non-Christian religions that, for them, may be equally as strong. But the discussion becomes strident and generates more heat than light when church leadership becomes resistant to dialogue on these issues with Catholic theologians, let alone with other faith traditions. In several documents, Vatican II, however, insisted on the importance of dialogue for evangelization, and, following the inspiration of the council, the late Cardinal Carlo Maria Martini of Milan emphasized it for the contemporary church.

The qualifier made in the paragraphs above *pertaining* to scholarship is deliberate and important because, at least or especially in Africa, multiple religious belonging is not merely an academic or theoretical issue. African converts to Christianity (and Islam) have always lived it, despite strong and persistent condemnation from Christian missionary spirituality, teaching, and practice. For a long time, many Christian theologians as well saw this as a "problem" of "dual religious consciousness" and described it as a phenomenon of negative syncretism. Even as recently as 2009, Pope Benedict XVI in his Apostolic Exhortation *Africae Munus* (*AM*), summarizing the deliberations of the second African Synod, feared that dual religious identity on

the continent would deprive Africans of "the fullness of the Gospel." Explicitly acknowledging that the phenomenon is a reality in Africa, however, the
pope, speaking for the African church, wants it removed through "profound
catechesis and inculturation." He gives belief in witchcraft as, to his mind, an
example of this danger:

> Witchcraft, which is based on the traditional religions, is currently expe-
> riencing a certain revival. Old fears are re-surfacing and creating para-
> lyzing bonds of subjection. Anxiety over health, well-being, children,
> the climate, and protection from evil spirits at times lead people to have
> recourse to practices of traditional African religions that are incom-
> patible with Christian teaching. The problem of "dual affiliation"—to
> Christianity and to the traditional African religions—remains a chal-
> lenge. Through profound catechesis and inculturation, the Church in
> Africa needs to help people to discover the fullness of Gospel values.
> It is important to determine the profound meaning of these practices
> of witchcraft by identifying the many theological, social and pastoral
> implications of this scourge. (*AM*, no. 93)

In practice, however, and contrary to this view, the acceptance of dual religious belonging among African Christians is now evident and has been institutionalized, without apology or embarrassment but with pride (as in the
case of Michael Amaladoss above) by the African Initiated Churches (AICs).
The question these churches have courageously addressed with different levels of success, as was pointed out at the beginning of this part of the book,
pertains to how to expunge cultural Eurocentrisms from the expression of the
Christian faith in Africa. How can the Christian faith be articulated, understood, and lived in an African way in the African environment? Of course,
the question faces all Christian churches everywhere and is addressed in various subtle and conspicuous ways. Again, this is the question of inculturation,
to which the response of the AICs' mainline churches has been much more
practical and radical in terms of acknowledging and appropriating African
values than has happened in the mainline Christian denominations.

Studies in interreligious dialogue point out that the encounter between
Christianity, grounded essentially in Eurocentric epistemology and other
religious epistemologies, including African Religion, necessitates four
options, which Paul F. Knitter enumerates: replacement, fulfillment, mutuality, and acceptance (Knitter 2002). In the African context, this amounts
in practice to a choice between total overthrow of African epistemology,
complete abandonment of European epistemology, reconciliation between
the two, or mutual tolerance between them. The first option is obviously

morally unconscionable, because it amounts to cultural genocide. It has hopefully become clear in the foregoing pages, further, that in this age of globalization, the second option is neither probable nor possible, if only, and especially, on account of the universal character of belief in Christ. The outstanding question for inculturation lies, therefore, in the last two alternatives: whether African and European epistemologies can be reconciled and whether, where this proves impossible, they can coexist in mutual acceptance of their differences.

The approach of the AICs seems to respect the sense of dialogue and cultural identity of peoples and to favor hyphenated Christian identity in Africa. What the early African converts to Christianity did clandestinely at the beginning, the AICs are doing boldly and openly now. In terms of living the Christian faith in Africa, this is a healthier situation. For the early African converts to Christianity, a complete break with their traditions and spirituality was required, coupled with the appeal to European culture as the only valid vehicle for interpreting and expressing the message of Christ. "Conversion" was understood as the process of severing the African people's connection to their spiritual roots. Naturally, as Fritz Stenger notes, not a few people internally defied this. "In order to protect their memory from the domesticating efforts of the colonizers and missionaries," according to Stenger, "the newly converted [African Christians] moved their most signifying practices to a hidden social space and restructured it in newly organised esoteric ways" (Stenger 2001, 38).

The AICs have captured this resistance and institutionalized it in productive ways that mainline Christianity in Africa has been unwilling to do, despite many theoretical propositions to the contrary. The inculturation process in its present form in the mainline churches is inadequate because "It only adapts some external signs of experiencing and expressing Christian faith and maintains, as an absolute rule, the being of Christianity as signified and historically actualised in the Western experience" (Stenger 2001, 42). Again, although it is official policy in the Catholic Church in Africa since the 1970s, inculturation has failed to make practical the theological insight of the Incarnation, that just as God became human in Jesus Christ to bring about the liberation of humanity, the Christian faith in its concrete expressions as church must enter thoroughly into its host African culture and become truly part of it to liberate it. Apart from this, the Christian faith cannot impact the "soul" of the people and culture being invited to explicitly acknowledge Christ as liberator.

When mere adjustment of foreign faith-expressions is made the basis of inculturation of African Christian spirituality, theology, and pastoral practice, it ignores the rootedness of every person in his or her context and becomes culturally alienating. Historically, adaptation has taken Western Christian perceptions and concepts of understanding the message of Jesus as starting points to which African perspectives must always conform. This is the sense one gets, for instance, from Pope Benedict's statement quoted above. But such procedure inhibits genuine dialogue, innovation, and insights into the gospel evoked by the African cultural and spiritual environment. Moreover, Western approaches are thereby disabled from the start from learning from this spiritual context with its God-given values. The shortcomings of this approach to inculturation has generally been recognized by the majority of African theologians; it is seen as inadequate in helping African Christian communities to become truly African and truly Christian, as we shall see below. Yet, on account of the Roman Catholic Church's centralized theological and administrative perception, it remains the dominant method in the ecclesiastical catechesis and pastoral practice of the mainline Christian churches in Africa.

The approach of the AICs to the activity of remembering (*anamnesis*), which we have referred to before, captures a fundamental spiritual trait of humanity. James B. Ashbrook and Carol Rausch Albright, students of the workings of the human mind, underline this when they recall how all human beings owe the amenities of their existence to the ingenuity and industry of their predecessors in this world. "All of us are indebted to a forgotten lineage of those who loved and worked and thought and dreamed—those who learned how to use fire, to domesticate animals and plants, to preserve food and weave cloth." There would be no progress in human life without this connectivity. Ashbrook and Albright continue: "We humans are indebted to those who developed written language and law, who labored to build the edifices of knowledge and culture that now support us. We also are indebted to those closer to us who personally loved and educated us" (Ashbrook and Albright 1997, 143). It is for this reason that ancestral traditions and customs and indigenous languages and symbols, on the one hand, and the language and symbols of the Bible, on the other, are important for the AICs in the expression of their faith in Jesus. One enriches the other.

For the AICs, Jesus is understood in both biblical and local images. This influences directly their approach to prayer and worship. When the AICs understand Jesus as God the Ancestor, Healer or Elder Brother, Chief, or Master of Initiation, prayer takes on a different character: it becomes an active conversation with an actual partner. Jesus becomes a member of the community who must be treated as such. So, although submission to Jesus as Ancestor is required as the attitude toward him in prayer, such responses as argument, reasoning, complaint, expression of disappointment, dissatisfaction, frustration, and perhaps even anger with him cannot be ruled out as inappropriate when the situation calls for it. Of course, this does not reflect negatively on the superior role of Jesus with the worshiper; it is rather a reflection of the human condition of the inadequacy of humanity in need of help in a relationship that Jesus has the power to mend. The center of prayer is for the vitality of the community in all dimensions, that it may grow, increase, and remain united. Jesus as Ancestor can supply these needs.

As the principal guardian of the community of those who believe in him, Jesus as the Proto-Ancestor is seen as the main focus and recipient of prayer and veneration. He is the senior partner in the spiritual conversation. The highest form of reverence is reserved exclusively for him alone and for God whom he represents. The spiritual vision of the AICs never attributes this honor to human ancestors (except in those rare cases where the founder arrogates to himself the name and position of Jesus as son of God), but the ancestors are not thereby superfluous. Because they possess immense power derived from their close association with Jesus in death, they are also acknowledged and venerated. It means that the ancestors and the elders of the community (parents and grandparents in their families, people with civil authority, experts in different fields of knowledge, religious leaders, and so on) who fulfill well their responsibility for the life of the community must also be honored for the reason that they share more intensely in the ancestral power of Jesus than the rest of the community.

Because for the AICs the central mission of Jesus is to bring fullness of life to the world in all its forms, their spirituality in prayer and in life in general is based on this goal. Human beings obtain the life that Jesus offers when they are freed from the invisible chains of evil, of hatred, anger, malice, pride, and contempt for God and one another, in a word, from witchcraft. They also experience this liberation when the chains of possession by evil spirits, disease, poverty and ignorance, phenomena that are all associated with witchcraft, are removed. The message of Jesus addresses all of these bonds and aims to break them so that abundance of life may prevail. For AICs, Christian prayer and activity are deficient if they do not address these issues that break the harmonious flow of life in the world.

The spirituality of the AICs arises out of the indigenous belief in the good life. Lack of desired offspring, sufficient food, and other material goods necessary for life, and especially the occurrence or recurrence of illness of whatever kind, are defects and threats against the good life. They are a sign of disfavor from divine and ancestral powers, and therefore from Jesus. As such, they are a clarion call for prayer and repentance before Jesus who alone can change the situation. In view of restoring life in its abundance, sickness must be healed, and any and every power that invades the individual or community to destabilize life must be expelled in the name and power of Jesus so that humanity may obtain divine favor to grow into wholeness.

The issue for the AICs in times of illness and suffering is not "why heal?" but how to do so. How should community leaders approach Jesus with the imperative for healing and deliverance? In the spiritual vision of the AICs, Jesus is ultimately the one who is the most potent vital energy. Although he sometimes gives his powers of healing and deliverance to certain "elders," this is to manifest his authority through their practice of medicine, counseling, peacemaking, prayers, and so on. In this way, God through Jesus comes into direct contact with his people. Anyone to whom God grants his power to heal bodies and souls in Jesus' name must be counted among the elders, who fulfill a function to which they are privileged by God.

A strong consciousness of the presence of the Divine Spirit characterizes the life of the AICs. Perhaps this is their most obvious quality and offers a balance to the overly Christological focus of Roman Catholic theology. The presence of God and Jesus in the community is manifested by the work of the Holy Spirit. The AICs believe in and experience the work of the Spirit of God in the universe through divine power which helps human beings in their affliction. This is the Spirit they believe Christ promised to send and who remains with the world as his manifestation. The Spirit, who is the power of God and Jesus for the life of the world, works to bring about the good life in the participation, unity, and solidarity of the Christian community. The spiritual power of God, the Holy Spirit, which leads to integration of the various forces of life in the world to sustain it, demands respectful silence as the proper response before its divine majesty. Recognizing the incomprehensibility of the Spirit who is "all in all" and who integrates everything, the AICs have generally preserved the splendor of God principally through celebration rather than explanatory theology.

By closely relating or combining spirituality with the experience of living, the AICs contribute to a genuine understanding of inculturation, not as a theoretical but a practical process. Although they are open to reform and transformation of certain indigenous traditions, sometimes in very radical ways, as they interact with the Bible, the indigenous tradition remains pivotal for their understanding of the Christian faith; they realize that if their faith in Jesus is to speak to them as Africans, it must retain the values of the African tradition and make it present with new meaning. Their creative innovation appears here, in the process of making the vision, acts, and values of the indigenous tradition respond to the requirements of the word of God, bringing about a creative synthesis of Christian existence rather than a completely novel construction unrelated to the African cultural and spiritual reality.

How in Africa might Africans understand the message of Jesus Christ and assimilate it as Africans? How can they relate to the God of Jesus in prayer and in worship, indeed, in the whole orientation of their lives, in a way that is affirming of their humanity as children of God and relatives of Jesus? This is the question the AICs try to answer; it is a question of meaning. What is involved in the process is the conviction, often till now intuited rather than theologically argued out, that a form of spirituality that is not affirming of African humanity and identity is alienating and, as such, cannot be Christian. In authentic Christian spirituality, relationship with the Absolute results in "abundance of life" for the community that believes in Jesus: "I came so they can have real and eternal life, more and better life than they ever dreamed of" (John 10:10).

At this point, the question arises: can some of these insights in the AICs' approach to "being Christian" contribute positively to interreligious dialogue?

The idea that the "church is mission," called and sent to the whole world to witness to the gospel of Jesus Christ, is familiar to most Christians in its exclusivist implications that, crudely put, Christianity is the only true faith to which God wants everyone to belong. In Africa, Christian mission was a unilateral movement from Europe, so much so that until only half a century or so ago it was unthinkable that Africans as a race could contribute anything to the understanding of the Good News of Jesus. Indeed, the term "missionary" was synonymous with "European." Today in some respects, this is changing; in the Roman Catholic Church numerous African priests and religious are going to the northern hemisphere as missionaries to minister to the faithful there. The universality or catholicity of the church would seem to call for this, and Christian theology affirms it.

However, in practice, many in the Western world are yet to come to terms with this development and would not like to see the flow of missionary work reversed. They therefore argue against mission from the South to the North. "The arguments used are all too familiar," A. Agbali notes: "African priests are unwilling to work with the laity . . . they are misogynists, they have accents, they are here to make money and gain status," and so on (http://www.utexas.edu/conferences/africa/ads/737.html). Many of these arguments are generalizations, of course, but the attitudes they produce are unfavorable to the emerging missionary process. What impact these attitudes will have in the long run on theological and pastoral cross-fertilization of the church universal through dialogue remains to be seen.

The dimension of mission as dialogue, one that is crucial today in the life of the church, is an underlying feature of the life of the AICs, evidenced by their readiness to bring the Bible and African culture into conversation. This forms part of the AICs' spirituality.

Christian mission inevitably involves spirituality; it is born out of, is impelled by, and is accomplished through a certain spiritual orientation. The first wave of Christian mission, which spread to northern Africa (c. 65–400 C.E.), based itself on the spiritual self-understanding of concern to spread the life-giving power of Jesus outward from a strictly and exclusively Mosaic Covenant to a universal one. The second and the third phases of Christian mission in Africa (respectively 1400–1800 and 1900 to the present), however, all but discarded the dialogical approach on account of prevailing historical circumstances, namely, the slave trade and colonialism. The church thus failed to reach out in respect and love to the African spiritual vision. In other words, it neglected the qualitative dimension of mission whose meaning is the desire for human and universal communion.

In practice, this dimension requires a degree of methodological clarity to help it to avoid the danger of ethnocentrism inherent in every missionary enterprise. The core of the process should be the recognition that intercultural and interreligious dialogue is necessary for genuine evangelization. Authentic Christian evangelization must be open to the riches offered by the divine presence in every culture, a presence that is itself responsible for enabling the message of Jesus to truly permeate and transform all cultures. What this demands on the part of the Christian evangelizer may be metaphorically described as bi- or multilingualism, the willingness to learn to "speak" more than one (exclusive) cultural-religious language. People who possess the facility to move from one world of language to another in thought and conversation usually have a wider horizon of reality beyond the restricted set of notions and concepts of their own culture and language. Without such multilingualism one will be confined within a certain "box" or framework of reality, and, therefore, possibly bigoted. True interreligious dialogue is a deep form of cultural-religious multilingual experience, spanning a whole horizon of perspectives relative to human fulfillment.

Another useful metaphor for interreligious conversation that can be obtained from the AICs is that of walking together. Herein is the meaning of the saying: "If you want to go quickly, go alone; if you want to go far, go together." Fruitful interreligious dialogue does not guarantee quick travel; it does, however, assure going the distance of hearing one another out through respectful mutual listening to shared stories of consequence, careful and unbiased evaluation of the meaning of these stories, and deep assimilation of the values they suggest. The journey that is dialogue is usually long because of the nature of the terrain to be traversed, but the destination aimed at is mutual understanding. The destination of unity ("one flock and one shepherd," John 10:16) should not necessarily be taken to mean uniformity of institutions or religious systems, but rather oneness of shared vision and the horizon concerning the sanctity of humankind and creation.

Some of the components that must form the content of the conversation between Christian and African spirituality, as the AICs demonstrate, include, first, the community-based experience of the holy, drawing from the spiritual experience and history of the community, its tradition. The authenticity of tradition is shown in the events of everyday life, above all in the fact that the community and every one of its members are alive and well, or can be restored to full life and health whenever things go wrong. The community in its tradition is the primary recipient of the experience of the holy. In it individual members participate. The church as a true assembly, the *ekklesia*, is the body of Christ at daily work, at play, in sadness and in joy or, in a word, in the dance of life in all its aesthetic components. The AICs try to make this the cardinal issue of church understanding and life. What kind of personal and communal activities and behaviors can be characterized as spiritually desirable and demonstrate the communion of people as church? Here we have the issue of the meaning and mission of church.

Second, the diffusion of sacred presence throughout existence, in human and natural events, and activities must be acknowledged. Although sacred power may be variously concentrated in certain elements and events, or more at certain times than others, the concentration simply proves the rule that everything is more or less a revelation of the divine. Everything is in the final analysis a spiritual force at its own level of existence. Since everything originates from and possesses divine force, it is capable of bestowing blessing or curse. Properly approached, handled, or used, everything in creation helps humanity's ongoing attempt to relate positively to all other life forces, animate as well as inanimate, to promote the good life. The contrary is equally true. The question for African Christian spirituality, inspired by the perspective of the AICs, is how to handle and accept the presence of the sacred in all things in the journey toward universal communion and community. The idea that the whole universe is sacred space, not to be polluted by excessive and destructive economic greed or human pride, thus becomes part of interreligious conversation. Where and how is this reality manifested most clearly? This is the question of morality and ethics.

The human quest for goodness implies the effort to avoid everything that indicates aversion against growth into human wholeness, or *Ubuntu*. This is another possible field for profitable conversation. The negation of growth into goodness, depending on how serious it is, is described in African spirituality as witchcraft. To the extent witchcraft grows, *Ubuntu* diminishes, so that, in the end, avoiding witchcraft and pursuing goodness or *Ubuntu* are one and the same struggle. Theologically, they belong in a similar system of language structure: one positive, "tracking" the right path, and the other negative, "avoiding" the wrong direction. The former implies welcoming into one's life safe and benevolent powers that protect life from destruction (the pursuit of *Ubuntu*); the latter calls for an expulsion of wicked and malevolent forces from one's thoughts and desires so as to let life's strength grow uninhibited (the rejection of witchcraft). In both cases, the process involves the language of rites and rituals whose ultimate meaning and goal is the good life. Only through symbolic language can human beings adequately imagine, image, and express the desire for the good life and make relatively accessible to human intellect. What kind of ritual language and symbol systems drive home the significance of human relationship with the spiritual powers? Here the concern is about liturgy, worship, and prayer.

None of these questions and issues can be fruitfully pursued in dialogue without the effort by all involved toward religious bi- or multilingualism. How can one arrive at this point in the context of Africa?

Ali A. Mazrui has suggested that dialogue for the sake of harmonious living in Africa must be carried out by taking into account the triad of indigenous African, Christian, and Muslim heritage (Mazrui 1987). In interreligious dialogue, therefore, besides the African indigenous and Christian spirituality that AICs are concerned with, it might be necessary at certain times, and increasingly today, to consider the contribution of Islamic spirituality as well (Kalu 2011).

The singular notion that captures the spirituality of Islam most comprehensively is none other than the name of the faith itself: Islam, submission or the readiness to give oneself completely over to God's will. In this sense of "self-yielding," Islam shares meaning with Christian surrender to God, so that God's will might be done (Dardess 2005, 22), and African fidelity to ancestral tradition. The Islamic testimony (*shahadah*) that "I bear witness that there is no god but God, and Muhammad is his Apostle [Messenger or Prophet]" signifies a creed as well as a way of life, shared by both African religionists and Christians, that trust in God offers a sense of security, assurance, and peace of mind as a consequence of personal surrender to God. As Ward J. Fellows explains, "the essence of Islam, its meaning and heart to believers, is that through submission to God Muslims (submitters) gain the peace and security of giving in to the one who is in control, who rules, and who judges all at the end" (Fellows 1979, 422).

However, surrender to God is not complete without correct action (*ihsan*), and correct worship (*ibadat*), the need for morality, ethics, and prayer in African Religion and Christianity. Because worship celebrates divine benevolence toward humanity, the Muslim is in turn required to be benevolent to others, especially the poor and destitute through almsgiving. The Prophet is reported to have declared that "He is not a believer who eats his fill while his neighbor remains hungry by his side." Here is the social dimension of Islamic spirituality, emphasizing sharing, solidarity, and egalitarianism. These are elements prominent during the month-long fast, the Ramadan. During Ramadan, as during the pilgrimage to Mecca, the *Hajj,* which Muslims are expected to perform at least one in a lifetime if possible, compassion is a basic theme. Divine compassion for human beings and the world stands as the criterion for human behavior, and it is something that every Muslim believer should emulate. This constitutes the greater *jihad,* the most important spiritual struggle for a Muslim, to bend the human heart and soul toward compassion (Dardess 2005, 146).

Islamic, Christian, and African spirituality share many fundamental links. Central among these is the emphasis on union with God through prayer and works of charity. All three underline the necessity of leading an ethical life in this world; the ethic of love, compassion, and care for human beings and the universe forms part and parcel of the fundamentals of these faiths. For African spirituality, for example, to respond to the voice of tradition is to enter into a relationship with God, the ancestors, and the universe at large. This relationship enables and brings about the attainment of the good life: happiness and peace in this world and contentment as an ancestor as a continuation of life in the world. But it is part of Christian belief as well that union with God transforms human life. It comes through prayer, whereby the person's entire outlook and behavior are orientated toward God. Christian mysticism refers to people whose life is totally in communion with God.

In Islam, the point of mystical union with God is highlighted in the Sufi tradition, where it is understood as enlightenment, or purification. One of its best-known representatives is the mystic Jalāl ad-Dīn Muhammad Balkhī, also known as Rumi (1207–1273). In the African indigenous context, the mystical experience is evident in the practice of divination and the occurrence of positive spirit possession. Moreover, to the extent that the presence of the ancestors and spirits is felt, every responsible adult is also in a sense a mystic in this tradition, especially as far as the responsibility of prayer for the well-being of the community under him or her is concerned, since this should bring him or her in communion with spiritual energies. In this tradition, perhaps more than in Christianity and Islam, prayer has a practical, almost utilitarian accent. As an example, the Sukuma people of northwest Tanzania honor their ancestors primarily because the latter must be beseeched or thanked for favors needed or granted. Frans Wijsen and Ralph Tanner argue that the insufficiency of this kind of spiritual pragmatism in Islam and Christianity makes these faiths unattractive to the Sukuma people (Wijsen and Tanner 2002).

An African hermeneutic and appropriation of Christian and Islamic spirituality reveal the fundamental requirement for living so as to be in right relationship with spiritual powers. Although African spirituality in the AICs tends to bend toward the legal dimension of biblical ethics—"If you live according to my laws and obey my commands ... I will be your God, and you will be my people" (Lev. 26:3-13), the deeper understanding of ethical life developed in Job and the prophets in the Hebrew Scriptures and advanced by Jesus in the Christian Scriptures with the emphasis on human-growth potential, *Ubuntu*, is similarly of central importance. This entails doing the divine (or ancestral) will (Matt. 26:39; Mark 14:36; Luke 22:42), and amounts to the attitude of total surrender to God in Islam to become a "submitter," the epitome of being human.

A good way to describe the central concern of all three faiths here under discussion, Islam, Christianity, and African Religion, is to describe it in terms of movement toward integration. It is, in other words, the desire of the human heart for transcendence, concern for love-justice, love of wisdom, and all the qualities that contribute to the excellence of human existence. Whether it is represented as *kenosis* (self-emptying in Christian theology), or *islam* (surrender in Islam), or *Ubuntu* (perfect humanity in African indigenous spirituality), the point of the spiritual pilgrimage for all three is for the human being to share as completely as possible in divine existence so as to achieve the good life. How can this be attained? Is it solely through Jesus Christ, as Christians believe, or only through *jihad*, as Muslims hold, or through faithfulness to ancestral tradition, as African spirituality perceives it? This, of course, is the question of religious multilingualism.

The suggestion in this chapter is that the beginning of a meaningful answer may be found in the approach that the AICs have taken. It is essentially based on the practical confession that the Spirit of God cannot be limited to one religious perspective alone. Participation in divine life and solidarity with one another as human beings and people of faith are the foundations for authentic religion and spirituality. Perhaps the best approach to true interreligious spirituality is loving-action in the world, a sentiment and method beautifully and pithily expressed by the prayer attributed to the best-known mystic, St. Francis of Assisi: "Make Me an Instrument of Thy Peace."

For St. Francis everything should incline toward reconciliation. For every negative situation there is a possibility of a positive: love for hatred, pardon for revenge, faith for doubt, hope for despair, light for darkness, and joy for sadness. But this requires a certain life-attitude, a certain personal spirituality, one of total self-giving to the other. Francis's conviction is that this spirit is contagious and is often reciprocated. As the prayer puts it, "for it is in giving that we receive, it is in pardoning that we are pardoned, and it is in dying that we are born to eternal life" (Dyer 2003, 139).

13

Politics and Governance

"A chief is like a swamp where fire ceases to burn."

It is no longer a trite argument that, for political and economic stability, Africa needs a new philosophy of governance based on its indigenous traditions. An increasing number of African thinkers, including Bénézet Bujo, Wamba-dia-Wamba, and Mogobe B. Ramose, have written to argue that a new, potentially liberating political dispensation in Africa must move "away from" the dominant paradigm of democracy as articulated and practiced in Western liberal political systems and into or toward indigenous modes of social organization. This amounts to a move from elitist to more egalitarian forms of political structuring. Ramose paraphrases Wamba-dia-Wamba saying, "the imperative to return to this tradition means that the tradition should function as a source from which to extract elements that will help in the construction of an authentic and emancipative epistemological paradigm relevant to the conditions in Africa at this historical moment" (Ramose 2009, 414).

There is nothing intrinsically wrong with different governance structures in different regions of the world. To point out that multiparty democracy as practiced in the Western world and insistently advocated for in Africa is inappropriate for the African context because it is divisive does not imply that the philosophy of democracy is wrong. Neither does it indicate, as is often insinuated, the desire to return to one-party systems of government that have so often failed Africa in a profound way. One-party rule in Africa was characterized by authoritarianism and dictatorship of a single person, the president, and consequently the cultivation of a dangerous personality cult. But to move judiciously into indigenous paradigms is not necessarily to embrace despotism. As Bujo has shown, absolute rule by an individual was foreign to many African traditional systems of governance. The position of the king or chief was sustained by common consent through a council of wise and also demonstrably ethical elders. This is exemplified by the powerful office of the

Mushigantahe (the incumbent ruler's advisor with genuine authority) among the Barundi of Burundi (Bujo 2009c, 393-94).

The considerable authority of the Queen Mother (*Ohenmaa*) among the Ashanti people of Ghana, the Baganda people of Uganda (where she was called *Nnamasole* or the king sister known as *Lubuga*), the Swazi people of South Africa (*Ndlovukati*), or the Yoruba people of Nigeria (*Iya Oba*) over the governance conduct of the ruler has already been discussed. It included subtle but real and effective veto power over a chief's rulings deemed by her not in the interests of the population as a whole. This woman, whoever she was, played the role of not only curtailing but eliminating extreme forms of autocracy and excessive forms of personality cult. Among the Yoruba, the *Iya Oba* was not even necessarily related to the ruler by blood but executed the same veto power as the Queen Mother.

Moreover, the "praise singer" played no insignificant role in the systems of governance of several African communities. Being accountable to no one but the ancestors, and relatively immune from the consequences of the eccentricities of the individual in power, the singer at court or in the village at large was able, in story, parable, song, and dance, to expose the weaknesses of the regime to the people and, conversely, the will of the people to the regime. Mvume H. Dandala likens this individual in the indigenous structure of governance to the media today (Dandala 2009, 269). Just as the praise singer was in the age of oral tradition, the institution of a free and independent mass media is essential for the good functioning of democracy today. The question, however, is how free and independent the media is in our time? To whom is it accountable? Is it ethical enough not to be bought?

On account of his social and spiritual-religious duties, the king or chief in African indigenous societies was expected to be *the* exemplar in both natural human and spiritual qualities. It is well known that sometimes the ruler was prevailed upon by custom to vacate the office if or when serious impairment in his physical, psychological, or spiritual faculties occurred and became evident; this is because the health of the ruler in any respect reflected on the respective health of the society. Nevertheless, everything being equal, the chief's position in governance was sacrosanct and unquestioned. He was a force of social cohesion and confidence. "A good chief knows how to listen to the views and feelings of his people," Dandala explains, "and with the finely-tuned skills to restate those views, drawing in even those who differ, so that the decisions he articulates are echoed by all his subjects." He was genuinely a corporate personality. "The chief is the embodiment of the nation; his voice is born of all different voices. His actions galvanise the entire nation's united force" (Dandala 2009, 267). Truly, a good ruler was "like a swamp where fire ceases to burn." Expected of the chief was the skill to settle disputes and bring about reconciliation. Like King Solomon in the Hebrew Scriptures, the African ruler's fame came not principally from his material wealth but from his wisdom in governance.

The contemporary president or religious leader who obliquely or openly appeals to "African tradition" to justify his or her authoritarian tendencies and activities is either ignorant of the political mechanisms of indigenous Africa or insincere. There is not much evidence in African indigenous systems of governance to back up undemocratic claims. Kwame Gyeke points out that generally in Africa, "the most important injunction was the chief should never ever act without the advice and full concurrence of his councilors, the representatives of the people." It was difficult for the chief to ignore or circumvent this requirement of ruling "with the consent of the people" in this manner, because acting against or without the tacit agreement of his advisors "was a legitimate cause for his deposition" (Ramose 2009, 425). Whether governance was by a chief or a council of elders, consultation at certain points and various levels formed the underlying political ideology in the ethnic groups of Africa. Nor did the advisors act on their own accord, impulse, or to their own advantage or material or social benefit; truly representing the mind and will of the population was what legitimated both their and the ruler's existence. This is the reason why the palaver, or *Indaba*, was given a central role in African indigenous systems of governance:

> The *indaba*, the traditional meeting for discussion of important matters affecting the life of the community . . . [has as underlying] conviction that the community has a common mind, a common heart. The purpose of the discussion is to discover that common mind, that common heart, in relation to the specific issue being debated. So the goal of the *indaba* is consensus. A mere majority vote on the issue is not enough. Discussion must continue until unanimity is achieved, a really common mind and heart. This is the only adequate sign that the truth of the matter has been discovered. It is also a valuable achievement in its own right. Achieving a common mind and heart on a specific issue builds up the community as such, intensifying the spirit of solidarity of its members. (Shutte 2009b, 95)

When various African scholars on the basis of African indigenous traditions suggest that the Western political paradigm of party politics is divisive, they are referring to the absence of this "common mind and heart," or what we might describe as the exercise of communal discernment. Current paradigms of Western democratic practice in Africa become even more inadequate given the reality of tribal affiliations within a single state because of the absence of a sense of genuine nationhood in many states, a colonial legacy. Parliamentary traditions of debate are hugely dissimilar to the African palaver, since their goal is ultimately not consensus but victory by one party over another, the rule of the majority. In the African context, this procedure is not conducive to harmony and communion but leads to an attitude of triumphalism on the part of the victorious majority and not infrequently bitterness on the part of the minority losers. What happens when the minority continues losing? Plotting to gain victory seems inevitable, even when this may not be for the benefit of the population as a whole.

"Adversarial politics," as this system has sometimes been described, undermines solidarity and community building. But these are elements crucial to African spirituality (Ramose 2009, 421-22). In the African indigenous paradigm, Metz has argued that "firstly, the search for unanimous agreement would demand identifying with others and acting for their benefit. Secondly, consensus decision making avoids minorities that repeatedly lose out to the majority until they become alienated" (Metz 2009, 348).

African indigenous paradigms of governance require freedom of speech on a level unimaginable in Western democracies, where the privilege is either manipulated or privatized. The palaver, or *Indaba*, with all its time-consuming "shortcomings," is the institution in indigenous Africa that supremely incorporates freedom of speech as a tool of governance. At the palaver, the word is respected; the "voice of the people" is truly cherished regardless of intellectual or social prowess or endowment. Here the wise as well as the "fools" have equal access to the word; they enjoy equal opportunity to express themselves without fear or hindrance. Even the unwise person, therefore, must also be allowed access to the word because in a palaver the process of accessing the word is completed only when consensus is reached. Ideally, everyone's word is sacred because the word is the expression of one's humanity and relationship with God, the ancestors, and all the universal powers that coalesce to make the life of the community possible. A speaker in a palaver may not be interrupted, much less summarily silenced, until he or she has had his or her say, regardless of the quality of the speech. To interrupt or stop someone's speech would amount to diminishing his or her humanity and, consequently, that of the entire community of which he or she is a member. It is not difficult to see how counterproductive this would be.

Can the palaver, or *Indaba*, approach form the basis of contemporary democratic discussion and governance on the continent? There are several difficulties with the approach, but they are not insurmountable. Bujo notes how colonial borders sometimes make the palaver paradigm very difficult. They were artificial constructions, often cutting across ethnic groups, so as to render many African "nations" at the time of independence virtually dysfunctional marriages (Bujo 2009c, 403-4). Nigeria, Democratic Republic of Congo, Somalia, and Sudan, even with the secession of the south, are obvious examples. In practice, no African state is totally free of this anomaly. Some failed or failing states in Africa are a result of the haphazard colonial border constructions, effected for the economic and political benefit of the colonial powers. Given the ancestral ties so vital to African spirituality of community and communion and so pivotal for the genuineness and effectiveness of the word, how can solidarity that is the motivation of the palaver paradigm of governance be inculcated?

As we shall see below with regard to economic structures as well, smaller social units of neighborhood, clan, and tribe will still be important as organizations in African states; they are where solidarity is mostly concentrated and felt, and from where it can radiate outwardly. These are structures that can cut across ethnic affiliations in the current political order to facilitate subsidiarity, where local issues of common concern and interest, such as health and education, water, and transportation needs, are addressed most realistically. At this level, it is possible for the palaver paradigm of direct democratic governance to play itself out most tangibly. It is clear that it would be naive in postcolonial Africa and in the context of today's globalized world to insist on strictly ethnic affiliations as ultimate for democratic organization. Ethnicity now claims wider implications to mean multi-ethnic *local* identities, with locality being the controlling dimension. When Augustine Shutte argues in this respect that "Genuine political community is now impossible unless it is global" (Shutte 2009a, 385), he is absolutely right. The village, the clan, and the ethnic group have to outgrow exclusive reliance on strictly autochthonous ethnic, economic, and political social units to embrace ethnicity that is multi-ethnic.

On the world stage, the Pastoral Constitution on the Church in the Modern World (*Gaudium et Spes* [*GS*]) from Vatican II acknowledges the growing and spreading "interdependence" among peoples and nations. "As a result the common good, that is, the sum of those conditions of social life which allow social groups and their individual members relatively thorough and ready access to their own fulfillment, today takes on an increasingly universal complexion and consequently involves rights and duties with respect to the whole human race." This makes it necessary that "Every social group must take account of the needs and legitimate aspirations of other groups, and even of the general welfare of the entire human family" (*GS*, no. 26). Where African ethnicity is concerned, this insight applies equally.

There can be no question that today there is need for an awareness of a wider, more complex sense of community than that warranted by the limits of clan or tribe (or indeed, even nation-state), as events in the world indicate. History demonstrates that the development from the family unit, to tribal enclave, to village community, to city, to state is a natural human process, dictated by the needs of security and material and social progress. But in its concrete realization, the movement is not automatic; it involves "thought and choice" as a rule for the sake of fuller human growth and maturity. But in the process of galvanizing humans together in these clusters and mega-clusters, positive human growth needs to be consciously inculcated (Shutte 2009a, 376). This is why it is now becoming evident that the notion of the nation-state, which for many centuries has formed the ultimate political community, is becoming more and more questionable in the contemporary context of the "global village." Strict adherence to the ideology of "national interests" is manifestly causing more harm than good in terms of the idea and ideal of "world community" which seems to be essential for the survival of the world in the long run.

For instance, Pope Benedict XVI, in his 2009 encyclical letter *Caritas in Veritate* (*CV*), on what it means today to have a human economy, built on the discourse of Pope Paul VI of 1967 on the true meaning of development (*Populorum Progressio*) and explicitly acknowledged the need for an international consciousness. "In our own day," Pope Benedict wrote, "the State finds itself having to address the limitations to its sovereignty imposed by the new context of international trade and finance, which is characterized by increasing mobility both of financial capital and means of production, material and immaterial." It is a fact that "This new context has altered the political power of States" (*CV*, no. 24). This insight might be one of the most important dimensions of the modern ethical evolution, the sense of a common humanity having priority over allegiance to the nation-state.

Rapidly accumulating evidence points unmistakably to the need for nation-states to be transcended in theory and practice in favor of a genuine international community, such as is suggested (though still very imperfectly) by the United Nations. Again, this seems unavoidable if human beings and the universe at large are to have any future. Nearly every village, and certainly every nation, mirrors not a single and homogenous unit but a multiple cultural (and religious) reality. What does this new situation impose on us? "What a pluralist world does . . . is to challenge people to include even more within the scope of their loving," Shutte writes. "To open oneself more widely, to other and alien influences . . . is not to lose one's identity but to enhance it and develop as a person" (Shutte 2009a, 383). In *Caritas in Veritate*, Pope Benedict addresses the same need. Although he grounds his argument in religious language, it is directly pertinent to modern politics and governance:

> Love in truth—*caritas in veritate*—is a great challenge . . . in a world
> that is becoming progressively and pervasively globalized. The risk for

our time is that the *de facto* interdependence of people and nations is not matched by ethical interaction of consciences and minds that would give rise to truly human development. Only in *charity, illumined by the light of reason and faith*, is it possible to pursue development goals that possess a more humane and humanizing value. The sharing of goods and resources, from which authentic development proceeds, is not guaranteed by merely technical progress and relationships of utility, but by the potential of love that overcomes evil with good . . . opening up the path towards reciprocity of consciences and liberties. (*CV*, no. 9)

In African ethical-spiritual terms, what Benedict was talking about here (and throughout the encyclical) is *Ubuntu*, with universal hospitality being its pivotal manifestation. Current policies in various countries of the economically developed regions of the world against immigration go directly against this spirit. So do xenophobic attitudes that seem to be gaining ground in some parts of the world. Policies based on xenophobia are not evenhanded; at the same time as they fight against immigration they promote emigration to poorer regions in the forms of economic dumping of cheap, even harmful, manufactured goods, and indiscriminate mining, oil drilling, and logging. Where these activities are destructive of the environment, the governments from where the corporations concerned originate are rarely called to task and punished.

Against an increasing global awareness, there are also those in Africa who advocate strict ethnicity. They propose a redrawing of the colonial-constructed borders currently in force into smaller "tribal" units to make the palaver paradigm of governance realistic, as they see it. But it is clear, taken the context of this argument as a whole, that this is not what many African scholars suggesting the palaver method of governance mean by it. When theologian Bénézet Bujo, for example, wonders whether, to reduce inter-state tensions over resources in Africa, it "might not be necessary, and possible, to realign the borders to give all states a fair share of resources" (Bujo 2009c, 404), he means "realignment" in a very different sense than that which comes immediately to mind, a physical redrawing of national boundaries. Such a move would not only be unrealistic and chaotic, but also retrogressive. "Realignment" of postcolonial boundaries has, for Bujo, more progressive, spiritual-attitudinal implications.

What the more enlightened thinkers such as Bujo share is what is increasingly universally recognized now, and what Pope Benedict wrote about in the encyclical just cited: it entails a move from smaller nonviable ethnic structures to larger multi-ethnic, multinational units that, while preserving solidarity of the smaller units—in the sense of the principle of "solidarity" delineated in Catholic social thought—at the same time allow the formation of larger and wider social engagements and commitments that facilitate an equitable distribution of resources to all. Throughout the world today there are developing examples of these social-political-economic formations that are more or less successful. Apart from the worldwide United Nations (UN), they include the European Union (EU), the North American Free Trade Agreement (NAFTA), the Organization of American States (OAS), the Association of Southeast Asian Nations (ASEAN), and the League of Arab States (Arab League). As just indicated, these unions and associations serve different purposes: some are purely economic, some are political, and some include both elements. In Africa, apart from the continent-wide African Union (AU), attempts at regional integration for the same purposes include the Economic Community of West African States (ECOWAS), the East African Community (EAC), and the Southern African Development Community (SADC).

The critique of these regional structures centers, of course, on who benefits from them. NAFTA, for example, faces criticism that it generally profits the already powerful and well-to-do. Yet this abuse cannot alter the principle that their main goal should be to satisfy the essential needs of all, the universal "common good" that smaller structures are increasingly unable to achieve.

In the church as well, an equivalent awareness is not lacking, so that one can see counterparts to many of these civil arrangements in the Christian churches. In Protestant Christianity there is the World Council of Churches (WCC), with a membership of 349 churches worldwide with the aim of attaining unity of Christian doctrine and witness. The WCC was founded in 1948, but its beginnings go back as far as 1911. In the Catholic Church also, national and regional associations of bishops exist worldwide. In Africa, the regional associations include the Association of Member Episcopal Conferences of Eastern Africa (AMECEA), Inter-Regional Meeting of Bishops of Southern Africa (IMBISA), and Regional Episcopal Conference of West Africa (RECOWA). The Symposium of Episcopal Conferences of Africa and Madagascar (SECAM) periodically gathers the hierarchy of the entire continent for deliberations.

The motto of EAC is "One People One Destiny." Deliberately or not, the motto expresses the African spirit of *Ubuntu*, where community is foundational, and the individual and primary human groupings find their individuality and identity within the community of people and goods. Still, within the community, the dignity of the individual cannot and must not be lost; as Vatican II states, it must be preserved in pursuit of the common good. The common good is not merely a principle, but a practical requirement of governance that takes into account human solidarity. "Therefore, there must be made available to all men everything necessary for leading a life truly human." The list includes access to "food, clothing, and shelter; the right to choose a state of life freely and to found a family, the right to education, to employment, to a good reputation, to respect, to appropriate information, to activity in accord with the upright norm of one's own conscience, to protection of privacy and rightful freedom even in matters religious" (*GS*, no. 26). To realize all of this fully, solidarity with creation on earth and the entire universe is of the essence. Humanity can grow wholly into the good life not in isolation from but in solidarity with the community of the universe.

Together with civic organization, ecclesial structures of administration, whose goal is likewise to promote human aspirations into the fullness of life, need to pay attention to the "growing awareness of the exalted dignity proper to the human person" (*GS*, no. 26). Within the expanding goal of larger social formations, primary groupings such as Small Christian Communities in the African churches should be cherished as privileged places where this awareness begins, and care must be taken that their identities are not carelessly swallowed up in the larger structures of the diocese, making the church an unhealthy monolith. There is no contradiction here with what has previously been said concerning the necessity and even inevitability of the welcome growth of the larger units in the modern world. In the governance of civil society, as in the church, both are complementary. Just as the individual and society must not be separated (a person is a person because of other persons), so also smaller local communities and larger units must always be considered together under the understanding that "the social order and its development must invariably work to the benefit of the human person" (*GS*, no. 26), all persons, and the universe at large.

The logic here, as formulated by Frank Sheed, is this: "By nature love is felt more intensely at the centre—most intensely for those who are close to us, less intensely as we move outwards. But the greater the love at the centre, the greater the radiation." This is a psychological reality. "Man has one will to love with, and one loving-power; and his loving-power grows by loving and is lessened by ceasing to love. The man who lacks love for his country is a diminished man: not so diminished as if he lacked love for his family, but there is less to him all the same" (Shutte 2009a, 383). To "think globally and act locally" is an important maxim. Charity begins at home. Human dignity, the common good, and the good life can be realized most concretely first on the local level. Here it is easier than at other levels of society to temper justice with mercy.

The Christian God and the message of Jesus are indeed universal, but, in practice, Christians believe that God's revelation was first directed to a particular group of people, the ancient Jewish nation, to the point that Jesus,

God Incarnate, was born a Jew. This is the logic of local charity that Sheed explains above. Simultaneously, however, God in the process of divine self-revelation made it clear in so many ways that God was God of all nations, not just Jews. When Jesus was born a Jew, and lived and taught under Jewish social conditions, which he cherished, he constantly worked to advance the Jewish environment to new spiritual heights. Contrary to Jewish ethnocentric sensitivities, convictions, and expectations, he learned to move it outward to "the nations." The example of the Canaanite (Matt. 15:21-28) or Syrophoenician (Mark 7:24-30) woman powerfully demonstrates this. After his ascension, the same ethnocentrism gripped his disciples, even after the dramatic descent of the Holy Spirit on them to send them forth without fear to speak to all peoples in their languages. Literally, they too had to learn to move outward to the "other," the "Gentiles," or the "nations." Pioneered above all by the Apostle Paul in the early church, this openness became the practical foundation of the universal mission of the church. This decision of the "Council of Jerusalem" in 48 or 49 C.E. was a momentous one, and it assured the survival of the church up to the present day.

Human "development" into solidarity and the common good implies at its core the coming-to-be of the human person in and with the world and the coming-to-be of the world with the human person. Neither the world nor humanity is a finished product. "The core of an historical consciousness is the recognition," according to Ben Meyer, "that man makes himself to be what he is, and that this self-making is a process whereby, acknowledged or not, all his acts of meaning enter into the forging of his selfhood" (Meyer 2008, 25). According to Vatican II, therefore, "social order requires constant improvement. It must be founded on truth, built on justice, and animated by love; in freedom it should grow every day toward a more humane balance." In our current social, political, and economic environment, "An improvement in attitudes and abundant changes in society will have to take place if these objectives are to be gained" (*GS*, no. 26). The council's conviction is that in all this the anchor is hope; the presence of God's Holy Spirit must be counted on, "who with a marvelous providence directs the unfolding of time and renews the face of the earth" (*GS*, no. 26).

Development and change should be a warning to any civil or ecclesiastical system not to make an idol of a particular form of democracy or any ecclesial structure. It is not possible in the long run to maintain such a stance of resistance to change without great harm to the human race and to the universe. It would entail a denial of the process of growth that is integral to authentic evolution of the human and all species. In social, political, and economic development, what must guide the process of change at all times is the goal of solidarity, the common good, and the good life.

14

The Economics of Affection
or "Eating Together"

*"Brotherhood or sisterhood does not mean physical resemblance
but mutual assistance."*

The African saying on relationships quoted above is sometimes also rendered as: "Being related does not mean looking alike but eating together." Its implications refer to the economic dynamics of solidarity, understood as a process or spiritual journey toward authentic hospitality and communion: the blessing and joy of sharing in respectful gratitude the resources necessary for life; in short, the imperative of "eating together."

The political scientist Ali A. Mazrui describes the idea of eating together in Africa in terms of economics of "prestige," in contrast to the economics of "production" in capitalist societies. Curiously, he disapproves of the former as inadequate for economic development today. In Africa, he warns, "Earnings are expended on entertainment and hospitality; on ostentatious weddings, expensive funerals and initiation ceremonies. In addition there is the crippling desire to fulfill obligations toward distant cousins and aunts" (see Murove 2009d, 233). This kind of "economics of affection," as some African economists have dubbed it, is in the eyes of Mazrui and others, responsible for the economic underdevelopment of Africa.

The contention by the critics of this economic culture is that, apart from obstructing incentive to produce, it invariably breeds nepotism and patronage at every level of society, the evil ghosts of which have widely haunted African political and economic administrative systems since independence, hampering economic performance as well as routinely violating procedural, distributive, and commutative justice. Kenya in the first decade of the twenty-first century may be taken as only one obvious example, where two instances of a breach of justice with impunity have been investigated and documented. One of these cases is described very powerfully and bluntly by

Michela Wrong in her book *It's Our Turn to Eat: The Story of a Kenyan Whistleblower,* pertaining to the problems of negative ethnicity. The other details the travesty of justice in that country by Christopher Goffard in his book *You Will See Fire: A Search for Justice in Kenya.*

That the "political instrumentalization of ethnicity and regionalism" is a major cause of Africa's political and economic woes is not in question. With Kenya in mind, Timothy Gachanga notes that this was partly the cause of the violence (mainly ethnic) that took place there following the 2007 general elections debacle in that country. Once considered one of the models of social stability and economic development on the continent, Kenya's economy and civic tradition of trust in the ability of political leaders to protect and advance the common good collapsed in the aftermath of the post-election violence fueled by negative ethnicity. "Successive Kenyan regimes politicized and 'ethnocized' state institutions," Gachanga argues, "and used the various offices as political tools for maintaining a system of ethnic patronage." As a consequence, he says, "the corruption at the highest level of governance created a political, economic, and social barrier between the citizens and their rulers" (http://www.africafiles.org/atissueezine.asp#art2).

This perception will take a long time to change in the Kenyan population. But Kenya is by no means alone in suffering in this way. Throughout Africa, nepotism and the politics of impunity create similar barriers between and among ethnic groups, as has been the case for a long time in Ivory Coast (Ngomba 2012). Inevitably, it results in inter-ethnic conflict and violence. In general, the tendency is to embezzle funds from public coffers to meet the "obligation" to entertain or the vanity to show off status. Ironically, in either case today, the individual concerned is seen as a "hero" by the beneficiaries, and if caught and disciplined, they consider it as victimization of "our son or daughter by people who do not want us to eat." In their villages, these individuals are invariably perceived with glory. Not that the injustice of this is lost to anyone, but it is subordinated to the limited solidarity of the ethnic group. But in a nation of many groups, this destroys harmony in the long run.

On one level, therefore, the validity of Mazrui's observation cannot be denied. Practically everyone with any kind of authority, earning a salary, or having financial and economic leverage in African societies will be faced with what many characterize as "the burden of appeasement," or what Mazrui describes as "the crippling desire" to discharge obligations of affection even toward distant relations who, without failure, will appear at the moment of one's actual or perceived success. Early in his career as President of Tanzania, Julius K. Nyerere admitted that this kind of social pressure by relatives and friends on public servants may drive them to engage in fraudulent activities with public property in order to satisfy them.

By their description of the psychological and emotional dynamics at play in this situation, however, Mazrui and others seem to acknowledge the complexity of the matter. Although, of course, the external elements of social pressure exist, the motivation to appease or conciliate relatives and friends by sharing one's "fortune," even to the extent of being dishonest, is not always an imposition from outside upon the individual. Rather, it often psychologically, emotionally, and even spiritually arises from within oneself, nurtured continually as a cultural value. Just like any other value, it can be and has been negatively exploited, as is evident on the African economic and political scene and as Mazrui and others testify. Nevertheless, it is necessary to point out that in the African context it forms part and parcel of the *Ubuntu* ontology, *being* defined not only as personal existence, but as participating and *interacting with* others. It calls for compassion as the ethical center of existence.

Do the negative effects of affective economics arise because of the values of *Ubuntu* that bestride these practices? Or in spite of them? Do the values of sharing necessarily lead to the culture of destructive nepotism, political impunity, and economic dishonesty, to the frustration of the common good in African states? Does the economics of affection necessarily destroy the vision of wider concern beyond the family or ethnic group now demanded by the idea of nationhood and the community of nations? How can one explain the fact that in some African countries the families of famous politicians own large tracts of land and exorbitant amounts of money (some stashed overseas), whereas the vast majority of their fellow citizens cannot eke out a decent existence?

It is not helpful to look for scapegoats to justify a deplorable situation. Yet in this matter, a thorough analysis is important so as to avoid superficial impressions and judgments as well as the danger of overlooking essential lessons for human solidarity. The question has therefore to be asked whether or not the capitalist economic system introduced into Africa by the slave trade and colonialism removes African understanding of ownership and sharing from its indigenous moorings and increases the potential to exploit them. A further question is whether, in the current world situation and for contemporary African economic development, it is unavoidable to copy Western capitalism to the letter. Is it not absolutely essential to cultivate, even today, the virtues of collective responsibility, solidarity, compassion, respect, human dignity, and unity to attain what Catholic social teaching describes as the essence of true development, the growth of the whole person and all persons?

Earlier in this book, it was noted that many of the first generation of African statesmen believed in the preservation and cultivation of these virtues and promoted them in their political and economic ideologies. Drawing on their African heritage, they argued that while material progress was important and necessary, it would be alienating and ultimately destructive to the human person if abstracted from the spirit of *Ubuntu*. The former should serve the latter. In the context of the Cold War in the 1960s and 1970s, this effort was interpreted by both ideological blocs as socialism or creeping Communism, despite the African leaders' professed ideological non-alignment. Nevertheless today, just as presidents Kwame Nkrumah, Julius Nyerere, Kenneth Kaunda, Leopold Senghor, and other founding fathers of various African states did then, some contemporary African scholars insist that "unless the development structures, strategies and processes can harness . . . *Ubuntu* values into a dynamic transformative force for reconstruction and development, failure [of social and economic development in Africa] will be almost certain. To succeed, African business practices should embrace *Ubuntu*" (see Murove 2009d, 233).

What is characterized in this chapter as the "economics of eating together" in Africa must be distinguished from and opposed to its abuse as just described. It is also different from the notion and practice of consumerism in laissez-faire, extractive capitalism. Simply explained, consumerism involves the production and distribution of goods for individual clients with the financial power to purchase them: the more the clientele for the goods, whatever their value for the necessities of life, the better for the economy. Therefore the emphasis is placed on advertising and packaging, for example, to entice more and more consumers and, consequently, more and more production. Although this is a very simplified view of the market economy, it accurately presents its basic approach. Capitalist consumerism is competitive and individual-oriented on the part of the producer and consumer, even if the producer is corporate. Its driving goal is maximization of profit, sometimes with very little regard for the common good.

The African economic perspective based on the philosophy of "eating together" emphasizes, in contrast, mutual dependence and cooperative success above competition and individual accomplishment in economic as in every activity. Its logic is the enhancement of common life through *communal* consumption. The accent is on the good life, the acquisition of the necessities of life, realized by all (or as many as possible) through the effort of all (or as many as possible). The sharp distinction between producers and consumers in this economic paradigm is blurred. Ideally, every able-bodied person must engage in the production of goods to satisfy the needs of the community. By this, he or she acquires the right to consume. On account of its emphasis on life lived now, this paradigm places little emphasis on personal or private savings, unless life's needs for everyone are first taken care of. The economic paradigm's practical expression is solidarity, which, as Pope John Paul II explains, "is not a feeling of vague compassion or shallow distress at the misfortunes of so many people, [but] a *firm and persevering* determination to commit oneself to the *common good* . . . of all and of each individual, because we are *all* really responsible for all." It means "a commitment to the good of one's neighbour with the readiness . . . to 'lose oneself' for the sake of the other instead of exploiting him, and to serve 'him' instead of oppressing him for one's own advantage" (*Sollicitudo Rei Socialis*, no. 38).

The propensity of this paradigm to lead to the extreme forms of parasitic dependence, on the one hand, and ostentatious prestige, on the other, must be acknowledged. A case study of the kind of possible abuse of *Ubuntu* in the economics of eating together is provided by Richard Tambulasi and Happy Kayuni with reference to Malawi under the regimes of Presidents Bakili Muluzi (1994–2004) and Bingu wa Mutharika (2004–2012). In order to act in a manner "befitting their position" as presidents, these leaders went around distributing food and money to people in a way that was excessively partial and lacked "accountability and transparency" (Tambulasi and Kayuni 2009, 432-34). On a larger national scale, this practice tended to fuel embezzlement and grand "corruption" in Malawi. Although it is perhaps not practiced so bluntly as in Malawi during the years in question, the phenomenon is widespread in many African countries at different levels of civil administration. One notices traces of it in the church as well.

Such practices cannot be entirely explained or justified on the grounds of the African economics of affection. As Metz explains, African moral theory would seem to "forbid state officials from awarding resources to individuals because they are related to them through family or political party" on account of the principle that "friendly relationships should not be promoted by unfriendly means." If the ultimate goal in economic as in all other relationships is harmony, strong partiality in the use of public resources to favor a section of the population destroys it and so cannot be justified. "A civil servant's duty not to be strongly partial derives from the state's need to realise harmony." Similarly, the use of public resources for self-benefit violates the principle of harmony, friendship, and solidarity. "'People first' should be the motto of a civil servant" (Metz 2009, 244-353). But who should be given priority and on what basis? Here the question of corruption arises. It needs a different nuance in the African cultural context of *Ubuntu*. What, in fact, does corruption entail in this environment? The answer may not be as obvious as it seems, and taking the standard definition at face value may deprive *Ubuntu* philosophy of a very important contribution toward harmony and solidarity.

"The Western-dominated interpretation of the 'corruption' phenomenon is to a greater extent determined by the canonical power of individualism," William De Maria notes. "Individual responsibility, and concomitant personal culpability, is positioned in the forefront of western consciousness. Family, village, history and ethnicity are pushed aside in the search for culprits that stand alone" (De Maria 2009, 362). But De Maria points to the study of African scholar P. Ekeh, who distinguishes the existence of "two publics" that translate into the existence of "two public moral universes" in colonial and contemporary postcolonial Africa. These are crucial to help place this problem in perspective. On the one hand, there is the indigenous (or "primordial") realm of the homogenous village; on the other, there is the modern (or "civic") heterogeneous realm. The indigenous realm is deeply morals-based, with all of its transactions founded on and tending to the fulfillment of harmonious relationships, community building, and communion with mystical powers. The civic realm, however, is basically "amoral" or at least "moral-free" or "moral-muted" in that sense. Structurally, the first demands execution of moral requirements within a well-known web of relationships that brings together the living, the dead, the unborn, and the community of goods. The second calls for execution of legal demands "impartially" in a basically impersonal way called "the rule of law" (De Maria 2009, 366).

As long as these two publics are not somehow integrated, as is the case in most African states until now, Ekeh suggests that many civil servants on the continent will continue to operate principally on the basis of the pull of the indigenous moral public. As already noted, they will feel internally that "it is legitimate to rob the civic public as long as the purpose is to strengthen the primordial public." Thus "practices defined in law as 'fraud' and 'embezzlement' are sanctioned or, at the very least, tolerated as long as the target is the government, not organic clusters, such as extended families and neighbourhoods" (De Maria 2009, 366). De Maria cites D. Smith, who captures with an example the substantive intellectual-moral operational process of indigenous ethics of connectedness which the legal understanding of corruption finds very difficult to see.

> Nneka [a Nigerian girl] scored well on her secondary school admission test but not well enough to guarantee entry to the school desired by her parents. Nneka's mother found out that her sister had a friend in the Federal Ministry of Education in Lagos. The friend said she would try to get Nneka admitted to the chosen school by having her name put on the minister's discretionary list. For this favour the parents had to pay the woman a considerable sum. (De Maria 2009, 368)

Was this an instance of corruption? It depends on the approach one takes between the two publics mentioned. From the legalistic point of view, there can be no question about it. In their heart of hearts, however, many Africans would not think so; Nneka's parents certainly did not. Rather they interpreted their action in terms of cultural codes of morality that require solidarity and material redistribution through gift giving. "To help your relation get admission when her scores were below the cut-off is expected and morally justified: the [moral] rules of kinship, community and reciprocity apply when the stakes are personal/communal" (De Maria 2009, 369).

In these rather ambiguous scenarios, how can this African economic paradigm be put forth as helpful in the contemporary world? The investigation is suggested at the level of the values inherent in it. The argument here is that the capitalist motivation of individual consumerism and the demand for communal sharing inherent in the African indigenous economics of affection, which are the basis for production in each of the two paradigms, can check and enrich each other in favor of a new economic paradigm for integral development. This will be an economic system of production with a human face and deep concern for the environment. To put the question simply: What can *Ubuntu* economics of eating together and extractive capitalism learn from each other? What model of economics, whatever the name, might emerge if the dialogue between them were taken and pursued seriously enough?

Barbara Nussbaum (2009a) points out that *Ubuntu* could contribute to the capitalist model the required respect for all human beings and nature. As essentially extractive and profit oriented, based on the principle of taking out of the human person and the environment (extracting) as much as possible at a minimum cost for as great personal profit as possible, capitalism tends to overlook one important aspect of the human economy: the primacy of the ethical principle of satisfying the human needs of all before the wants of the few. If one cuts through the economic jargon, the theory currently advanced in response to this concern, essentially that once the well-to-do are satiated, resources will "trickle down" to and take care of the needs of the poor majority in the population and in the world, is seen to be intrinsic to the capitalist paradigm. Often it does not work well, and the poor remain poor; and even if it does, it is obviously demeaning for the masses. There is more to human dignity than satisfying the belly with "crumbs that fall from the master's table" (Matt. 15:27). The ethics of human dignity require equitable participation by all in various dimensions of the economy. As a requirement of a human economy, this requirement can never be seen as outdated, as it is often claimed.

Another troubling issue that arises in the capitalist economic paradigm concerns the environment. Mining, drilling, or logging concessions in Africa, for example, extract nonrenewable natural resources. These activities create "a win/lose situation," according to Nussbaum. The community where the extraction takes place "is left with nothing." When this happens, "the [extracting] company will leave that area for cheaper labor elsewhere" in a vicious cycle with similar consequences (Nussbaum 2009b, 251). The host community not only hardly shares in the profits made on its soil but suffers great harm from the activities as well. The Texas-based oil-drilling multinational corporation Shell can be taken as an illustration of extractive procedures that ignore human and environmental welfare in favor of the priority for commercial gain. Shell's destructive presence in Nigeria has been widely publicized and is well known.

Since 1958, Shell has been drilling for crude oil in the Ogoni area of the Niger Delta, in Rivers State, Nigeria. In the process, it has devastated the land by pollution and, with the tacit consent of successive Nigerian governments, has marginalized the Ogoni population, leading them into extreme poverty while repatriating most of the oil profits. When in the 1990s activists like Ken Saro Wiwa and his Movement for the Survival of the Ogoni People (MOSOP) tried to draw attention to this unjust situation, they were branded as "terrorists" and dealt with as such. For his activities in defense of the Ogoni people and the protection of the Niger Delta, Ken Saro Wiwa was eventually arrested, tortured, and executed for murder with dubious evidence, in spite of international calls to abrogate the sentence.

The story of Royal Dutch Shell in the Niger Delta is an example of corporate capitalist insensibility to human and environmental dignity and rights, as the United Nations Environmental Program (UNEP) reported in a statement in 2011. After fifty years of pollution by Shell in the Niger Delta, UNEP stated in the report, it would require more that U.S. $1 billion and up to thirty years just to begin the cleanup. According to UNEP, it would be the most extensive operation of its kind in the world. But for a long time, Shell has admitted neither the fact of pollution as a result of its oil-drilling activities nor responsibility for the cleanup.

Ubuntu as a moral theory of solidarity and mutual sharing would seem to check the purely capitalist motivation underpinning this practice on a number of counts. Although the extraction of crude oil (and other resources) is understandable and justifiable as an economic activity, stripping the land or the forests bare is irresponsible in that it ignores the welfare of the human and natural communities left behind. A lesson from *Ubuntu* moral philosophy and spirituality in a case like this would be, according to Nussbaum, to help "foster the human qualities of humility over arrogance, co-operation over domination and generosity over greed." The *Ubuntu* approach would avoid unilateral decisions by multinational corporations in collusion with corrupt governments but would "place inclusive dialogue and discussion at the heart of . . . [the] economic agenda" (Nussbaum 2009b, 249). Taken seriously, *Ubuntu* would act as a bridge-builder between the notional and practical separation that exists between "profit and people, politics and economics, material and spiritual" dimensions of life, bringing together economic and other forces to be "mutually reinforcing, fair and cooperative" (Nussbaum 2009b, 250).

Consequently, frugality in consumption becomes an issue of economic human dignity and rights as well as an environmental issue. Consumption must be balanced between needs and wants; the basic needs of the majority should temper the insatiable wants of some. Moreover, all human consumption must be judicious at the risk of the destruction of the environment. The depletion of the ozone layer and consequent global warming, for example, which is to a great extent the result of burning fossil fuels in factories and motor vehicles in industrialized countries, is now a matter of common knowledge. But global warming and its consequent calamities know no borders, and the least developed regions of the world, least prepared to deal with such disasters, usually suffer most from them.

Even if economic processes everywhere are marked by a certain degree of human greed, the point of *Ubuntu* economics of affection concerns the level of greed ethically acceptable in terms of its consequences on the common good. *Ubuntu* moral theory would not justify a situation where the majority of people are dying of hunger while a minority is rolling in luxury. The economic situation in the world today, nationally and internationally, is unacceptable by the principles of *Ubuntu,* which is founded on "prizing harmonious or friendly relationships between people, where such relationships are construed to be a matter of sharing a life with others and exhibiting solidarity towards them" (Metz 2009, 353). The principle of the common good also has this as its center, as we have seen, and the foundations of social teaching of the Catholic Church in the Scriptures and the early Doctors of the Church make the same point unambiguously. In the preceding chapter, examples were drawn from the teaching of the Second Vatican Council. Among numerous other documents dealing with the social question in Catholic Christianity, writings by popes since Leo XIII are rich resources for this position, as are relevant documents from other Christian churches.

Sharing may not lead to individual personal success; that is, it may not in itself have instrumental value, but it possesses the intrinsic value of human solidarity. And it need not be blatant; in indigenous Africa it was subtle and often took the form of "teaching a person to fish" rather than merely handing out the fish. Mvume H. Dandala explains that when a person with plenty of cattle knew a poor relative, he would go to him to ask if the latter would agree to help him tend one of his cows as a favor. Without his dignity being affected in any way, the poor man would agree to "help" his relative, and would benefit from the milk. When the owner returned to reclaim his cow, the poor relative would have started a herd of his own with the calves that the cow had borne.

"This is a way of sharing wealth that is positive, affirming and characteristic of *Ubuntu*. It is dignified, productive and embedded in African culture" (Dandala 2009, 275). It also respects the dignity and responsibility of the person to whom the cow is lent. If he fails to take care of the cow, he will remain without any, and few would be willing or ready to help him out again. In the hands of a responsible person, however, "A cow never dies"(Dandala 2009, 276).

At its very beginning, the book of the Acts of the Apostles paints a picture of how the Eucharist was incorporated into the daily spiritual, political, and economic life of the faithful in the early Christian community. "They met constantly to hear the apostles teach, and to share the common life, to break bread, and to pray." Concomitant with this and essential to it was that "all whose faith had drawn them together held everything in common: they would sell their property and possessions and make a general distribution as the need of each required" (Acts 2:42, 44-46). This practice of common prayer, eating together "with unaffected joy," and common life earned the community the respect of the population. It distinguished them as a group that "put their money where their mouth is" or "walked the walk," as the current expression goes. They preached mutual love and practiced mutual love as much as their circumstances allowed.

This was never meant to be a blueprint on which to construct an exact edifice, brick by brick for all times, and to suggest this for our time from the text would be naïve in the extreme. Like the washing of the feet of the disciples by Jesus at the Last Supper, it is a symbol, and a powerful one at that, whose meaning is ignored at the risk of loss of the *meaning* of the Eucharist and of the Christian faith in general. The celebration of the Eucharist makes no sense *in itself* except as a memorial, a making present, of the life, teaching, suffering, death, and resurrection of Jesus: "Do this in memory of me" (Luke 22:19; 1 Cor. 11:24). However, the Eucharist is a symbol of empathy and solidarity that is constructed depending on the times. But the effectiveness of the symbol, and therefore the sharing of the body and blood of Jesus, is realized in practice only in the act of "eating together" in the widest sense of this phrase as mutual assistance. It is the cardinal virtue that *Ubuntu* asserts.

In *Ubuntu* moral theory, eating together is an act, or, more exactly, a process, of constant transformation; it is why it should be repeated ritually, like the Eucharistic celebration. As much as the food eaten transforms the bodies of the partakers as it is itself transformed into each one's body, so too sharing food transforms the relationships of those who eat together and binds them into one, beyond table, to life fellowship. Eating together bodes friendship, realized or intended. It is an expression of the parity that underlies the Christian celebration of the sacraments, mindful that "If one part suffers, every part suffers with it; if one part is honored, every part rejoices with it" (1 Cor. 12:26). As Cathy C. Campbell writes, eating "opens to the Sacred." Perhaps more than anything else, it is the sacrament of divine presence in the world open to everyone to read. "The ways we eat—the food we eat when, with whom, with what, the etiquette of eating, the tables we gather around— reveal much about our material, social, and spiritual culture" (Campbell 2003, 61; also Jung 2006). "Give us today the food we need" (Matt. 6:11) is not a petition for some; it is a request for all.

If economic structures move people away from the practice of eating together, of gift giving in accordance with the spirit of the Eucharist, they move them away from God and from the Christian enterprise (see Campbell 2003, 68). In the scene of the Last Judgment that the Gospel according to Matthew depicts, it is not for nothing that the "Son of Man," the final judge, is surrounded by "all the nations." It is in this inclusive context that the words of judgment are pronounced: I was in need of food, and so on, and you did not provide for me. "Truly I say to you, to the extent that you did not do it to one of the least of these, you did not do it to Me" (see Matt. 25:31-46). Further, when he feeds the hungry, Jesus does not discriminate: all five and four thousand are fed (see Matt. 14:13-21; Mark 6:31-44; Luke 9:10-17; John 6:5-15; and Matt. 15:32-39; Mark 8:1-26). And at a dinner, Jesus urges his host to do the same: "But when you give a banquet, invite the poor, the crippled, the lame, the blind, and you will be blessed" (Luke 14:13-14). This kind of sharing is the essence of Christian mission, according to Wolfgang Vondey. It is a mandate "to turn strangers into neighbors, lepers into partners, outcasts into followers, enemies into allies, addicts into friends, and homeless into brothers and sisters at the table of bread" (Vondey 2008, 138).

It is tempting in current dominant economic structures to interpret all this as a kind of unrealistic sentimentalism, but the point these and other scriptures make cannot be more pragmatic or more spiritual. It is a wake-up call not only to the church to realize herself as church, as a Eucharistic assembly locally and universally, but to the world, as the only way to justice, peace, and reconciliation. The brotherhood and sisterhood of all peoples cannot be achieved through the current economic structures of competition and exclusion, but only through radical restructuring of the extraction and use of resources with respect for the dignity of everyone and the environment (Katongole 2011, 167-69). There should be no need for an invitation card for a banquet. Everyone is assumed to be welcome, and the bigger the attendance the better. In the conceptual framework of *Ubuntu*, the idea of "gatecrashing" does not exist (see Marks 2000, 183). At initiation ceremonies, marriage feasts, funerals, and ordinary meals, this is the spirit that guides the African perspective of eating. *Ubuntu* ethics demands that one should produce to share.

15

$\mathcal{R}$econciliation as $\mathcal{P}$eace

"I have never heard someone say,
'Let's go visit a person wounded in a fight.'"

Colonial attitudes ridiculed the African psychosocial temperament of tolerance, describing it generally as "thick-skinned," very slow to take offense, too ready to forgive, and rather quick to forget injury. Ali Mazrui describes this disposition among Africans in terms of a "low level of hate-retention" or a "short memory of hate." He exemplifies it with reference to the Nigerian civil war (1967–1970), whose wounds were soon forgotten; the experience of Nelson Mandela who spent twenty-seven years in prison under the South African apartheid regime and emerged to integrate the nation; or indeed the experience of colonialism itself, under which Africans suffered humiliation but later were willing to live with their oppressors. These experiences, according to Ali A. Mazrui, illustrate that "Africanism recommends a return to normality without hate after each conflict" (Mazrui 2009, 37). Jomo Kenyatta, the first president of Kenya, similarly described the effect of his imprisonment at Lokitaung Prison in Kapenguria, West Pokot District, by the British colonial administration in a 1968 book titled *Suffering without Bitterness*.

Ideally, therefore, fights were to be avoided, and anyone who provoked or recklessly engaged in one hardly deserved sympathy. When interethnic conflicts occurred or turned into blood feuds, they were not allowed to last for too long or claim unnecessary lives or destruction of property. If a person killed a member of your clan, you were not expected to avenge with random killings. The *lex talionis* certainly existed and was accepted and practiced, but in a strictly proportionate way. Beyond a certain level, retaliation was censured and condemned (on both sides of the divide). The ideal in every case, however, was reconciliation, and detailed rituals were developed toward this end. Some of these rituals were temporary, addressing the specific occasion;

many were nonetheless permanent, including those sealed by marriage or blood pacts between the conflicting parties.

Perhaps the most enduring form of interethnic reconciliation as peace is the joking relationship whereby the expression of verbal and other mild forms of hostility is mutually (that is, symmetrically) or one-sidedly (asymmetrically) permitted without retaliation. In any of its three recognized forms (as a means of social sanction, intergenerational affection, or ritual avoidance), a joking relationship prevents any emergence of actual conflict on a permanent basis. Its social implications need no explanation, but it has a spiritual message as well. Rituals leading to this kind of relationship are meant to emphasize the humanity of every human being as sacred because it contains divine power, and that destruction of anyone's life ultimately means diminution of one's own. It interferes with the fulfillment of earthly life on which ancestral life is premised.

This is why among many ethnic groups, after a serious conflict, especially one involving the spilling of blood, the elders or "healers from each side would arrange for a cleansing ceremony that involved all those who had fought." According to Nussbaum, "They believed that, because people had died, the ancestors on both sides would be aggrieved, and that the hands, hearts and spirits of all the killers needed to be cleansed. This profoundly mature skill," Nussbaum writes, "demonstrated an inbuilt capacity for post-war reconciliation" (Nussbaum 2009a, 103). Mbiti describes in some detail one example of such rituals, among "thousands that take place daily all over Africa," between the Luo and Maasai people of Kenya and spells out its implications. As many members of the warring parties as possible assembled in one place, at a border of the territories in question. A fence of poisonwood trees, a symbol of existing hostility, was constructed there. The two communities stood facing each other across the fence. Against it on either side all the weapons of war were laid.

> Then they took a black dog and laid it across the fence. The dog was cut into two and blood was allowed to flow through the fence and onto the ground, on both sides of the fence. Then the mothers with suckling babies exchanged their young back and forth across the fence, so that Maasai mothers could suckle Luo babies and Luo mothers suckle Maasai babies. Prayers followed this, in which the respective elders beseeched God to bless the covenant of peace. The participants pronounced anathemas on any one who ever crossed that fence to do evil. (http://www.upf.org/component/content)

Beyond being merely a peace pact, this ritual symbolized and actually signified the establishment of blood ties, which allowed the former adversaries to eat together as brothers and sisters. The commitment was made unmistakably evident by the exchange and suckling of the babies, the icons of peace and joy, between the two communities. The willingness to form this bond is assured by the presence of all of the members, men and women, young and old, of both parties, who are asked in prayer to give up "bitterness, grudges, hatreds, mutual fears, and suspicions" and all things that could in any way "injure, damage, or destroy the other." The blood of life of the "innocent" and "neutral" animal, the dog, is deliberately shed to symbolize the end of the spilling of human blood. The prayers offered recognize the will of God and the ancestors for peaceful coexistence, so that the party that breaks the bond offends not only a legal but also a deeply spiritual and sacred norm. Thus, the formal curse's overseers are the spiritual powers. The message to everyone is clear: may anyone who breaks the bond meet the fate of the dog whose blood has flown on both sides of the fence.

As can be seen from the action of suckling babies, women, who are the carriers of life, played a central role in peacemaking and reconciliation. Among the Zande of South Sudan, for example, in the case of hostilities between clans, the grandmothers and mothers of one clan would deliberately stand between the fighters to make them stop. When in the heat of passions this did not work, Mbiti reports, the women "would threaten to expose their nakedness or to go down on their knees. In either case, the gesture signified a curse for those who bore the responsibility for such grave acts." This usually sufficed to make the warriors put down their weapons. Otherwise, "the old women, naked and on their knees, would crawl toward the foolhardy combatants [verbally forbidding them to advance for battle]. And if the assailants still refused to see reason and marched on the village, they would suffer the ultimate punishment for having disobeyed and obliged their 'grandmothers' to expose their nakedness" (http://www.upf.org/component/content). This punishment was loss of vital force in various ways. An elder's nakedness symbolizes life; it is where life comes from. To deliberately see the source of life is tantamount to the presumption of wanting to see the face of God itself, a sacrilegious act. As the Hebrew Bible puts it, "no one can see the face of God and live" (Exod. 33:20).

Incidentally, the same strategy was used in Kenya in 1992 by women followers of Professor Wangari Maathai, founder of the Green Belt Movement and the first African woman to receive the Nobel Peace Prize, protesting the imprisonment without trial of their sons. As the *East African Standard* of April 2, 2008, recalled, while their leader was writhing on the ground in pain, hit by a tear-gas canister during a demonstration at Freedom Corner in Uhuru Park, "the outraged mothers stripped bare in an effort to shame the charging police officers." Others shook their breasts at them as a sign of a curse, knowing that no man would lay hands on his own mother.

Similarly, when a young white American peace and pro-integrationist activist, Amy Biehl, was attacked and killed by a gang of black youths in Guguletu township in South Africa in August 1993, just before Nelson Mandela's accession to power as president, mothers marched through the township's streets to atone for the life lost (Marks 2000, 188); by their public march they wished to show that they regarded Biehl as their daughter for the life-giving activities she had done for the community. They were also making a statement about their hope for the youth who had committed the crime, that they, like Biehl, might change to become agents of life rather than of destruction.

What is the point? The essence of all of this is that the legal approach to reconciliation alone, devoid of the transcendental, sacramental dimensions, is highly unsatisfactory and unsustainable in the long run. Without an inner spirit of forgiveness, procedural and restorative forms of justice do not serve the cause of peace in a lasting way (Tutu 1999). Susan Colin Marks remarks that "tools, and techniques, and mechanisms" do not suffice for genuine reconciliation. "Reconciliation is about people and about their willingness to bring spirit and truth and feeling to the reconciliation table to give it meaning" (Marks 2000, 181). Perhaps it was something similar that the philosopher Jacques Maritain had in mind when he wrote in 1943 that justice in its full and authentic sense requires "friendship . . . [as] its very life-giving form." Authentic justice, Maritain maintained, "tends towards a really human and freely achieved communion. It lives on the devotion of the human persons and their gift of themselves." For Maritain, true justice is attained only when people "are ready to commit their own existence, their possessions and their honour for its sake." For him, "The civic sense is made up of [both] this sense of devotion and mutual love as well as the sense of justice and law" (see Shutte 2009a, 379).

In the African context this is perhaps best exemplified by the Rwanda experience. In the aftermath of the 1994 genocide, the new government of Rwanda instituted the Gacaca courts to seek redress for the crimes of the pogrom. Within and outside Rwanda there are numerous criticisms of this institution, many of which are justified given the immensity of the events and the emergent cultural confusion as a result of a long colonial experience. Still, the system is obviously and fundamentally inspired by the African vision of attaining justice as reconciliation.

Customarily in the Gacaca court system, all conflicting parties would assemble before well-respected elders called *Inyangamugayo,* or "people of integrity," representing the village. The *Inyangamugayo* would attempt to pinpoint the wrongdoers for the purpose of bringing about mutual accord. The system emphasized not primarily retributive justice but a sense of forgiveness on the side of the wronged based on admission of wrongdoing by the proper side. Although this did not preclude restitution of one kind or another, this was understood merely as a sign of the genuineness of the offender before the assembled community and the ancestors. Central to the system procedurally was the involvement of the entire community as an impartial assessor and jury. As with the palaver, or *Indaba*, processes, every member of the assembly could speak for one side or the other vocally or by bodily attitudes in the interests of promoting collaboration between everyone since all have a stake in the ultimate outcome of the process: harmony in the community (see Kubai 2010, 264-72).

The centrality of forgiveness as the determining dimension of reconciliation, justice, and peace is illustrated by the personal experience of a young girl from Burundi, Justine, and a young Rwandese priest, Marcel Uwineza. Both lost many close relatives during ethnic violence in their respective countries and narrowly escaped death themselves.

Ethicist Emmanuel Katongole heard the story of nine-year-old Justine from Maggy Barankitse of Burundi. Justine insisted to Maggy, who had taken her in after her father and other members of her family had been killed, that she wanted to visit her family's killer, express her forgiveness of him, and ask him to ask forgiveness of her. Only in this way, Justine confided to Maggy, could she *live*, "Because the hatred prevents me from continuing to live." That's exactly what Justine did; nay, she did more. She asked the unbelieving man to become her substitute father. He agreed and together they rebuilt her father's house. When the man got ill, Justine took care of him; and she bitterly wept at his death and arranged flowers on his grave. But the man's dying words to Maggy, Justine's guardian, are perhaps even more touching: "Thank you, Maggy. Because now I am dying like a human person, not like a killer. Your forgiveness [through Justine] gave me back hope, love, life" (Katongole 2011, 181-82).

A similar situation occurred with my former student Marcel Uwineza (now a priest, but in 1994 a mere child). In a private correspondence, Uwineza narrates his horrifying experience as well as his journey to forgiveness and reconciliation. It is worth quoting in full:

> The 1994 genocide against the Tutsi was not just a tragedy for me; it left me with wounds that took time to heal. I remember after July 1994 when the genocide ended, it was so hard to love or see anything good . . . [in] a Hutu.

Some of our Hutu neighbours killed my father, buried him and later exhumed his body for [the] birds of the air and dogs to feast on. . . . They threw my two brothers and my sister in a pit latrine alive and [they] died inside. They led my maternal grandma and many cousins to the big River Nyabarongo and threw them there [to drown]. I am sure the fish of Lake Victoria ate them. They raped my aunt and gave her HIV. They seriously beat and wounded my mother . . . this was to develop into something she would not survive after the genocide. How on earth was I to live and love these people again? No! This was not something I was ready to do. The God who asks us to love our enemies, no I was not ready to listen to him! Why had he let my beloved people be killed like cockroaches? Why had Nkurunziza and Kanani killed my beloved relatives? I . . . remember how my father had given them land and paid school fees for their kids.

Yet this God got hold of me! Why did I survive? Why was I still alive? Am I better than those who were killed? Why had they [the *genocidaires*] not discovered Mr. Kabera's big empty beehive in which he hid me during the genocide? These questions troubled me for years. I could not see a future without my father, mother and brothers. I had become a prisoner in myself. It was not until I read Psalm 116:12, where the Psalmist says: "How can I repay the Lord for all the good done for me . . . ?" that I realised that I have been given more time [to live] and so I should use it well for God.

A few years later I went back to the village (Kabirizi, Gitarama) where we lived and to my surprise I met one of the killers of my brothers and sister. I could not believe my eyes. Upon seeing me, he came towards me. I thought he . . . [was] coming to kill me too. But I could not believe what happened . . . ; it appeared like a movie . . . ; he knelt before me and asked me to forgive him. If there is one time I felt God invading my life [it] was this time. I . . . [took] him and embraced him and said: I forgive you; the Lord has been good to me. Ever since [then] I [have] felt free! My wounds were able to heal the wounds of others. That is how I later found myself desiring to give the gift of my very self to the Lord as a Companion of Jesus [Jesuit], who I am as I write. . . . (Uwineza, personal communication with author, 2012)

Side by side with Justine's story, Marcel's experience is haunting. At any rate, here we have but two examples of what Pope Benedict XVI has described in *Africae Munus* (*AM*) as "moving testimonies from the faithful of Africa, 'accounts of concrete suffering and reconciliation in the tragedies of the continent's recent history' [which] have shown the power of the Spirit to transform the hearts of victims and their persecutors and thus to re-establish fraternity" (*AM*, no. 20). The total healing power in the dynamics of acknowledgment of wrong, penitence for it, and free granting of forgiveness is beautifully illustrated in this account. So is the spiritual liberating power it gives to the wronged person to recognize the wrongdoer again as a person, a member of the human communion. The social and spiritual effects of mutual acceptance that must have followed this encounter in both Uwineza and his relative's killer are the substance of genuine, healing justice.

Another touching illustration of integral healing comes from the United States. In April 1995, Timothy McVeigh deliberately drove a truck full of explosives in front of the Murrah Federal Building in Oklahoma City, Oklahoma. In the subsequent explosion, 168 people lost their lives, including Julie Welch, the bright and promising twenty-three-year-old daughter of Bud Welch. For this atrocious act, Bud Welch was full of a desire for revenge and wanted nothing for Timothy McVeigh but the death penalty. "I was so full of revenge," he narrates, "All I could feel was hate and revenge. I didn't want trial for [McVeigh and his accomplice Terry Nichols]. I simply wanted the bastards to fry. I'd have killed them myself if I'd been given the chance" (Philpot 2012, 8).

After a long time of engaging in self-destructive behaviors like excessive drinking and smoking because of this feelings of hate, something began to change in Bud Welch. He slowly came to the realization that the execution of the perpetrators of the crime would contribute nothing to his healing process. He decided to embark on a path of forgiveness: he met Timothy's father to express this feeling and wanted to (but was prevented from) meeting Timothy himself for the same purpose. Moreover, he joined a nationwide campaign against the death penalty. It had taken him a long time to forgive his daughter's murderer; but "forgiveness is not an event, it's a process," he explained, "and I started feeling that process in June 2000, and finally in October or November I realized that I was really beginning to move forward. By the time that Tim was executed in June 2001, I had fully forgiven him. It was a release for me rather than for him" (Philpot 2012, 10).

In Zimbabwe, many of those who participated in the atrocious war of liberation lived in constant fear that the spirits of the people killed during the struggle would bring them misfortune in the form of illness and death unless they sought healing. Healing in this sense is something more than "curing." Because the war itself and the spilling of blood meant a perversion of the human heart and spelled breakdown of the desired order in creation, healing sought to establish right order on the "physical, psychological, social, and spiritual levels; it involves work on the individual, the group and surrounding environment and cosmos" (see Maenzaise 2009, 187).

Pope Benedict XVI asserts in *Africae Munus* that "unless the power of reconciliation is created in people's hearts, political commitment to peace lacks its inner premise." Because "inner purification . . . is the essential prior condition for building justice and peace," it precedes and is a condition for authentic human political order. As the pope puts it, "Reconciliation is a pre-political concept and a pre-political reality, and for this very reason it is of the greatest importance for the task of politics itself" (*AM*, no. 19).

"If it is to be effective," as Pope Benedict explains, "this reconciliation has to be accompanied by a courageous and honest act: the pursuit of those responsible for these conflicts, those who commissioned crimes and who were involved in trafficking of all kinds, and the determination of their responsibility." The other component of true reconciliation involves the need for victims to know the truth. "It is important for the present and for the future to purify memories, so as to build a better society where such tragedies are no longer repeated" (*AM*, no. 21). Thus, from the African social and spiritual point of view, there is no "cheap" reconciliation, so to speak. Some form of restitution to the wronged, however symbolic, is not a priori ruled out in these processes. In fact, it seems required as a sign of true repentance leading toward the reestablishment of harmony. Geared toward this goal, justice becomes a concretization of love, for the most important quality of justice is "the justice of love" (see *AM*, no. 25). Anyone caught in an adulterous affair, for example, was expected to pay a fine to the husband or, in case of the woman, suffer some form of temporary public censure. Such compensation is institutionalized in the joking relationship where the parties, within established and recognized limits, may take and use each other's property without permission and without legal consequences.

At many points in the preceding pages, passing reference has been made to the importance of individuation and identity in the process of human self-understanding and growth at all levels of existence. Emmanuel Katongole explains that identity, whether personal, ethnic, or national, is not based primarily on techniques or "strategies and skills" but by "stories and imagination." War and peace, economics, political and social organization, and self-perception all result from stories; it is the "myths," as we might call them, that we tell and believe about ourselves (as well as those that others tell and believe about us) and upon which we place certain emphasis, that circumscribe and for the most part define who and what we think we are and can become, and therefore, largely determine how we act. "Stories not only shape our values, aims, and goals; they define the range of what is desirable and what is possible." According to Katongole, therefore, in a very basic way our foundational stories construct our "social ecology" (Katongole 2011, 2). Tradition is important for any human community for this reason.

But the illustrations above are the myths, the stories of reconciliation for African ethnic groups; they are the African narratives about methods of performances toward justice and peace. These narratives are based on the principle or *vision* that demonstrates both the theory and practice of African spirituality, morality, and ethics. They emphasize and have as their goal inclusion, community, and communion.

Katongole narrates the stories of three contemporary Africans who have lived out, against considerable odds, this vision, this spirituality of inclusive reconciliation as the only way to peace: namely, Bishop Paride Taban of Sudan, in the context of ethnic and religious persecution; Ms. Angelina Atyam, in the midst of Joseph Kony's indiscriminate and unpredictable terror in northern Uganda; and Ms. Maggy Barankitse, in the face of tribal discrimination, oppression, and violence in Burundi (see Katongole 2011, 135-92). Imagining and establishing visible structures of inclusion regardless of persecutor and persecuted, each in his or her own small way, have demonstrated the spirit of forgiveness and inclusion as the only path to peace. Katongole frames these stories within the Christian story of the spirit of Jesus of the Gospels because he aims to show the meaning of Christian ethics in contemporary Africa. Our point, however, is that the essence of these narratives is intrinsically contiguous with the African indigenous narrative of the spirit of reconciliation, justice, and peace. Within situations where the foundational "African values of community and solidarity" have become "subverted to serve the story of hatred and revenge" (Katongole 2011, 175), Taban, Atyam, and Barankitse serve as reminders of their lasting persistence in African communities.

16

The Universe as the "Divine Milieu"

"No one shows a child the sky."

"But ask the animals, and they will teach you,
or the birds in the sky, and they will tell you;
or speak to the earth, and it will teach you,
or let the fish in the sea inform you.
Which of all these does not know
that the hand of the LORD has done this?"
(Job 12:7-9)

Since the publication in 1859 of *The Origin of the Species* by Charles Darwin, there has been an ongoing debate between two sides of the theological divide concerning the origin of the cosmos. In the book Darwin raised the question of how the universe and life in it came into existence. Was it through the direct action of God, as religious faith (specifically Christianity) believed then, or "naturally" by gradual evolution through its own internal dynamics, as Darwin now claimed?

This long-standing debate has therefore been between what is generally simplified as the hypotheses of religion and science, or creation and evolution. The advocates of the theory of the direct intervention by God in creation, or "creationism," on the one hand, argue that the origin of all life, including life in human form, comes "as is" from a single act of God at the beginning of time. The same theory is nuanced by others, called moderate creationists, who replace the role of God by some "Intelligent Design" within or directing the activity of creation, but to the same basic effect. On the other hand, there are the evolutionists, or proponents of evolution, who contend that life in the world evolved through the dynamics of its own internal "natural selection," producing diverse forms of beings, without necessarily the intervention of an external force. The debate between these two persuasions has often been as interesting as it has been acrimonious and confusing, sometimes with tragicomic consequences destructive of mutual tolerance. But it is important to appreciate that whatever position is held is important for spirituality and universal survival, because it influences how men and women approach and behave toward the universe. It is for this reason we mention it for consideration here.

African spirituality, which takes neither of these sides, seems to hold a specific view in this debate. Instead, it indicates that constructing these opinions in such a reciprocally hostile and mutually exclusive way is perhaps a little too simplistic. In the African spiritual understanding, the religious belief that God created life and the universe is a distinct issue; it does not purport to answer the question *how* or *when* exactly creation happened. The scientific discovery articulated by people such as Darwin that life, including human life, came into existence through the process of evolution by natural selection over billions of years until *homo sapiens* or the human species as we know it today emerged does not necessarily preclude the religious belief, according to African spirituality, that God was or is involved in creating life. If we understand well the African perspective, it seems that for it the scientific and the religious views are to be taken not as mutually exclusive but complementary.

The myths of creation both in the Hebrew Scriptures and in African traditions are much too rich theologically to be deprived of their symbolizing intent by being reduced to a literal creationist or scientific signification, exclusive of each other. A warning must be sounded for those who would take them literally and dogmatically: it is naïve to imagine that when these theories originated people understood, or should have understood, what is known today about the cosmos. Today, faith in the divine origin of the universe should not be taken to imply demonstrable molding of the universe by some pre-existent supreme being in six days. Yet, on the other hand, the notion of evolution and natural selection is much too complex to be limited to provable material evidence alone, completely devoid of spiritual considerations. Even if scientific experiments are successfully conducted to ascertain the *how* and *when* of the origins of the universe and life, it is equally naïve to imagine that modern science should be required or able to express its discoveries and findings in the language of religious symbolism, which concentrates on the question of *by whom* and *why* the universe came into being. It is now generally realized that to restrict understanding of the issue of creation exclusively to one or the other of these perceptions is to radically impoverish both.

Given contemporary understanding of the development of the universe, Ilia Delio is amazingly in line with the basic sentiments of African thinking when she maintains that compilers of something similar to the Genesis myth today would not eliminate the divine element from the conception of the process of creation. Similarly, she argues, modern science should not. "If the book of Genesis were rewritten today," Delio asks, "how would the story begin?" She suggests the broad outlines of a possible rendition, which takes into account divine agency and power, as well as the principle of evolution. Thus, the first sentences of the account might be a variation of something like this: "In the beginning was God, filled with power and mystery, and God spoke one Word, and the Word exploded into a tiny, hot, dense ball of matter that gave rise to forces and fields, quarks and particles, all joined together like a single strand of thread" from which eventually, through many millennia, life as we know it unfolded" (Delio 2008, 15).

It would seem that African spirituality preserves this complexity of the process of creation by, in principle, not rejecting either the activity of the divine Word or the dynamics of natural selection in it, because elements of both are essential to it and true. This stance reveals the African approach to reality, one that proceeds from a both-and, not an either-or view in all complex life-giving considerations. This is a perception of existence that looks for, finds, and accepts whatever is good and true in life-enhancing processes wherever it is to be found. Thus, again, for African spirituality, there is no necessary contradiction between the theory of God's creative Word in the universe and the scientific hypothesis of evolution as a way of approaching the question of the existence of the universe and life in it. The two are complementary. Evolution does not remove divine agency in creation; rather, it reinforces the Mystery that is divine power behind and within the entire process. The fact of evolution, on the other hand, gives creation the supernatural quality of an unfolding divine energy underlying existence, coalescing everything that exists into one. This causative and sustaining energy, however, may be understood as God's Word or spirit, which breathes forth everything that exists (see Garon 2006, 130-36). In the human person the divine spirit achieves its climax, but though distinct, it is not completely separate from matter.

The African perspective on creation finds clarification and confirmation in Pope John Paul II's reflections in his 1996 "Message to the Pontifical Academy of Sciences on Evolution." Acknowledging that "new findings lead us toward the recognition of evolution as more than a hypothesis," he nevertheless called for two epistemological approaches to the fact of human existence:

With man, we find ourselves facing a different ontological order—an ontological leap, we could say. But in posing such a great ontological discontinuity, are we not breaking up the physical continuity which seems to be the main line of research about evolution in the fields of physics and chemistry? An appreciation for the different methods used in different fields of scholarship allows us to bring together two points of view which at first might seem irreconcilable. The sciences of observation describe and measure, with ever greater precision, the many manifestations of life, and write them down along the time-line. The moment of passage into the spiritual realm is not something that can be observed in this way—although we can nevertheless discern, through experimental research, a series of very valuable signs of what is specifically human life. But the experience of metaphysical knowledge, of self-consciousness and self-awareness, of moral conscience, of liberty, or of aesthetic and religious experience—these must be analyzed through philosophical reflection, while theology seeks to clarify the ultimate meaning of the Creator's designs. (http://www.ewtn.com/library/PAPALDOC)

The links between, or connectedness of, all existence is itself something God-like; it can be described as "consciousness," or what African spirituality refers to as life force or vital energy. S. A. Thorpe comments on Rabbi Harold Kushner's view on this matter to the effect that essentially creation is one; it belongs together in its origin and development. The substance that constitutes humans as conscious beings is most likely the same that constitutes all creation, and it goes back to the beginning of time in a way that we can say that everything contains a mind of force of life (Thorpe 1991, 120). Accordingly, African spirituality speaks of the energy, *manna, anima,* power, or spirit that is in every creature and that connects every creature with all others. In a sense, African spirituality understands the universe as one whole, a point that the pioneering Catholic paleontologist Pierre Teilhard de Chardin also strongly made in his writings.

This connection cannot be ascribed simply to natural selection alone; it obviously precedes and transcends it. And so, when Bénézet Bujo reflects on this issue, he draws the inevitable conclusion that because of the essential connectedness of all creation, it is ethically incumbent on human beings to respect and preserve nature. Since humanity is intrinsically and inextricably bound up with, and consequently implicated in, the rest of creation and vice versa, he points out, "conservation needs no other argument than the unity of the whole." In Bujo's opinion, "It is not [only] other beings' sensitivity to pain, or their capacity to communicate, that establishes an ethical obligation for human beings towards nature." From the African point of view, as Bujo interprets it, "The cosmic community itself, including all beings, not just animals, is the essential foundation of African ecological ethics" (Bujo 2009b, 296). Care and respect for all of creation are, consequently, the main principles that should guide human behavior in life. Balance that preserves the harmony of creation is the fundamental ethical criterion. In the words of Bujo, "human greed and blind confidence that anything can be achieved, however unnatural, is likely to lead to destruction of self and the cosmos. By failing to distinguish between life's friends and enemies, the human person can lead himself and all humanity to death and destruction" (Bujo 2009b, 285).

"The deepest cause of the present devastation [of the universe]," Thomas Berry writes in amazing correspondence with African ecological-spiritual concerns, is found in a mode of consciousness that has established a radical discontinuity between the human and other modes of being and the bestowal of all rights on the humans" (Berry 1999, 4). It is a cause of great anxiety that the dominant present-day "political, economic, intellectual, and religious establishments" push the perspective that denies rights for "other-than-human modes of being." In fundamental agreement with African spirituality, once again, Berry confirms the oneness of creation. "In reality," he writes, "there is a single integral community of the Earth that includes all its component members whether human or other than human," in which every member has its proper "role," "dignity," "spontaneity," and "voice." According to Berry, "Every being declares itself to the entire universe. Every being enters into communion with other beings." For Berry, "This capacity for relatedness, for presence to other beings, for spontaneity in action, is a capacity possessed by every mode of being throughout the entire universe" (Berry 1999, 4), a fundamental consciousness of African spirituality.

The African totemic system (as discussed previously) demonstrates this concretely on the level of attitudes. It is a source of inspiration for respect for other-than-human modes of existence in that it perceives the "presence" of the human spirit in animals, plants, and other beings depending on the myth of the clan or ethnic group. Through identification of a particular animal or object with the ancestral spirit, the representation of the totem with the particular clan is established. Although the totem and clan are not strictly identical, they represent each other in the sense that the spirit of the one exists in a real and present way in the other. The prohibition or taboo of violating the integrity of the totem or the totem the human counterpart follows naturally from this, so that the totem must not be harmed just as much as the totem cannot harm any member of the relevant clan. The relationship is mutual. The basic spiritual lesson in the clan-totemic relationship is that of the communion of every being with all other beings in existence, which Berry speaks about. "A plant, then," as Mark Hathaway and Leonardo Boff continue the argument, "is not just something before me—it is a resonance, a symbol, and a value within me. There is within me mountain, vegetable, animal, human, and divine dimensions" (Hathaway and Boff 2009, 314). The totemic relationship is the microrepresentation of the macrocosm. Its deeper meaning and significance are relevant and indispensable to ecological spirituality today. It may be compared to the explanation found in classical Catholic Christology.

John C. Haughey argues that the Christology of the Council of Chalcedon (421) "takes seriously the humanity of Jesus, not allowing this to be absorbed by his divinity. It holds that, in the person of Jesus, an uncreated divine nature and a created human nature came into a wholly unique ('hypostatic') union . . . without either being annihilated." Thus the human and divine in Jesus exist together "to bring all created reality to its completion and fullness" (Haughey 2009, 55). We may take this Chalcedonian Christology to reflect the spiritual perspective of Africa. The spiritual reality of existence is understood in Africa to be integrated in the physical, completely and truly, but without one annihilating the other. When we see visible substance or matter, we cannot but feel the invisible spiritual power within it, which completes and brings it to perfection.

By the divinity within him, Jesus in his human physical form leads creation, as Chalcedon postulated, to a much deeper meaning beyond physical existence to the spiritual character and power that are an inseparable property of the being of each. In African Christian spirituality, if allowed to be enriched by African indigenous spirituality, the mystery of Christ's incarnation, which is the concrete expression of the unity of the divine and the earthly, the invisible and visible forces, implies and requires a certain manner of human existence in the world. Jesus' "hypostatic union" must therefore not be robbed of its symbolic and actual significance by fossilizing it into a merely notional doctrine restricted to the "nature" of Jesus alone, understood in a unchanging way and localized at a certain historical time. This is true, but Jesus, as the Scriptures tell us, enters the world as dynamic "Word" (see John 1:1), who, with the Father from the beginning of time, speaks reality into existence. For African Christian spirituality, this is of cardinal importance; it inspires and calls for a positive attitude toward the universe, one that, based on Jesus' activity as self-giving Word, can bring about full communion of every aspect of the universe.

It is essential for contemporary Christianity to recover the wisdom of the "cosmic Christology" already intuited by theologians such as Origen (c. 183–254), Irenaeus (c. 115–200), and Maximus the Confessor (c. 580–662). This intuition was lost in the subsequent Christological controversies and dogmatic declarations. Elizabeth A. Johnson proposes that even the doctrine of the Holy Trinity can and should profitably be understood in a similar "cosmic" way. For her, trinitarian teaching makes sense only within the context of the saving mystery. This pertains to African Christian spirituality. The Trinity within this context is not about numbers, Johnson insists, for this leads easily to the misconception of tritheism. On account of their own misleading reading of the teaching on the Trinity, Christians have erroneously yet justifiably been accused of this heresy. On the contrary, the Trinity is about communion. God in everything and everything in God (or "panentheism") are symbolically, analogously, and metaphorically expressed in three ways or modes of understanding the divine presence in, and relation to, the universe in the history of salvation. These correspond to the mode of creation from the very beginning of time, articulated in always-inadequate human language as God Father; the mode of redemption in concrete earthly time and space as God Son; and in the mode of complementarity, in the sense of ever-ecstatic fulfillment of goodness in the "dance" of life as God Spirit. All language about God as Trinity, Johnson insists, regardless of whether it is understood "as analogy, metaphor, or symbol . . . is talk that points to God's being as a communion of love" (Johnson 2007, 214) and abundance of life. This is the point of African spirituality.

From the African spiritual worldview, what demonstrates lack of the full flowering of life, or the absence of the spiritual "communion of love," are practical matters of disease, pain, suffering, lack of offspring, witchcraft, and disharmony among people and between human beings and the rest of creation manifested in these phenomena. Afflictions like these are understood to be a consequence of the human failure to act well before and toward others and the universe, a contravention of right order in the spiritual realm. Wrongful living is therefore ultimately a matter of harm to the well-being of the human community and creation. But the mission of Jesus, in Christian and African Christian spirituality, is to reverse this. Consequently, various analogies, symbols, and metaphors in African Christian theology are now employed to capture adequately this mission for the African imagination—one that corresponds to the African people's experience of integral freedom (see Mugambi and Magesa 1989; Schreiter 1991; Gibellini 1994; Stinton 2004). They include (as mentioned earlier) Jesus as Proto-Ancestor or Ancestor *par excellence*, as Healer (*Nganga*), Elder Brother, Chief, and Master of Initiation. Activities pertaining to these categories of people are central to African life and literally move the African world in the direction of the appropriation of fullness of life. If this is the mission of Jesus, to bring life in its completeness to the world, then it is not inappropriate to see him and his mission in terms of these and similar African analogies. These analogies pertain to the African understanding of family and kinship relationships, which also evoke the mystery of the Holy Trinity, as Johnson explains it. They indicate likewise that salvation in Jesus implies that all creation is indeed a family community and that to survive, it must exist as such, as communion.

It is inspiring that a Christian saint, Francis of Assisi, so closely connected in Christian hagiography with the spirituality of the ecosystem and the environment, perceived the universe not only in terms of family relationships, as reflected most cogently and radically in his *Canticle of Creation,* but also lived and acted accordingly (see Delio et al. 2008, 65-108). Francis in the *Canticle* refers fondly to nature as "brother" and "sister." As Delio and her colleagues put it, "If the *Canticle* speaks to us of creation as family, it is because the notes of brotherhood and sisterhood resound harmoniously throughout it: brother wind, sister stars, Sister Mother Earth" (Delio et al. 2008, 84). But these notes, for Francis as for African spirituality, evoke creation's spiritual character: "all remind us that we come from the fountain of the Most High, the Father's overflowing love, which flows through the Word into creation" (Delio et al. 2008, 84). Mark Hathaway and Leonardo Boff report that St. Basil, many centuries before Francis, had prayed in recognition of this fact in this manner: "O God, enlarge within us a sense of fellowship with all living things, our brothers and sisters the animals, to whom you gave the Earth as their home in common with us" (Hathaway and Boff 2009, 320).

The spirituality of communion with all existence liberates. It makes one "relaxed" about one's relationship with nature; we are all one intimate sacred community. It simultaneously lets creation "be at ease" in its integrity as well as enhances the integral development of the entire human person and the human community. Thomas Berry has argued, in warning against senseless exploitation, that humanity risks a stunted existence at all levels if the physical universe is senselessly and insensitively vitiated: "what happens to the nonhuman happens to the human," he states. "What happens to the outer world happens to the inner world" (Berry 1999, 200). Concurring intrinsically with the perception of African spirituality, Berry argues strongly that "The human and the Earth are totally implicated, each in the other. If there is no spirituality in the Earth, then there is no spirituality in ourselves" (Berry 2009b, 69). What follows from this?

> If the outer world is diminished in its grandeur then the emotional, imaginative, intellectual, and spiritual life of the human is diminished or extinguished. Without the soaring birds, the great forests, the sounds and coloration of the insects, the free-flowing streams, the flowering fields, the sight of the clouds by day and the stars at night, we become impoverished in all that makes us human. (Berry 1999, 200)

From a different spiritual perspective, antagonistic to both the African and orthodox Christian orientations, much energy is expended in fighting the forces of the universe to subdue them and dominate the earth. Apart from the relative benefit of bringing about material transformation in the last five hundred years, something that today is also referred to as "development," the attitude that subjects the whole of creation to the primary aim and goal of human consumption has also caused great harm to the universe. It continues to do so today. More and more, it is becoming clear that this kind of exclusive, exploitative development in favor of supposedly unlimited human consumption cannot be sustainable in the long run. African spirituality as contained in the African people's myths and traditions prescribes a degree of limit of flow in the relationship of humanity with nature, suggesting respect for nature's sacred character. In times past, for example, no one was allowed to trespass in certain locations or make use of certain things in the village because tradition said that these places and things were sacred, that is, reserved as clear symbols of the autonomy and balance of human and cosmic energy (see Magesa 2010b, 127-52). What can only be referred to as the tyranny of mindless exploitation of the earth in favor of humanity alone is thereby checked.

The issue is, of course, once again, our basic human attitude toward the world. The traditional African attitude in general portended an atmosphere of peaceful coexistence rather than hostility between humans and the rest of creation in the universe. A unique case that exemplifies this is that of the Maasai people who for centuries lived in harmony with wild game, respecting their space in an intuitive recognition of universal communion or interdependence.

What leads to the spirituality of exploitation and expropriation of the world for the sole purpose of human consumption and pleasure is basically the self-perception and understanding of the human being as an entity separated, first of all, from other human beings and, second, as an extension of this, from the community of the universe. This is a result of the philosophy, anthropology, psychology, and, indeed, religion into which any human group is predominantly socialized. This has much to do with the understanding of the meaning of the person unraveled through practical life. The *Ubuntu* perspective I have previously discussed at some length understands freedom and fulfillment of the human person in all dimensions and at all levels within the context of the community of persons and goods, something that necessitates belonging and sharing, as well as through participation in the community of creation. A person becomes authentically such only in community with others under these processes. The implications of this way of perceiving and actualizing personhood and basic humanity have immense consequences on ecological spirituality.

If personhood is understood apart from community, individualism reigns. One of the most destructive psychological-spiritual consequences of individualism is the belief that the sacred is centered in the individual, and in the community merely as an aggregation. It means what life has to offer has only the individual as its primary and most important purpose and can be exploited without loss for that purpose. In strictly religious terms, this translates into a vertical relationship between the individual and God to attain (as is sometimes misconstrued in Western Christian theology) personal salvation. Ecological concerns as part of the activity of redemption feature as tangential issues of the process, if at all in such theological imaginations. When personhood is understood in the context of community, however, one's mental and spiritual conceptualization and life-action change. The sacred is no longer perceived to exist primarily in the individual, who then sanctifies the community. The inverse now becomes the case, where the individual draws sacredness from the larger and more original and originating sacredness of the entire community. And since humanity cannot exist without and apart from the universe, this must include the sacredness of the universe.

Religion and spirituality in this view have much to do with community attitudes and behavior; as we mentioned, true religion and spirituality become the way of appropriating reality. This is principally a question of morals, how to (continually) construct and structure the universal community so that it remains integral and harmonious, reflecting pragmatically the harmony and integrity of the Trinity. From the perspective of African spirituality, this is the challenge that human beings are faced with now more than before in their social, political, economic, and religious arrangements: seeing the sacred in all things and appreciating the sacredness of all things. In *The Divine Milieu*, Teilhard de Chardin is clear about this same point that African spirituality emphasizes: the sanctification of human action is part of the transformation of the universe in the sense of all matter. Creation shares with humanity in this process of sanctification since humanity is united to creation and serves as the "voice" of its evolving consciousness, the manifestation of the Divine Spirit in the universe (Teilhard de Chardin 1968, 49-73).

17

Mission in the Age of Globalization

"The place where you stand is holy ground."

D rawing from the understanding of community as a sacred communion of creation, of humanity and nature, the process of fulfilling life in the world (which is the purpose of Christian mission) calls every follower of Christ to live in solidarity with other human beings and with the universe as a sacrament or sign of God's love. The sense of mission as sign of God's universal love defined the self-identity of the first followers of Jesus. Soon after Jesus' resurrection and ascension, the disciples came to the awareness that their mission was not restricted only to the "house of Israel" but extended to the Gentiles as well, that is, "to every nation" (Matt. 28:19-20).

Of all the disciples, this was the specific and special intuition of Paul of Tarsus not long after his conversion. We find here already the recognition that the frontier of mission is everywhere, every nation, the whole world, the entire creation. Thus it necessarily includes activity in different geographical, environmental, and cultural locations worldwide. Consequently, the issue of social and cultural justice cannot be overlooked in the evangelization process.

The history of Christian mission in Africa by the mainline Christian churches, however, shows precisely this neglect. This is well known. In fact, perhaps it was worse than neglect in Africa; rather, it was active contempt for African culture and the glorification of European cultures as the only vehicles worthy of containing the gospel. From reading the New Testament, we know that a similar attitude existed in St. Paul's time, referred to in the Acts of the Apostles as "Judaization." The "Judaizers" were Jewish Christians who wanted to foist Jewish customs on non-Jewish converts to Christianity. In Africa, "Westernizers" or, in Catholic Christianity specifically, "Latinizers" are the equivalent of the Judaizers. Their attitude is the same; they are a legion of gospel preachers, both Western missionaries and Western-trained Africans, who insist that African Christians must conform to Western symbols, forms, and expressions of the Christian faith. They can be found everywhere in the continent.

As in Paul's time, the conditions for conversion the Westernizers impose on people are culturally oppressive. Bible readers are familiar with Paul's outburst and challenge against Peter in Galatia who, in the view of Paul, seemed to be promoting this attitude (Gal. 2:14). In a similar way, in 1914, one Bishop Le Roy, challenging the Catholic missionary methods, wondered "whether it is actually necessary, in order to convert the world [to Christ], first of all to Latinize it" (Bridston 1965, 49). Beyond theory, the question has in practice not been satisfactorily resolved. In 1955, the South African Afrikaner author Laurens van der Post articulated the injustice and oppression of current mission theology when he complained in his book *Dark Eye in Africa* that Christian mission was equated with forcing Africans to deny their identity, to alienate themselves from their divinely endowed cultural and religious sensitivities and imitate Europe. For this reason, van der Post observes, African Christians remained inwardly resentful (see Bridston 1965, 42).

The approach of St. Paul to mission was different, and so too, quite soon afterward, was Peter's. After a special revelation, Peter learned that doing violence to other people's cultures in the name of the gospel was unacceptable to God himself. As Peter told Cornelius, the Roman centurion, and his household: "You know that it is unlawful for a Jewish man to associate with, or visit, a Gentile, but God has shown me that I should not call any person profane or unclean. And that is why I came without objection when sent for" (Acts 10:28). But how often and in how many ways have Africans historically been considered as such by Christian missionaries? Peter's conversion was strengthened by the inner realization that "God shows no partiality. Rather, in every nation whoever fears him and acts uprightly is acceptable to him" (Acts 10:34-35). In other words, God accepts people as they are, in their full identity, provided that guided by the ubiquitous Divine Spirit they do what is right.

Cultural oppression in evangelization can be aggravated by various developments in the contemporary world. The issue of cultural identity is closely related to the globalization movement, which, perhaps inadvertently, often tramples on the identities of people and cultures. Of course, the phenomenon of globalization has many positive facets, such as the ease of movement of people from one region of the world to another by modern means of travel. Still, it is important to point out, lest this fact be unduly magnified, that this movement tends to be easier in one direction, from the rich northern hemisphere to the less economically privileged southern hemisphere.

For our discussion, the most dangerous effect of globalization is the attempt at homogenization. In its most common form, globalization involves a sort of mindless transfer of ideas and goods from the industrialized regions of the world. Through the power of money and the influence of mass communication, it generally imposes a sort of uniformity in material and intellectual consumption that has now become very hard to resist. Unfortunately, it appears that resistance against this attempted annihilation of identity and diversity, when it happens, often manifests itself in the form of violence, because it emerges as the underdog, as powerlessness struggling against power. In order to make any headway, resisters therefore think they must resort to desperate measures of sabotage and terrorism. In the process, great disruption occurs at many levels in personal as well as national and international harmony. By such action and reaction the spirit of communion is broken.

Most such resistance appropriates religious symbolism in some way (see Huntington 1996; Sacks 2002). This seems to indicate that there is something within human religious consciousness that rejects human alienation and oppression for any reason whatsoever. If Christian churches could recognize their history in this regard in many areas of the world since the fifteenth century, they could yet become peaceful agents of harmony through respect of the divine presence in the universe. They can engage in mission that eliminates the tendency to violent resistance by safeguarding the cultural dignity of peoples and by preserving what we can only describe as divinely willed human diversity. This calls for theological courage and a drastic change in the understanding of mission. A pedagogical or catechetical change must be made from the view of mission as imposing concepts, even biblical concepts, and particular, time- and culture-conditioned doctrines to eliciting divinely endowed goodness in people as cultural beings. This is what the Christian gospel, and, therefore, authentic Christian mission is all about.

The imperative of preserving cultural identity and diversity and the values embedded there is now recognized even by civic institutions such as the *African Charter on Human and Peoples' Rights* (ACHPR, Article 29.7) and the *United Nations Declaration on the Rights of Indigenous Peoples* (UNDRIP, Article 11.1). "This includes the right to maintain, protect and develop the past, present and future manifestations of . . . [peoples'] cultures, such as archaeological and historical sites, artifacts, designs, ceremonies, technologies and visual and performing arts and literature." In Article 12.1 the document also emphasizes the right of peoples "to manifest, practice, develop and teach their spiritual and religious traditions, customs and ceremonies; the right to maintain, protect, and have access in privacy to their religious and cultural sites; the right to the use and control of their ceremonial objects; and the right to the repatriation of their human remains" (http://www1.umn.edu/humanrts/instree/z1afchar.htm).

The *Universal Declaration on Human Rights* (UNDHR, Article 1) declares without any ambiguity that "all human beings are born free and equal in dignity and rights. They are endowed with reason and conscience and should act towards one another in a spirit of brotherhood" (http://www.un.org/esa/socdev/unpfii/documents/DRIPS_en.pdf). Although some of these sentiments meet with resistance from some quarters, from the consequences in terms of the degree of freedom they have engendered in different parts of the world, the documents can be seen to have contributed a positive dimension to the appreciation of the spirituality of communion.

The churches as part of the human and universal family cannot ignore this voice despite its flaws. The Christian churches are called to embrace as their own whatever value comes out of authentic human experience. The dignity of human cultures as part and parcel of the dignity of the human person in the world, something intrinsically recognized by these declarations and conventions, must today be counted as one such value. From the perspective of the churches, these and similar values are steeped not only in human reason, but in belief in transcendence, the essence of universal communion, which is the basis of religion.

Fundamental human values, which are also by definition Christian values, are directly and fundamentally related to Christian belief in the incarnation of God as a human being in Jesus Christ. Roland de Pury explains that "in Jesus Christ divine and human rights are conjoined and become inseparable. To violate the rights of a creature of God in the name of divine right is thus to serve another god—to commit idolatry" (see Montgomery 1986, 215). Through the Christian perspective of creation, we must accept that although cultures are human constructions, they incorporate within them a divine element or spirit, called "breath" in the Hebrew myth of creation, or *nommo* in the mythology of the Dogon people of Mali. This is the reason why, from the Christian point of view, they must be respected and esteemed. Without appealing to religious sentiments as such, this, again, is the point captured by the documents cited above.

Of course, the churches cannot take these documents as end-points that conclude the discussion of the cultural dignity of persons and communities; faith in Christ cannot take anything short of Jesus himself revealed in glory as the end-point of all endeavor. God does not reveal neat conceptual propositions about the divine self; God reveals the divine self continuously in history, and humanity must discover it always partially through historical processes by the procedure, conscious or intuitive, of a balance of values, of yes and no. From the point of view of Christian faith, humans are called to this process until they see Jesus "face to face," when he will be for all humanity the embodiment of the fullness of truth (1 Cor. 13:12).

In the same way, the churches must take their own articulated teachings on the divine reality. Everything should be seen as a starting point for a deeper understanding of the gospel demands for cultural rights and the dignity of the human person and human groups. In terms of mission, this relates to the fundamental issue of how to impart the "truths" of the gospel, how to evangelize. In this light, the notion advanced by Søren Kierkegaard and Bernard Lonergan that "'truth is subjectivity' and that one must discover it in the particulars of experience, not in any alleged universal, timeless generalities" (see Montgomery 1986, 192) must be taken seriously in Christian mission activity if it is to avoid the danger of cultural oppression and violence, especially during this era of globalization.

But Pope Benedict XVI repeatedly expressed the concern that this approach leads to what he described as the "tyranny" or "dictatorship" of relativism. In his view, subjectivity leads to a situation where there are no ethical values, which, as he sees it, implies an "anything goes" approach to life. "A large proportion of contemporary philosophies, in fact, consist of saying that man is not capable of truth," he says. "But viewed in that way, man would not be capable of ethical values, either. Then he would have no standards. Then he would only have to consider how he arranged things reasonably for himself, and then at any rate the opinion of the majority would be the only criterion that counted" (Benedict XVI and Seewald 2010, 50).

"Subjectivity" as a methodological principle applied to Christian mission does not mean what Benedict describes and fears here. Since the Christian mission is to impart the values of the gospel, it does and must insist on certain values. But the point for mission today is that these are not principally propositional values "out there," so to speak, unrelated to human experience and meaning. The point, as Bernard Lonergan would put it, is rather that, for any value to be a value *for the subject*—whether that subject is an individual or a group—the subject must somehow "own" it, must bring it from inside of oneself, to make meaning out of it, and meaning more or less freely arrived at (Crowe and Doran 1988, 225-26, 232-45). This is perhaps what Jesus' question to his disciples implies when he inquires of them who they perceive him to be (Mark 8:29). Apart from this, the alleged "value" can become an imposition from outside the subject in question, a form of oppression, an assault on, or disregard and infringement of human rights and dignity.

Lonergan again explains this point well by pointing out that because it is the mind of the person that makes judgments on phenomena, in the final analysis truth is subjective because it exists in minds, in consciousness (Ryan and Tyrrell 1974, 71-72). The truth that impacts human social construction of structures and attitudes can be perceived only by paying "close attention to the data of consciousness." Only then is it possible to "discover insights, acts of understanding with the triple role of responding to inquiry, grasping intelligible form in sensible representations, and grounding the formation of concepts" (Ryan and Tyrrell 1974, 74). Apart from this there is the danger of falling into what Lonergan calls "conceptualism," or abstract, conjectural "objectivity of truth," of mistaking dry, uprooted concepts for understanding—an approach that, according to Lonergan, has for a long time marked Catholic dogmatic approaches to evangelization. The "widespread alienation from dogma," he argues, "is not unconnected with a one-sidedness that so insisted on the objectivity of truth as to leave subjects and their needs out of account" (Ryan and Tyrrell 1974, 71). This has certainly been the case with traditional methodologies of mission in Africa.

Instead, Lonergan urges the recognition of the role the historical, social, and psychological limitations and determinations of human beings plays in the perception and reception, if not "construction," of truth, out of which concepts and doctrines arise and which influences each individual's horizons. As he puts it, we experience different realities in our existence as human beings, and these realities construct our practical social, psychological, and spiritual worlds of truth. But even when we experience the same reality, we often interpret it differently (see Ryan and Tyrrell 1974, 69). The particular interpretation of our reality most fundamentally gives direction to our ways of living, which can be modified or changed most effectively only through dialogue. Dialogue in its various forms broadens the intellect, and by thus expanding horizons can modify or change judgments. The importance of diversity in humanity and creation as divine intention can be seen and appreciated in this context.

For Christians this should not be too difficult to appreciate because of the Christian understanding of the implications of divine creation of all existence. Specifically, *all* human beings in their particularities reflect in a special way God's image, necessitating the conviction that there is an element of the divine in every culture and circumstance. Consequently, God, through the Divine Spirit, precedes human mission, and, as M. A. C. Warren reminds everyone, mission ministry means standing on "holy ground" on account of the prior and, indeed, primordial presence in human cultures and generally in creation (see Warren 1963, 10-11).

In other words, subjectivity is part and parcel of creation and must be seen as a necessary element of the divine plan. In a sense, each creature has been endowed with this quality and can be properly understood and appreciated only on the basis of the subjectivity it possesses. It is the essence of each creature's relative autonomy. The respect that humans owe to one another as human beings, and to the rest of creation in the community of the universe, is based on this principle. This respect of persons and cultures in their subjectivity must be the foundation of and must extend to every facet of the evangelization activity of the church.

In this sense subjectivity has nothing to do with relativism when the latter is taken as a denial of the existence of overarching values and truths. Subjectivity necessitates the process of looking at reality from different possible angles, so as to gain ever more comprehensive horizons into the divine presence and activity in the subjectivity of the other. The genius of the early church lay precisely here: it decided at the Council of Jerusalem that "if the unity of the church was to be maintained it had to have a form sufficiently comprehensive and flexible to encompass the full reality of the Body as living, expanding, and changing" (Bridston 1965, 111). In this recognition too lay the realization of the universality of the church.

Pope John Paul II (1978–2005), undoubtedly one of the most dynamic of missionary popes of the twentieth century, admitted (and had the exceptional courage to confess publicly) that in the process of evangelization, "sins" had been committed against the cultural integrity of peoples. In his 1994 Apostolic Letter "On the Preparation for the Jubilee of the Year 2000" (*Tertio Millennio Adveniente* [*TMA*]), the pope regretted "the acquiescence given, especially in certain centuries, to intolerance and even the use of violence in the service of truth." Even "the consideration of mitigating factors," according to the pope, cannot completely excuse missionary work of the past from this shortcoming. Mission in the future, the pope demanded, must "adhere fully to the sublime principle stated by the [Second Vatican] Council: 'The truth cannot impose itself except by virtue of its own truth, as it wins over the mind with both gentleness and power'" (*TMA*, no. 35).

On October 10, 2012, Fr. Adolfo Nicolás, the Superior General of the Society of Jesus, made the following remarks to the Thirteenth Ordinary General Synod on "The New Evangelization for the Transmission of the Christian Faith":

> By not paying sufficient attention to how God was present and had been working in the [non-European] peoples we encountered, we missed important clues, insights and discoveries. It is now, therefore, the time to learn from this history, from what was missing in the First Evangelization, before we move ahead in the New. Many good things have happened, that we want to keep, develop and celebrate. At the same time, we know that many mistakes have also taken place, particularly in terms of not listening to the people, in judging with great superficiality the merits of old and rich cultures and traditions, in imposing

forms of worship that did not, in the least, express the relationship and
sensibility of the people in their turning to God in prayer and praise.
(http://www.sjweb.info/imagesNews/121007%20Intervention.pdf)

In the theology of mission, David Bosch insists that to be genuinely Christian, the starting point and end point of Christian evangelization must be the
acknowledgment that mission is principally God's activity; it must be based
on the truth of God. Bosch argues that the time is long past when mission
could be seen in terms of the church's effort to save souls from "eternal dam-
nation," or to introduce uncivilized peoples "to the blessings and privileges
of the Christian West," or even in terms of exclusively geographical catholicity to spread the church throughout the world (Bosch 1991, 389). Mission, as Bosch understands it, is "an attribute of God." Prior to the Council
of Trent, "mission" referred to the inner and external life of the Trinity. God
is a missionary God who essentially inclines toward the universe in love.
Thus, mission must now be conceived and done primarily in terms of divine
concern for creation, the entire universe. By the presence of the Holy Spirit
throughout creation, this divine universal concern or mission precedes and
anticipates any other form of Christian evangelization, including the church's
participation in and mediation of it (Bosch 1980, 239-48). It is God the
Father in Christ through the Spirit that is the "fountain" of mission in which
the church "bathes," so to speak (Bosch 1991, 390).

This comprehensive and theologically more accurate understanding of
mission is captured as well in the Pastoral Constitution on the Church in the
Modern World (*Gaudium et Spes*) of Vatican II, where mission is understood
most fundamentally as witness (*GS*, no. 1). Since, as we have seen, mission
flows from the love of God toward creation, nothing of creation is left out of
its embrace. Mission therefore includes many forms, such as the quest for
justice and peace, liberation, ecumenism, and inculturation (Bosch 1991,
368-510; Thomas 1995, 81-322; Bellagamba 1992, 48-69). Whether from
this perspective everything can be seen as mission depends on the premise upon which Christian mission finds its justification: "the participation of
Christians in the liberating mission of Jesus . . . wagering on a future that veri-
fiable experience seems to belie. It is the good news of God's love, incarnated
in the witness of a community, for the sake of the world" (Bosch 1991, 519).

On the basis of this theological understanding of mission, Lonergan
makes two fundamental claims relevant to freeing mission. First, mission
seen as "Being in Christ Jesus is not tied down to a place, culture or epoch.
It is catholic with the catholicity of the Spirit of the Lord." The second point
is equally important for authentic mission. Inasmuch as it is universal, and
perhaps because of this fact, mission must inescapably take subjectivity into

account. Mission is not "an abstraction that dwells apart from every place and time, every culture and epoch. It is identical with personal living, and personal living is always here and now, in a contemporary world of immediacy, a contemporary world mediated by meaning, a contemporary world not only mediated but also constituted by meaning" (Crowe and Doran 1988, 231).

This realization is more crucial than ever in our present time on account of new developments taking place in the world, including the ubiquitous phenomenon of globalization (Friedman 2005). The church's responsibility is to help the faithful become servants of God's mission in the contemporary world situation. It is, once again, to call every follower of Christ to affirmative action, to live in solidarity with other human beings and with the universe as a sacrament or sign of God's love. With the experience of the past in mind, as Pope John Paul II recalled at the threshold of the twenty-first century, Bosch suggests that doing mission today is concurrently for the church a form of admission and confession of guilt "before God and man" for past oppressive approaches that wounded people's subjectivity and dignity. Now "mission is the Church-crossing-frontiers-in-the-form-of-a-servant" (Bosch 1980, 248). It calls for the realization that, according to Adolfo Nicolás, "The fullness of Christ needs the contribution of all peoples and all cultures." The essence of mission may lie in "acknowledging the work of God in the life and history of people, accompanied by sincere admiration, joy and hope whenever we find in others goodness and dedication" (http://www.sjweb.info/images-News/121007%20Intervention.pdf).

18

Where Is Inculturation Going?

"The fetus that is afraid of criticism is never born."

What lies between creation and eschatology? Risk. Humanly speaking, God took a risk in creating the universe. Further, God took a risk in letting the human species evolve, culminating in self-consciousness. It is a risk that, theologically, resulted in human rebellion against the Creator, putting the entire universe at risk of diminishment. However, it is also the same risk that, again theologically, we know provided the opportunity for the liberation of humanity and the universe from destructive situations and structures, the "structures of sin," through the work of Jesus Christ. The Incarnation was itself an informed risk, one that portended not only the suffering and death of the Messiah but the extension of the practical lesson of loving justice for the completion of the universe by the agency of the Holy Spirit. If salvation history teaches us anything, it is that without the process of risk, nothing, and certainly not human redemption, is attained.

Inculturation, contextualization, interculturation: whatever name is given to describe the positive and beneficial process of cross-fertilization of thought and life for the culmination or completion of the universe in love is similarly risky at any and every stage of its realization when peoples and cultures encounter one another. Will people accept or reject one another? This is always the question. Inculturation demands that people move away from what modern popular psychologists have called their "comfort zones" into often unfamiliar territories. Sometimes the hurdles against positive and respectful encounter may seem insurmountable, thereby making the process uncertain, even destabilizing. Perseverance, however, often promises rewarding and life-enhancing results. At any rate, nothing tried, nothing gained. As the people of Rwanda say, "A fetus that is afraid of criticism is never born." Taking risks to make genuine the inculturation of Christian spirituality in Africa is what this book has been all about.

After decades of talk about inculturation in the African church, sometimes with strong encouragement from the authorities of the church, the question still remains: How real is inculturation in Africa? Adapting the question that John C. Haughey asks regarding the goal of Catholic higher education (Haughey 2009), one might be forgiven for wondering: *Where is inculturation going in Africa?* If we as the church in Africa are committed to being "fully Christian and fully African," and theologically there seems to be no alternative, and if the African church is to go beyond appearances in self-governance, self-propagation, and self-reliance, how should we go about it?

It is important for self-governance, but not enough, to have black faces in positions of authority in the church (see Thiong'o 1986). For genuine inculturation, minds must be attuned to the work of the Divine Spirit within Africa. It does not suffice for inculturation to don monkey-skin hats and hold buffalo-tail fly whisks and dance in church buildings during worship to the rhythm of the tom-tom. It is true that inculturation includes these gestures, but deep inculturation must revisit and reinterpret dogma in the light of the divine self-revelation existent in Africa. As far as self-reliance is concerned, it is a violation of simple justice to require that people support top-heavy church structures that are inherently beyond their economic means. In their triple calling and role as priests, prophets, and kings by baptism, Christians in Africa must become involved in the reformation of church structures so that they reflect where they are economically. At the same time, they should inspire these and civil economic structures to be "universe-friendly," for the human race to live wholesomely with the earth and the entire creation. For this the church needs an African theology geared toward these goals, the most fundamental area of self-propagation.

It is not that nothing has been done. There has been some development, different from the time when, as some people above sixty or so years of age will remember, every African expression of faith in God, or in other words African spirituality, was ridiculed and dismissed as pagan or worse. There are still many critics of African spirituality, but generally it is no longer strange to attend liturgies and experience an African-inspired ambiance in church. Vestments like the *kitenge* cloth (largely used in East and Central Africa) or *kente/nwentoma* garb (mainly in West Africa) worn by a priest celebrating the Eucharist are no longer considered sacrilege. Drums and African stringed instruments are often played during worship services. African musicians have composed liturgical songs that respond to the sentiments of African performance. Occasionally, liturgical dance with a message is performed by some worshippers. Although this is not enough, it is nevertheless a good sign.

As far as art (painting and sculpture) is concerned, a "black" Jesus or Virgin Mary does not raise many eyebrows today as it would have, say, fifty years ago. There are innovative efforts in this sphere from artists all across the continent. Perhaps the best known is the "Life of Jesus Mafa," an illustration of the life of Jesus in the Gospels based on African day-to-day life and painted in Cameroon. P. Dondy, Director of Catholic Schools in Yaounde, explains the attempt as "urgent and necessary" for the meaningful proclamation of the gospel in Africa, because it takes into account "our language," "our life," and "our culture." Just as others have done in this area honoring their environment, Dondy suggests that we in Africa must also continue to do so, in full faithfulness to the historical Jesus. As he puts it:

> We must not restrict ourselves to the historical and cultural forms of a particular people or period. The creation of a black Christ in Africa does not diminish at all the historical Christ, on the contrary, it [enriches] the universal meaning of the message of God. This God who became one of us in order to proclaim Christ as the Lord of all nations of the world, through all their authentic riches: their languages, their gestures, their art, their whole life and culture. Evangelization means to give the message of the historical and eternal Christ to all nations, following the apostles who made themselves Jews with the Jews, Greeks with the Greeks, similar to their Master who identified himself with every weak and persecuted human being when he said to Saul the persecutor: "Saul, why do you persecute me?" Doesn't this daring and unspeakable identification go far beyond what we are trying to express by these pictures? It shows not only their legitimacy but their necessity. (http://www.jesusmafa.com/anglais/accuei)

Inculturation, however, extends to the area of day-to-day living. What are the external manifestations of inner spirituality? As it implies, inculturation must become a culture, and culture is lived. We might take the example of religious life in Africa. In many religious congregations of Africa, members still wear the "habit" inspired by European traditions, climatic conditions, and culture. This is, of course, a choice, but it is one that speaks volumes. It is stretching the point when the European-inspired habit is almost equated with loyalty to Christ, as it is sometimes claimed! But *Cucullus non facit monachum* ("the cowl does not make the monk"), nor does it necessarily detract from their ministry. The institutes that have opted for an African style of dress survive very well and minister in the same fields as the others. According to reports, their number of "dropouts" is no greater than any other. The more important question, however, is how much African spirituality has influenced missionary institutes with a long-time presence here on the continent that now host numerous African members. How can it enrich the charisms originally envisioned by their founders and foundresses? When this question is answered properly, it will address even these external aspects of life.

What is there to learn from African spirituality for general church governance? It is rare to find genuine palaver, or *Indaba,* procedures as a paradigm of church governance in African dioceses, despite the established and widespread systems of consultation that we have seen were customary in indigenous forms of leadership. This was leadership "with wide ears," as Elochukwu E. Uzukwu, following the Manja tradition of the Central African Republic, describes it. Very close "to God, to the ancestors, and to the protective spirits of the community," as the chief is taken for granted to be, he never replaces these powers in this paradigm, for, in a sense, they permeate the community. The chief is, however, necessary because "along with other elders, he makes . . . [these powers] present (represents them) [concretely] in his person and behavior." The role of the chief goes even further, however:

> The Manja underline listening as the most dominant characteristic of the chief. His "large ears" bring him close to God, ancestors, and divinities and close to the conversations taking place in the community. He has the last word because he speaks after having assimilated and digested the Word in the community. He is the guardian of the dynamic, life-giving Word which creates and recreates the community. "Word" means truthfulness, fairness, honesty, communication. (Uzukwu 1996, 127)

The "Word" is too immense to be contained in or by one person, however elevated in the community the person may be. As the Bambara people of Mali see it, the individual leader can only be a mouthpiece of the community, and even then just partially, for the word is "too large" for any mouth. "Each sacred speech (of the community leader or of the representative of the community) [only] approximates this Word" (Uzukwu 1996, 126-27). This concretizes the church as the family of God in Africa.

While in various ways church authorities in Africa urge the practice of democracy on civil society as a necessary and ethical matter of justice, they are incongruously too quick to retort that "the church is not a democracy" when questioned about what sometimes appears to be authoritarian, top-down, decision-making procedures and judgments. It appears too much like the tendency "to confuse dignity with . . . sheer pomposity," something that Julius K. Nyerere condemns in political leaders (see Nyerere 1966b, 223) and which Cardinal Carlo Maria Martini also decried in the church (Martini 2012, 8-9). One sometimes questions the genuineness of diocesan synods, for example, as well as other parish and diocesan bodies such as parish councils or diocesan pastoral councils, when this procedure is closed to all but the most banal and inconsequential of issues. Where is the *sensus fidei* or the *sensus fidelium*, the sense of the faith of the believer within the community of the faithful, that the early fathers of the church insisted on and wrote so much about? How is the faith of the church made manifest? Or is "the church" the leader at any level of the institutional structure, a perception that is still prevalent among many? One is not unaware that many documents of the Catholic Church subordinate the *sensus fidei/fidelium* under the authority of the hierarchy (for example, see *Lumen Gentium*, no. 35). Such ecclesiology departs significantly from that of the early church. It is necessary to recover the balance between the voice of the leaders and the voice of the people within the church which, together, is the voice of God. The two must proceed side by side; one does not replace the other (see Chiwanga 2011; see also Nyerere 1966b, 223-26; Nyerere 1968b, 136-42). Hierarchy acting alone fails to respect the work of the Holy Spirit in the whole church.

> The image of the chief or community leader with "large ears" . . . highlights two salient points. First of all, authority is exercised fundamentally for the integral well-being of the community. Second, this style of exercising authority is capable of mobilizing the community for its integral development and the achievement of its aims and objectives. This perception of leadership has the potential for facilitating relationship not only within the local church but also on the supralocal (universal) level of the church. (Uzukwu 1996, 141)

While justice has always been held to be a cardinal virtue by the church, what structures for due process for employees can be found in African dioceses and other institutions? According to the synodal document "Justice in the World" (*Justitia in Mundo*) of 1971, which nowadays appears to be rarely mentioned in church official circles, "action on behalf of justice and participation in the transformation of the world fully appear to us as constitutive dimensions of preaching the Gospel, or, in other words of the Church's mission for the redemption of the human race and its liberation from every oppressive situation" (Synod of Bishops 1971, Introduction). Whether or not this synod is accepted as genuinely one of the general synods of the church since Vatican II, what the document says is part of the authentic prophetic teaching of the church with its foundations in the Scriptures and must infuse the entire process of inculturation in the African church.

Structurally, Small Christian Communities (SCCs) are capable of manifesting the sense of being church in Africa in many of its dimensions. Genuine inculturation requires that SCCs become truly respected as *theological* expressions of the presence and activity of the Holy Spirit. They should exercise freedom in terms of ministry and governance. The practice of justice in the church is best realized in SCCs when they are allowed to develop as the Spirit directs them. They should be allowed to develop structures of justice in society, with new ministries dictated by the needs of the place and hour. Again, the threefold qualities and mission of Jesus of kingship, priesthood, and prophecy, received by every Christian at baptism, are most practically and realistically exercised at this level (see Healey 2012, 67-108, 125-35). What we are engaged in with SCCs are not "political" but theological considerations, relating to *the* most fundamental principle of Christian life: the presence of the Holy Spirit in the church and in the world. The faith of Christians in the God of Jesus becomes concrete only through serious attention to the performance of the Holy Spirit among the faithful, guiding all creation toward the fulfillment of love and universal communion.

Where, then, is inculturation going? It must involve the political sphere as much as other spheres of life. As Ghanaian founding president Kwame Nkrumah thought, foreign contact with Africa must not be allowed to determine the articulation of African history. On the contrary, any such contact "needs to be assessed and judged from the point of view of the principles animating African society and from the point of view of the harmony and progress of this society" (Nkrumah 1964, 63). The same can be said of the church. Can we—indeed, must we—not state with the same conviction that Western Christian spirituality in contact with Africa must be "assessed and judged" from the basis of African spirituality, that is, on the basis of principles animating and harmonizing African society, and not vice versa? A fundamental act of faith in the power and performing presence of the Holy Spirit in the African church and wider society is once again involved here.

Is there anything to "retrieve" from African indigenous spirituality for contemporary African Christian living? If so, does retrieval involve only insignificant and superficial elements of appearances or, rather, fundamental aspects of vision and orientation, a matter of foundational horizons? If the former, would it not be better to save the time and effort expended in the charade of "inculturation" for more serious undertakings? The truth is, however, that there is something of substance "to retrieve and preserve" from African indigenous spirituality for contemporary African Christian life (Ramose 2009, 417). "The teaching of Jesus Christ and His redemption are, in fact, the complement, the renewal, and the bringing to perfection, of all that is good in human tradition," Pope Paul VI wrote in his message to the countries of Africa (*Africae Terrarum*, [*AT*]) in 1967. "And that is why the African who becomes a Christian does not disown himself, but takes up the age-old values of tradition 'in spirit and in truth'" (*AT*, no. 14). Africans who become Christians do not abandon their indigenous spirituality. Their spirituality always remains as a foundation of acceptance of any other religion. African Christians "take with them some of the elements of their old religion and culture, which they consider to be 'noble', 'beautiful' and representing the highest values of human expression in relation to God or the Supreme Being" (Ucko 2004, 5). One cannot insist too much that here we have, once again, the foundation of a rich theology of the Holy Spirit, which is at the basis of authentic inculturation.

The proper development of this foundation in Africa has been stunted by the inattentiveness of medieval-centered Christian theology, fixed overwhelmingly on a certain static understanding of God, one that has tended to weaken the horizons of divine salvific action in the world. There seems to be a tragic loss of consciousness of the Spirit, or cosmic animism in the positive sense of the concept. In Christian theology we might describe the current phenomenon (along with theologians Walter Kasper and Yves Congar) as an underdeveloped or sick pneumatology whose equivalent in scientific endeavors is overextended materiality. Both indicate the progressive failure to recognize the power of the Spirit, and Divine Spirit, in human affairs and creation. Both weaken humanity and endanger the world. Could the power of the Spirit, or "soul force," "be a beautiful quality deeply inherent in all human beings that, through the forces of times, urbanization, industrialisation and concomitant alienation, tends to be denied, suppressed and temporarily forgotten" (Nussbaum 2009a, 104; see also Johnson 2007)?

What picture emerges concerning the spirituality of inculturation? What is the spirituality, practically speaking, of the African person who is also a Christian? As we have indicated, the mainline Christian churches in Africa can draw a lesson about this from the perspective and practices of many of the African Initiated Churches (AICs). AICs have their shortcomings, including lack of a coherent theology, weak institutional structures, inadequate responses to poverty, and insufficient engagement against oppression and discrimination in the modern globalized world. Yet their overall basic spiritual orientation responds much better to African religious yearnings. The question these churches address is how to respond to Christ's call to love, a call that can only be answered properly based on all circumstances surrounding a particular person or community. The proper response always takes place in context; its practical expression is never predetermined and cannot, therefore, in the strict sense, be adapted wholesale from one context to another.

When adaptation is made the basis of inculturation, the process ignores the rootedness of every person in his or her context and becomes alienating. Historically, adaptation in Africa has invoked Western Christian concepts as starting points to which African perspectives must conform. But this inhibits genuine dialogue: Western approaches are disabled from the start from learning from African spiritual perceptions, on the one hand; and, on the other, African approaches are denied free self-expression. The approach has generally been recognized by the majority of African theologians as dysfunctional and innately incapable of helping African Christian communities to become truly African and truly Christian. Nevertheless, and paradoxically, it remains the dominant one in Africa in the catechesis and pastoral practice of the mainline Christian churches.

Inculturation by its various designations respects the sense of dialogue and cultural identity of peoples. Just as God became human in Jesus Christ and so concretely united himself to the human historical process of growth in consciousness so as to bring about the liberation of the universe, the Christian faith and its concrete expression (or sacrament, as expressed at Vatican II in *Lumen Gentium*, nos. 48-51) as church must enter thoroughly into any of its host cultures and become truly part of it. Apart from this, Christian faith runs the risk of not making any deep impact on the people being invited to explicitly acknowledge Christ as Lord, the most potent vital energy of the universe.

The basic and most fundamental question of inculturation is how to interpret the God of Jesus Christ based on the identity of the African person. How can Africans relate to the God of Jesus in prayer and in worship, indeed, in the whole orientation of their existence, in a way that is affirming of their humanity as Africans? This is, of course, a question of meaning. Spirituality that is not affirming of the humanity of the human and the essential sacredness of creation is by that very fact alienating and, as such, cannot be Christian. In authentic Christian spirituality, relationship with the Absolute results in "abundance of life" for humanity and for the universe.

The success of inculturation in Africa will depend on whether or not the process addresses the way of living of Africans, mainly the African indigenous traditions. Although these traditions are open to reform, even in very radical ways as they interact with the Bible, they remain pivotal in the African reception of the gospel. If the Good News is to stay African in character, it must be enriched by the essential values of the indigenous tradition. The emerging worldview must *remember*, in the sense of making present in some fundamental way, the original spiritual perceptions of life. This is where creative innovation can take place. Inculturation will be a process in which the vision, acts, and values of the old tradition are kept in the forefront of intellectual-spiritual consciousness in creative tension with the word of God already embedded in a different culture, in order to bring about a creative synthesis rather than a completely *ex nihilo* construction.

Genuine inculturation, then, cannot be anything but a pilgrimage of return home, back to familiar waters of God's primordial presence in African culture. "The crocodile is only strong in the water," they say in Angola; similarly, African Christians will be strong when they are steeped in the Spirit of God in African cultural experience. The Spirit that Christ promised to remain with the world to sustain it works in African culture to bring about the good life through unity and solidarity between humans and the rest of creation. This power of God, which leads to integration of the various forces of life in the world to uphold it, calls for an attitude of awe before God who is "all in all" and who integrates everything. The Spirit preserves the splendor of God, before whom human beings and the entire creation must bow in humble stillness.

Epilogue

"Even the best dancer on the stage must retire sometime."

The time to retire from the stage has come; but let us emphasize a few points before we go. This study has attempted to demonstrate the following ideas:

1. No type of spirituality, whether it is in the form of personal piety or a religious system of a community, can endure without firm roots. Throughout the fluctuations of history in Africa, in good times and in bad (recall, as examples, the slave trade, colonialism, the experience of brutal dictatorships after independence, the HIV/AIDS pandemic, and several genocides), the resilience of the African spirit has been remarkable. It has relied heavily on the personal and communal assurance of ancestral benevolence, which directly mediates the never-ending divine love upon the world. Despite mutations of various kinds, ancestral spirituality is the root of the enduring African spirituality, its belief in the basic goodness of life. To destroy the African ancestral heritage is, therefore, to annihilate the existence of the African people.

2. Spirituality for the people of Africa is not a passive "given"; it is played out in day-to-day life, through observance of moral codes, rites and rituals, and patterns of relationships. Relationships among all elements of creation, physical and nonphysical, visible and invisible, are the essence of African spirituality, because Africans believe that only through harmonious relationships is cosmic existence possible and its vital force preserved. Africans believe that the universal life-force inherent in the totality of creation "is transmitted effectively within the domain of the physical universe. Life comes where nothing had been, and everything is constantly being sublimated into something beyond the reach of time" (Kobia 2003, 17-18). Human participation in this process of continual "sublimation" constitutes the essence, meaning, and requirement of spirituality. The foundation of the vital force that makes universal existence possible is God, whose being the human mind can never completely fathom. God is God.

3. The cosmos is a "moral" reality in the African worldview; it is a performance or experience "nurtured not only through the relational value of all life within the cosmos but especially by the [active] network of human relation-

ships that define moments of transition to new life" (Kobia 2003, 18). These moments are marked by indispensable prescribed rituals without which the vital force of humanity and the cosmos may be seriously threatened. These are rituals of transition and integration. They continually establish connections that lead to an ever-fuller realization of life: they range from conception to birth; from initiation ceremonies to marriage; from elderhood to death and ancestorhood; from war to peace; from wrongdoing to repentance and forgiveness, and so on. Again, lack of these ritual performances diminishes both humanity and the rest of creation.

4. Relationships for the promotion of the force of life must embrace "others" in all their differences, for all creation and the various ways it is experienced and expressed contain the spark of divine, "spiritual" life. Plurality or multiplicity of the experience and expression of belief, for instance, poses no innate problem for African spiritual life. On the contrary, it facilitates the practical application of an essential component of African spirituality. Elochukwu Eugene Uzukwu has described it as "the principle of duality or plurality or the combination of twinned components . . . [which] obliges one always to take a second look at everything, to question all assumptions without exception, including the African tradition itself" (Uzukwu 2012, 20). The "Word" that represents the Truth of the Universe is too big for one mouth only, even where the physical sciences are concerned. To have fuller access to the reality of the universe, its "twinness" or "multiplicity" must be constantly recognized and acknowledged (see Uzukwu 2012, 10). The principle of multiple significations of reality, elaborated as *Sic et Non* (Yes and No) by the medieval theologian Peter Abelard, leads to the same realization.

5. Patient dialogue rather than forced conversion, therefore, is the direction indicated by the awareness of "twinning" reality; multiple signification is the only acceptable path into the wider and deeper world of the divine presence in this multidimensional universe. In dialogue with the other culture, with the other religion, with the other artistic expression, and so on, it is possible to construct the kind of communion or harmony that is central to the preservation and enrichment of life that happens by way of expanded consciousness. The inclusive "both-and" (rather than "either-or") attitude that characterizes so much of the African approach to life expresses not only the complexity of but also the grace inherent in the universe. Rooted in one's personal and cultural view of reality, which must remain distinct, genuine dialogue provides the possibility of transcending oneself; it avails one of wings by which to fly to new landscapes, with sharper eyes with which to see further horizons, and, hopefully, with stronger resolve and commitment to deeper communion with the vital powers and, of course, from the Christian perspective, with the God of Jesus Christ.

6. The goal of African spirituality, and African *Christian* spirituality for that matter, is the good life (John 10:10). In this millennium, where growth and development continue to be global catchphrases, Africa still grapples with scarcity in a number of key sectors. Few policies have translated into good practice with positive results. More than ever before, the church and nation-states must make peace and justice a reality for millions in Africa, people who have systematically been robbed of their dignity through conflicts, lack of basic needs, and a general disregard for human rights. This rupture in normal life has led to increasing disintegration of family and community ties and values. Deprivation breeds alienation. In order to respond adequately to people's realities, material and spiritual needs must be met satisfactorily, for in the end both converge. This is the message that African spirituality, in conversation with other worldviews in a spirit of respect for diversity and inclusivity, bears for contemporary humanity. Africa's contribution to humanizing the world remains relevant.

7. African spirituality can inspire Christian theology and pastoral approaches to "unbind the Spirit," the very same Spirit or Advocate whom Christ promised that he would send into the world to enlighten and ever guide it to complete truth (John 14–16). Saint Paul, writing to the Christian community at Ephesus, similarly reminds them that they have been "sealed with the promised Holy Spirit," and in the Spirit, together with the entire universe, must continually grow deeper into "a dwelling place of God" (see Eph. 1:11–2:22). The Ephesians are us. Saint Paul's bidding is for us.

Works Cited

Addo, Peter Eric Adotey. 2004. "Origins of African American Spiritualism," in *Yale Journal for Humanities in Medicine*. http://info.med.yale.edu/intmed/hummed/yjhm/essays/ paddo1. html. Accessed on October, 31, 2011.

Amaladoss, Michael. 2011. "Attaining Harmony as a Hindu-Christian." In John C. Haughey, ed., *In Search of the Whole: Twelve Essays on Faith and Academic Life*. Washington, DC: Georgetown University Press, 99-110.

Ashbrook, James B., and Carl Rausch Albright. 1997. *The Humanizing Brain: Where Religion and Neuroscience Meet*. Cleveland, OH: Pilgrim Press.

Awolalu, J. Omosade. 1979. *Yoruba Beliefs and Sacrificial Rites*. London: Longman.

Ayoade, John A. 1979. "Time in Yoruba Thought." In Richard A. Wright, ed., *African Philosophy: An Introduction*. Washington, DC: University Press of America, 71-89.

Barrett, David B. 1968. *Schism and Renewal in Africa: An Analysis of Six Thousand Contemporary Religious Movements*. London: Oxford University Press.

Baur, John. 1994. *2000 Years of Christianity in Africa: An African Church History*. Nairobi: Paulines Publications Africa.

Belcher, Stephen. 2005. *African Myths of Origin*. London: Penguin Books.

Bellagamba, Anthony. 1992. *Mission and Ministry in the Global Church*. Maryknoll, NY: Orbis Books.

Benedict XVI, and Peter Seewald. 2010. *Light of the World: The Pope, the Church and the Signs of the Times*. San Francisco: Ignatius Press.

Berry, Thomas. 1988. *The Dream of the Earth*. San Francisco: Sierra Club Books.

———. 1991. *Befriending the Earth*. Mystic, CT: Twenty-Third Publications.

———. 1999. *The Great Work: Our Way into the Future*. New York: Bell Tower.

———. 2006. *Evening Thoughts: Reflections on Earth as Sacred Community*. Edited by Mary Evelyn Tucker. San Francisco: Sierra Club Books and University of California Press.

———. 2009a. *The Christian Future and the Fate of the Earth*. Edited by Mary Evelyn Tucker and John Grim. Maryknoll, NY: Orbis Books.

———. 2009b. *The Sacred Universe: Earth, Spirituality, and Religion in the Twenty-First Century*. Edited by Mary Evelyn Tucker. New York: Columbia University Press.

Berry, Thomas, with Brian Swimme. 1992. *The Universe Story*. San Francisco: HarperSanFrancisco.

Beyaraza, Ernest. 2000. *The African Concept of Time: A Comparative Study of Various Theories*. Kampala: Makerere University Press.

Blakely, Pamela A. R., and Thomas D. Blakely. 1994. "Ancestors, 'Witchcraft', & Foregrounding the Poetic: Men's Oratory & Women's Song-Dance in

Hemba Funerary Performance." In Thomas D. Blakely, Walter E. A. van Beek, and Dennis L. Thomson, eds., *Religion in Africa: Experience and Expression*. London: James Currey, 398-442.

Bongmba, Elias K., ed. 2009. "Aesthetics in African Art: Implications for African Theology." In Anthony B. Pinn, ed., *Black Religion and Aesthetics: Religious Thought and Life in Africa and the African Diaspora*. New York: Palgrave Macmillan, 187-203.

Booth, Newell S. 1993. "Time and African Beliefs Revisited." In Jacob. K. Olupona and Sulayman S. Nyang, eds., *Religious Plurality in Africa: Essays in Honour of John S. Mbiti*. Berlin: de Gruyter, 83-94.

Booth, Newell S., ed. 1977a. *African Religions*. New York: NOK Publishers.

———. 1977b. "An Approach to African Religions." In Newell S. Booth, ed., *African Religions*. New York: NOK Publishers, 1-11.

———. 1977c. "The View from Kasongo Niembo." In Newell S. Booth, ed., *African Religions*. New York: NOK Publishers, 31-67.

Bosch, David J. 1980. *Witness to the World: The Christian Mission in Theological Perspective*. Atlanta: John Knox Press.

———. 1991. *Transforming Mission: Paradigm Shifts in Theology of Mission*. Maryknoll, NY: Orbis Books.

Bowie, Fiona. 2000. "Witchcraft and Healing among the Bangwa of Cameroon." In Graham Harvey, ed., *Indigenous Religions: A Companion*. London: Cassell, 68-79.

Bravmann, Rene A. 1977. "Contemporary Dimensions in African Art." In Phyllis M. Martin and Patrick O'Meara, eds., *Africa*. Bloomington: Indiana University Press, 348-66.

Bridston, Keith R. 1965. *Mission, Myth and Reality*. New York: Friendship Press.

Brown, Duncan. 2009. "Religion, Spirituality and the Postcolonial: A Perspective from the South." In Duncan Brown, ed., *Religion and Spirituality in South Africa: New Perspectives*. Scottsville: University of KwaZulu-Natal, 1-24.

Bujo, Bénézet. 2009a. "Is There a Specific African Ethic? Toward a Discussion with Western Thought." In Munyaradzi Felix Murove, ed., *African Ethics: An Anthology of Comparative and Applied Ethics*. Scottsville: University of KwaZulu-Natal Press, 113-28.

———. 2009b. "Ecology and Ethical Responsibility from an African Perspective." In Munyaradzi Felix Murove, ed., *African Ethics: An Anthology of Comparative and Applied Ethics*. Scottsville: University of KwaZulu-Natal Press, 281-97.

———. 2009c. "Springboards for Modern African Constitutions and Development in African Cultural Traditions." In Munyaradzi Felix Murove, ed., *African Ethics: An Anthology of Comparative and Applied Ethics*. Scottsville: University of KwaZulu-Natal Press, 391-411.

———. 2011. "Reasoning and Methodology in African Ethics." In James F. Keenan, ed., *Catholic Theological Ethics Past, Present, and Future: The Trento Conference*. Maryknoll, NY: Orbis Books, 147-59.

Bynum, Edward Bruce. 1999. *The African Unconscious: Roots of Ancient Mysticism and Modern Psychology*. New York: Teachers College Press, Columbia University.

Cambridge Dictionary of Christianity. 2010. Edited by Daniel Patte. Cambridge: Cambridge University Press.

Campbell, Cathy C. 2003. *Stations of the Banquet: Faith Foundations for Food Justice*. Collegeville, MN: Liturgical Press.

Chiwanga, Simon E. 2011. *Mhudumu: Episcopacy in Africa Reconsidered*. Nairobi: Acton Publishers.

Christensen, Thomas G. 1990. *An African Tree of Life*. Maryknoll, NY: Orbis Books.

Coetzee, P. H., and A. P. J. Roux, eds. 2002. *The African Philosophy Reader. Second Edition. A Text with Readings*. Cape Town, South Africa: Oxford University Press of Southern Africa.

Cox, James L. 2000. "Characteristics of African Indigenous Religions in Contemporary Zimbabwe." In Graham Harvey, ed., *Indigenous Religions: A Companion*. London: Cassell, 230-42.

Crowe, Frederick E., and Robert M. Doran, eds. 1988. *Collected Works of Bernard Lonergan*. Toronto: University of Toronto Press.

Daley, James, ed. 2006. *The World's Greatest Short Stories*. Mineola, NY: Dover Publications, 226-29.

Dandala, Mvume H. 2009. "Cows Never Die: Embracing African Cosmology in the Process of Economic Growth." In Munyaradzi Felix Murove, ed., *African Ethics: An Anthology of Comparative and Applied Ethics*. Scottsville: University of KwaZulu-Natal Press, 259-77.

Dardess, George. 2005. *Meeting Islam: A Guide for Christians*. Brewster, MA: Paraclete Press.

De Maria, William. 2009. "Does African 'Corruption' Exist?" In Munyaradzi Felix Murove, ed., *African Ethics: An Anthology of Comparative and Applied Ethics*. Scottsville: University of KwaZulu-Natal Press, 357-74.

Deacon, Moya. 2002. "The Status of Father Tempels and Ethnophilosophy in the Discourse of African Philosophy." In P. H. Coetzee and A. P. J. Roux, eds., *The African Philosophy Reader. Second Edition. A Text with Readings*. Cape Town, South Africa: Oxford University Press of Southern Africa, 97-111.

Delio, Ilia. 2008. *Christ in Evolution*. Maryknoll, NY: Orbis Books.

Delio, Ilia, Keith Douglas Warner, and Pamela Wood. 2008. *Care of Creation: A Franciscan Spirituality of the Earth*. Cincinnati, OH: St. Anthony Messenger Press.

Dhavamony, Mariasusai. 1997. *Christian Theology of Inculturation*. Rome: Editrice Pontificia Universita Gregoriana.

Donovan, Vincent J. 1982. *Christianity Rediscovered*. Maryknoll, NY: Orbis Books.

Dreyer, Elizabeth A., and Mark S. Burrows, eds.

———. 2005. *Minding the Spirit: The Study of Christian Spirituality*. Baltimore: Johns Hopkins University Press.

Dube, Musa W. 2009. "'I Am Because We Are': Giving Primacy to African Indigenous Values in HIV&AIDS Prevention." In Munyaradzi Felix Murove, ed. *African Ethics: An Anthology of Comparative and Applied Ethics.* Scottsville: University of KwaZulu-Natal Press, 188-217.

Dulles, Avery. 1978. *Models of the Church.* Garden City, NY: Doubleday.

———. 1992. *The Craft of Theology: From Symbol to System.* New York: Crossroad.

Dupuis, Jacques. 1997. *Toward a Christian Theology of Religious Pluralism.* Maryknoll, NY: Orbis Books.

Dyer, W. D. 2003. *There's a Spiritual Solution to Every Problem.* New York: Quill.

Eliade, Mircea. 1960. *Myths, Dreams and Mysteries: The Encounter between Contemporary Faiths and Archaic Realities.* New York: Harper Torchbooks.

———. 1969. *Fantastic Tales.* London: Dillon's.

Ellis, Stephen, and Gerrie ter Haar. 2004. *Worlds of Power: Religious Thought and Political Practice in Africa.* New York: Oxford University Press.

Ephirim-Donkor, Anthony. 2011. *African Spirituality: On Becoming Ancestors.* Lanham, MD: University Press of America.

Equiano, Olaudah. 1999. *The Life of Olaudah Equiano, or Gustavus Vassa, the African.* Mineola, NY: Dover Publications.

Fellows, Ward J. 1979. *Religions East and West.* New York: Holt, Rinehart & Winston.

Fisher, Robert B. 1998. *West African Religious Traditions: Focus on the Akan of Ghana.* Maryknoll, NY: Orbis Books.

Fortes, Meyer. 1987. *Religion, Morality and the Person: Essays on Tallensi Religion.* Cambridge: Cambridge University Press.

Friedman, Thomas L. 2005. *The World Is Flat: A Brief History of the Twenty-First Century.* New York: Farrar, Straus & Giroux.

Garon, Henry A. 2006. *The Cosmic Mystique.* Maryknoll, NY: Orbis Books.

Gibellini, Rosino, ed. 1994. *Paths of African Theology.* Maryknoll, NY: Orbis Books.

Gill, Sam D. 1982. *Native American Religions: An Introduction.* Belmont, CA: Wadsworth Publishing Company.

Goffard, Christopher. 2012. *You Will See Fire: A Search for Justice in Kenya.* New York: W. W. Norton.

Gore, Charles. 2007. *Art, Performance and Ritual in Benin City.* London: International African Library.

Griaule, Marcel. 1965. *Conversations with Ogotemmeli.* Oxford: Oxford University Press.

Griaule, Marcel, and Germaine Dieterlen. 1954. *The Dogon.* London.

Gutiérrez, Gustavo. 1984. *We Drink from Our Own Wells: The Spiritual Journey of a People.* Maryknoll, NY: Orbis Books.

Gyekye, Kwame. 1998. "The Relation of *Okra* (Soul) and *Honam* (Body): An Akan Conception." In Emmanuel Chukwudi Eze, ed., *African Philosophy: An Anthology.* Malden, MA: Blackwell Publishers, 50-65.

Haight, Roger. 1999. *Jesus Symbol of God.* Maryknoll, NY: Orbis Books.

Hallen, Barry. 2006. *African Philosophy: The Analytic Approach*. Trenton, NJ: Africa World Press.

Hamminga, Bert, ed. 2005. *Knowledge Cultures: Comparative Western and African Epistemology*. Amsterdam: Rodopi.

Harris, Grace Gredys. 1978. *Casting Out Anger: Religion among the Taita of Kenya*. Prospect Heights, IL: Waveland Press.

Harvey, Graham. 2000a. *Indigenous Religions: A Companion*. London: Cassell.

———. 2000b. "Art Works in Aotearoa." In Graham Harvey, ed., *Indigenous Religions: A Companion*. London: Cassell, 155-72.

———. 2000c. "Introduction." In Graham Harvey, ed., *Indigenous Religions: A Companion*. London: Cassell, 1-19.

Hathaway, Mark, and Leonardo Boff. 2009. *The Tao of Liberation: Exploring the Ecology of Transformation*. Maryknoll, NY: Orbis Books.

Haughey, John C. 2009. *Where Is Knowing Going? The Horizons of the Knowing Subject*. Washington, DC: Georgetown University Press.

Healey, Joseph G. 2012. *Building the Church as Family of God: Evaluation of Small Christian Communities in Eastern Africa*. Limuru, Kenya: Kolbe Press.

Huntington, Samuel P. 1996. *The Clash of Civilizations and the Remaking of World Order*. New York: Simon & Schuster.

Irwin, Lee. 2000a. *Native American Spirituality: A Critical Reader*. Lincoln: University of Nebraska Press.

———. 2000b. "Native American Spirituality: An Introduction." In Lee Irwin, ed., *Native American Spirituality: A Critical Reader*. Lincoln: University of Nebraska Press, 1-8.

Isichei, Elizabeth. 2004. *The Religious Traditions of Africa: A History*. Westport, CT: Praeger Publishers.

Johnson, Elizabeth A. 2007. *Quest for the Living God: Mapping Frontiers in the Theology of God*. New York: Continuum International Publishing Group.

Jung, L. Shannon. 2006. *Sharing Food: Christian Practices for Enjoyment*. Minneapolis, MN: Fortress Press.

Kalu, Ogbu. 2000. "Ancestral Spirituality and Society in Africa." In Jacob K. Olupona, ed., *African Spirituality: Forms, Meanings, and Expressions*. New York: Crossroad, 54-84.

Kalu, Hyacinth. 2011. *Together as One: Interfaith Relationships between African Traditional Religion, Islam, and Christianity in Nigeria*. Bloomington, IN: iUniverse.

Kaphagawani, Didier N. 2000. "Some African Conceptions of the Person." In Ivan Karp and D. A. Masolo, eds., *African Philosophy as Cultural Inquiry*. Bloomington: Indiana University Press, 66-79.

Katongole, Emmanuel. 2011. *The Sacrifice of Africa: A Political Theology for Africa*. Grand Rapids, MI: Eerdmans.

Keim, Curtis. 2009. *Mistaking Africa: Curiosities and Inventions of the American Mind*. Philadelphia: Westview Press.

Kenyatta, Jomo. 1968. *Suffering without Bitterness.* Nairobi: East African Publishing House.

———. 1978. *Facing Mount Kenya: The Traditional Life of the Gikuyu.* London: Heinemann.

Kimaro, Lucy R. 2011. *The Role of Religious Education in Promoting Christian-Muslim Dialogue in Africa.* Nairobi: Catholic University of Eastern Africa.

Kinoti, H. W., and J. M. Waliggo, eds. 1997. *The Bible in African Christianity: Essays in Biblical Theology.* Nairobi: Acton Publishers.

Kirk-Greene, Anthony H. M. 1998. "'Mutumin Kirki': The Concept of the Good Man in Hausa." In Emmanuel Chukwudi Eze, ed., *African Philosophy: An Anthology.* Malden, MA: Blackwell Publishers, 121-29.

Kirwen, Michael C., ed. 2005. *African Cultural Knowledge: Themes and Embedded Beliefs.* Nairobi: MIAS Books.

———. 2006. "Newsnotes." Maryknoll Institute of African Studies of Saint Mary's University, Minnesota and Tangaza College 18, no. 2. Nairobi: Mimeo.

———. 2008. *African Cultural Domains: Life Cycle of an Individual.* Nairobi: MIAS Books.

———. 2010. *African Cultural Domains. Book 2: Cycle of Family & Interpersonal Relationships.* Nairobi: MIAS Books.

Kisembo, Benezeri, Laurenti Magesa, and Aylward Shorter. 1977. *African Christian Marriage.* London: Geoffrey Chapman.

Knighton, Ben. 2005. *The Vitality of Karamojong Religion.* Aldershot, England: Ashgate Publishing.

Knitter, Paul. 2002. *Introducing Theologies of Religions.* Maryknoll, NY: Orbis Books.

Kobia, Samuel. 2003. *The Courage to Hope: The Roots for a New Vision and the Calling of the Church in Africa.* Geneva, Switzerland: World Council of Churches Publications.

Kubai, Anne N. 2010. "*Gacaca* and Post-Genocide Reconstruction in Rwanda." In Frans Wijsen and Sylvia Marcos, eds., *Indigenous Voices in the Sustainability Discourse: Spirituality and the Struggle for a Better Quality of Life.* Berlin: LIT Verlag, 261-80.

Kushner, Harold S. 1997. *When Bad Things Happen to Good People.* New York: Anchor Books.

Lawson, Thomas E. 1985. *Religions of Africa: Traditions in Transformation.* San Francisco: Harper & Row.

Lovell, Nadia. 2002. *Cord of Blood: Possession and the Making of Voodoo.* London: Pluto Press.

MacGaffey, Wyatt. 1986. *Religion and Society in Central Africa: The Bakongo of Lower Zaire.* Chicago: University of Chicago Press.

Maenzaise, Beauty R. 2009. "Ritual and Spirituality among the Shona People." In Dwight N. Hopkins and Marjorie Lewis, eds., *Another World Is Possible: Spirituality and Religion for Global Darker Peoples.* London: Equinox Publishing, 183-89.

Magesa, Laurenti. 1997. *African Religion: The Moral Traditions of Abundant Life.* Maryknoll, NY: Orbis Books.

———. 2004. *Anatomy of Inculturation: Transforming the Church in Africa.* Maryknoll, NY: Orbis Books.

———. 2010a. *African Religion in the Dialogue Debate: From Intolerance to Coexistence.* Vienna: LIT Verlag.

———. 2010b. "African Indigenous Spirituality as a Paradigm for Environmental Conservation." In Frans Wijsen and Sylvia Marcos, eds., *Indigenous Voices in the Sustainability Discourse: Spirituality and the Struggle for a Better Quality of Life.* Berlin: LIT Verlag, 127-52.

Magesa, Laurenti, and Michael C. Kirwen. 2012. *Exploring the Future of Mission in Africa: In Celebration of Maryknoll's 100 Years in Mission.* Nairobi: MIAS Books.

Maillu, David G. 1988. *Our Kind of Polygamy.* Kenya: East African Educational Publishers.

———. 2011. "Trying to Understand One Another: African Religion versus Christianity." Public Lecture at Hekima College, Nairobi, Kenya, on January 29.

Malinowski, Bronislaw. 1948. *Magic, Science and Religion and Other Essays.* Boston: Beacon Press.

Marks, Susan Collin. 2000. *Watching the Wind: Conflict Resolution during South Africa's Transition to Democracy.* Washington, DC: United States Institute of Peace Press.

Martin, Phyllis M., and Patrick O'Meara, eds. 1977a. *Africa.* Bloomington: Indiana University Press.

———. 1977b. "Africa: Problems and Perspectives." In *Africa.* Bloomington: Indiana University Press, 3-8.

Martini, Carlo Maria. 2012. "The Pope and the Bishops Should Find 12 Unconventional People to Take On Leadership Roles." *Tablet,* September 8, 2012, 8-9.

Mazrui, Ali A. 1987. *The Africans: A Triple Heritage.* New York: Little Brown.

———. 2009. "Africa's Wisdom Has Two Parents and One Guardian: Africanism, Islam and the West." In Munyaradzi Felix Murove, ed., *African Ethics: An Anthology of Comparative and Applied Ethics.* Scottsville: University of KwaZulu-Natal Press, 33-59.

Mbiti, John S. 1969. *African Religions and Philosophy.* Oxford: Heinemann Educational Publishers.

———. 1970. *Concepts of God in Africa.* London: SPCK.

———. 1971. *New Testament Eschatology in an African Background: A Study of the Encounter between New Testament Theology and African Traditional Concepts.* Oxford: Oxford University Press.

———. 1975a. *The Prayers of African Religion.* London: SPCK.

———. 1975b. *Introduction to African Religion.* London: Heineman.

———. 2012. *Concepts of God in Africa.* Second edition. Nairobi: Acton Publishers.

McVeigh, Malcolm J. 1974. *God in Africa: Conceptions of God in African Traditional Religion.* Cape Cod, MA: Claude Stark.

Merriam, Alan P. 1977. "Traditional Music of Black Africa." In Phyllis M. Martin and Patrick O'Meara, eds., *Africa*. Bloomington: Indiana University Press, 243-58.

Metz, Thaddeus. 2009. "African Moral Theory and Public Governance: Nepotism, Preferential Hiring and Other Partiality." In Munyaradzi Felix Murove, ed., *African Ethics: An Anthology of Comparative and Applied Ethics*. Scottsville: University of KwaZulu-Natal Press, 335-56.

Meyer, Ben F. 2008. *The Early Christians: Their World Mission and Self-Discovery*. Eugene, OR: Wipf & Stock.

Milingo, Emmanuel. 1984a. *The Demarcations*. Mimeo.

———. 1984b. *The World In Between: Christian Healing and the Struggle for Spiritual Survival*. Gweru, Zimbabwe: Mambo Press.

Miller, William Ian. 1997. *The Anatomy of Disgust*. Cambridge, MA: Harvard University Press.

Montgomery, John Warwick. 1986. *Human Rights and Human Dignity*. Grand Rapids, MI: Zondervan.

Morrison, Kenneth M. 2000. "The Cosmos as Intersubjective: Native American Other-Than-Human Persons." In Graham Harvey, ed., *Indigenous Religions: A Companion*. London: Cassell, 23-36.

Mugambi, J. N. K., and Laurenti Magesa, eds. 1989. *Jesus in African Christianity: Experimentation and Diversity in African Christology*. Nairobi: Initiatives.

Mulago, Vincent. 1991. "Traditional African Religion and Christianity." In Jacob K. Olupona, ed., *African Traditional Religion in Contemporary Society*. New York: Paragon House, 119-34.

Mundele, Albert Ngengi. 2012. *A Handbook on African Approaches to Biblical Interpretation*. Limuru, Kenya: Kolbe Press.

Munyaka, Mluleki, and Mokgethi Motlhabi. 2009. "*Ubuntu* and Its Socio-moral Significance." In Munyaradzi Felix Murove, ed., *African Ethics: An Anthology of Comparative and Applied Ethics*. Scottsville: University of KwaZulu-Natal Press, 63-84.

Murove, Munyaradzi Felix, ed. 2009a. *African Ethics: An Anthology of Comparative and Applied Ethics*. Scottsville: University of KwaZulu-Natal Press.

———. 2009b. "Beyond the Savage Evidence Ethic: A Vindication of African Ethics." In Munyaradzi Felix Murove, ed., *African Ethics: An Anthology of Comparative and Applied Ethics*. Scottsville: University of KwaZulu-Natal Press, 14-32.

———. 2009c. "African Bioethics: An Explanatory Discourse." In Munyaradzi Felix Murove, ed., 2009. *African Ethics: An Anthology of Comparative and Applied Ethics*. Scottsville: University of KwaZulu-Natal Press, 157-77.

———. 2009d. "The Incarnation of Max Weber's *Protestant Ethic and the Spirit of Capitalism* in Post-Colonial African Economic Discourse." In Munyaradzi Felix Murove, ed., *African Ethics: An Anthology of Comparative and Applied Ethics*. Scottsville: University of KwaZulu-Natal Press, 221-37.

Naipul, V. S. 2010. *The Masque of Africa: Glimpses of African Belief*. New York: Vintage Books.

Neil, Stephen. 1961. *Christian Faith and Other Faiths: The Christian Dialogue with Other Religions*. London: Oxford University Press.

Ngomba, Teke. 2012. "Ethno-Regionalism and the Governance Challenge in Africa: Lessons (Again) from Ivory Coast." In *AfricaFiles: At Issue Ezzine*. http://www.africafiles.org/atissueezine.asp#art2. Accessed on April 3, 2012.

Nicolás, Adolfo. 2010. "Interreligious Dialogue: The Experience of Some Pioneer Jesuits in Asia." *The Way* 50, no. 4 (October 2010), 7-33.

Nida, Eugene A., and William A. Smalley. 1959. *Introducing Animism*. New York: Friendship Press.

Nielssen, Hilde. 2012. *Ritual Imagination: A Study of Tromba Possession among the Betsimisaraka in Eastern Madagascar*. Leiden: Brill.

Nkrumah, Kwame. 1964. *Consciencism: Philosophy and the Ideology for Decolonization*. London: Heinemann.

Nussbaum, Barbara. 2009a. "*Ubuntu*: Reflections of a South African on Our Common Humanity." In Munyaradzi Felix Murove, ed., *African Ethics: An Anthology of Comparative and Applied Ethics*. Scottsville: University of KwaZulu-Natal Press, 100-109.

———. 2009b. "Ubuntu and Business: Reflections and Questions." In Munyaradzi Felix Murove, ed., *African Ethics: An Anthology of Comparative and Applied Ethics*. Scottsville: University of KwaZulu-Natal Press, 238-58.

Nyamiti, Charles. 1984. *Christ as Our Ancestor: Christology from an African Perspective*. Gweru, Zimbabwe: Mambo Press.

———. 1987. "Christ's Ministry in the Light of African Tribal Initiation Ritual." *African Christian Studies* 3, no. 1 (1987), 65-87.

———. 1990. "The Incarnation Viewed from the African Understanding of Person." *African Christian Studies* 6, no. 1 (1990), 3-27.

Nyerere, Julius K. 1966a. *Freedom and Unity/Uhuru na Umoja: A Selection from Writings and Speeches 1952–1965*. Dar es Salaam: Oxford University Press.

———. 1966b. "Pomposity." In Julius K. Nyerere, *Freedom and Unity/Uhuru na Umoja: A Selection from Writings and Speeches 1952–1965*. Dar es Salaam: Oxford University Press, 223-26.

———. 1968a. *Freedom and Socialism/Uhuru na Ujamaa: A Selection of Writings and Speeches 1965–1967*. Dar es Salaam: Oxford University Press.

———. 1968b. "Leaders Must Not Be Masters." In Julius K. Nyerere, *Freedom and Socialism/Uhuru na Ujamaa: A Selection of Writings and Speeches 1965–1967*. Dar es Salaam: Oxford University Press, 136-42.

———. 1981. "Tujisahihishe." In *Honest to My Country*. Tabora, Tanzania: TMP Book Department, 54-63.

Obiego, Cosmas Okechukwu. 1984. *African Image of Ultimate Reality: An Analysis of Igbo Ideas of Life and Death in Relation to Chukwu-God*. Frankfurt am Main: Peter Lang.

O'Murchu, Diarmuid. 1997. *Reclaiming Spirituality*. New York: Crossroad.

Opoku, Kofi Asare. 1993. "African Traditional Religion: An Enduring Heritage." In Jacob K. Olupona and Sulayman S. Nyang, eds., *Religious Plurality in Africa: Essays in Honour of John S. Mbiti*. Berlin: de Gruyter, 67-82.

Parrinder, Edward Geoffrey. 1967. *African Mythology*. London: Hamlyn.

Peel, John D. Y. 1968. *Aladura: A Religious Movement among the Yoruba*. Oxford: Oxford University Press.

Perman, Tony. 2011. "Awakening Spirits: The Ontology of Spirit, Self, and Society in Ndau Spirit Possession Practices in Zimbabwe." *Journal of Religion in Africa* 41, no. 1 (2011), 59-92.

Phan, Peter C. 2004. *Being Religious Interreligiously: Asian Perspectives on Interfaith Dialogue*. Maryknoll, NY: Orbis Books.

Philpot, Terry. 2012. "Freedom of Forgiveness." *The Tablet* (October 20, 2012), 8-10.

Plancke, Carine. 2011. "The Spirit's Wish: Possession Trance and Female Power among the Punu of Congo-Brazzaville." *Journal of Religion in Africa* 41, no. 4 (2011), 366-95.

Platvoet, Jan G. 2000. "Rattray's Request: Spirit Possession among the Bono of West Africa." In Graham Harvey, ed., *Indigenous Religions: A Companion*. London: Cassell, 80-96.

Principe, Walter. 2000. "Toward Defining Spirituality." In Kenneth J. Collins, ed., *Exploring Christian Spirituality: An Ecumenical Reader*. Grand Rapids, MI: Baker Books, 43-59.

Ramose, Mogobe B. 2002a. "The Ethics of *Ubuntu*." In P. H. Coetzee and A. P. J. Roux, eds., *The African Philosophy Reader. Second Edition. A Text with Readings*. Cape Town, South Africa: Oxford University Press of Southern Africa.

———. 2002b. "The Philosophy of *Ubuntu* and *Ubuntu* as a Philosophy." In P. H. Coetzee and A. P. J. Roux, eds., *The African Philosophy Reader. Second Edition. A Text with Readings*. Cape Town, South Africa: Oxford University Press of Southern Africa, 230-38.

———. 2009. "Towards Emancipative Politics in Modern Africa." In Munyaradzi Felix Murove, ed., *African Ethics: An Anthology of Comparative and Applied Ethics*. Scottsville: University of KwaZulu-Natal Press, 412-26.

Rasmussen, Susan J. 1995. *Spirit Possession and Personhood among the Kel Ewey Tuareg*. Cambridge: Cambridge University Press.

Ray, Benjamin C. 1976. *African Religions: Symbol, Ritual and Community*. Englewood Cliffs, NJ: Prentice Hall.

———. 2000. "African Shrines as Channels of Communication." In Jacob K. Olupona, ed., *African Spirituality: Forms, Meanings, and Expressions*. New York: Crossroad, 26-37.

Richardson, Neville. 2009. "Can Christian Ethics Find Its Way and Itself in Africa?" In Munyaradzi Felix Murove, ed., *African Ethics: An Anthology of Comparative and Applied Ethics*. Scottsville: University of KwaZulu-Natal Press, 129-54.

Ruel, Malcolm. 1997. *Belief, Ritual and the Securing of Life: Reflexive Essays on a Bantu Religion*. Leiden: Brill.

Rwiza, Richard. 2010. *Ethics of Human Rights: The African Contribution*. Nairobi: CUEA Press.

Ryan, William F. J., and Bernard J. Tyrrell, eds. 1974. *A Second Collection: Papers by Bernard J. F. Lonergan, S.J.* Toronto: University of Toronto Press.

Sacks, Jonathan. 2002. *The Dignity of Difference: How to Avoid the Clash of Civilizations.* London: Continuum.

Schneiders, Sandra M. 2000. "Spirituality in the Academy." In Kenneth J. Collins, ed., *Exploring Christian Spirituality: An Ecumenical Reader.* Grand Rapids, MI: Baker Books, 249-69.

———. 2005a. "Approaches to the Study of Christian Spirituality." In Arthur Holder, ed., *The Blackwell Companion to Christian Spirituality.* Oxford: Blackwell Publishing, 15-33.

———. 2005b. "The Study of Christian Spirituality." In Elizabeth A. Dreyer and Mark S. Burrows, eds., *Minding the Spirit: The Study of Christian Spirituality.* Baltimore, MD: Johns Hopkins University, 5-22.

Schreiter, Robert J., ed. 1991. *Faces of Jesus in Africa.* Maryknoll, NY: Orbis Books.

Sheldrake, Philip. 2000. "What Is Spirituality." In Keith J. Collins, ed., *Exploring Christian Spirituality: An Ecumenical Reader.* Grand Rapids, MI: Baker Books, 21-42.

———. 2007. *A Brief History of Spirituality.* Oxford: Blackwell Publishing.

Shivji, Issa. 1973. "Tanzania—The Silent Class Struggle." In Lionel Cliffe and John S. Saul, *Socialism in Tanzania, Vol. 2. Policies: An Interdisciplinary Reader.* Dar es Salaam: East African Publishing House, 304-30.

Shorter, Aylward. 1975. *Prayer in the Religious Traditions of Africa.* Nairobi: Oxford University Press.

Shutte, Augustine. 2009a. "Politics and the Ethics of *Ubuntu.*" In Munyaradzi Felix Murove, ed., *African Ethics: An Anthology of Comparative and Applied Ethics.* Scottsville: University of KwaZulu-Natal Press, 375-90.

———. 2009b. "*Ubuntu* as the African Ethical Vision." In Munyaradzi Felix Murove, ed., *African Ethics: An Anthology of Comparative and Applied Ethics.* Scottsville: University of KwaZulu-Natal Press, 85-99.

Sieber, Roy. 1977a. "Some Aspects of Religion and Art in Africa." In Newell S. Booth, ed., *African Religions.* New York: NOK Publishers International, 141-57.

———. 1977b. "Traditional Arts of Black Africa." In Phyllis M. Martin and Patrick O'Meara, eds., *Africa.* Bloomington: Indiana University Press, 221-42.

Some, Malidoma Patrice. 1993. *Ritual: Power, Healing & Community: The African Teachings of the Dagara.* Bath, UK: Gateway Books.

Spear, Thomas, and Isaria N. Kimambo, eds. 1999. *East African Expressions of Christianity.* Oxford: James Currey.

Stenger, Fritz. 2001. *White Fathers in Colonial Central Africa: A Critical Examination of V. Y. Mudimbe's Theories on Missionary Discourse in Africa.* Munster: LIT Verlag.

Stenger, Fritz, et al., eds. 2005. *Africa Is Not a Dark Continent.* Nairobi: Paulines Publications Africa.

Stinton, Diane B. 2004. *Jesus in Africa: Voices of Contemporary African Christology.* Maryknoll, NY: Orbis Books.

Stringer, Christopher, and Robin McKie. 1996. *African Exodus: The Origins of Modern Humanity*. New York: Henry Holt & Company.

Sundermeier, Theo. 1998. *The Individual and Community in African Traditional Religions*. Hamburg: LIT Verlag.

Sundkler, Bengt G. M. 1961. *Bantu Prophets in South Africa*. London: Oxford University Press.

———. 1976. *Zulu Zion and Some Swazi Zionists*. London: Oxford University Press.

Taiwo, Olu. 2000. "Music, Art and Movement among the Yoruba." In Graham Harvey, ed., *Indigenous Religions: A Companion*. London: Cassell, 173-89.

Tambulasi, Richard, and Happy Kayuni. 2009. "Ubuntu and Democratic Governance in Malawi: A Case Study." In Munyaradzi Felix Murove, ed., *African Ethics: An Anthology of Comparative and Applied Ethics*. Scottsville: University of KwaZulu-Natal Press, 427-40.

Tarimo, Aquiline. 2005. *Applied Ethics and Africa's Social Reconstruction*. Nairobi: Acton Publishers.

Taylor, John V. 1963. *The Primal Vision: Christian Presence amid African Religion*. London: SCM Press.

Teilhard de Chardin, Pierre. 1968. *The Divine Milieu*. New York: Harper & Row.

———. 1978. *The Heart of Matter*. San Diego: Harcourt.

———. 1999. *The Human Phenomenon*. Portland, OR: Sussex Academic Press.

———. 2004. *The Future of Man*. New York: Image Books.

Ter Haar, Gerrie. 1992. *Spirit of Africa: Healing Ministry of Archbishop Milingo of Zambia*. London: Hurst & Company Publishers.

———. 2009. *How God Became African: African Spirituality and Western Secular Thought*. Philadelphia: University of Pennsylvania Press.

Thiong'o, Ngugi wa. 1986. *Decolonising the Mind: The Politics of Language in African Literature*. Nairobi: Heinemann.

———. 2009. *Something Torn and New: An African Renaissance*. New York: Basic Books.

Thomas, Norman E., ed. 1995. *Classic Texts in Mission and World Christianity*. Maryknoll, NY: Orbis Books.

Thorpe, A. A. 1991. *African Traditional Religions: An Introduction*. Pretoria: University of South Africa.

Tutu, Desmond. 1999. *No Future without Forgiveness*. New York: Doubleday.

Tylor, Edward B. 1958. *Religion in Primitive Culture*. New York: Harper.

Ucko, Hans. 2004. "Africa's Contribution to the Religious and Spiritual Heritage of the World." *Current Dialogue* 44 (December 2004).

Uzukwu, Elochukwu E. 1996. *A Listening Church: Autonomy and Communion in African Churches*. Maryknoll, NY: Orbis Books.

———. 2012. *God, Spirit, and Human Wholeness: Appropriating Faith and Culture in West African Style*. Eugene, OR: Pickwick Publications.

Vondey, Wolfgang. 2008. *People of Bread: Rediscovering Ecclesiology*. Mahwah, NJ: Paulist Press.

Warren, M.A.C. 2010. "General Introduction." In John V. Taylor, *The Primal Vision: Christian Presence amid African Religion*. London: SCM Press, 5-12.

Welbourn, F. B. 1961. *East African Rebels: A Study of Some Independent Churches.* London: SCM.

Welbourn, F. B., and B. A. Ogot. 1966. *A Place to Feel at Home: A Study of Two Independent Churches.* London: Oxford University Press.

Wijsen, Frans, and Ralph Tanner. 2002. *"I Am Just a Sukuma": Globalization and Identity Construction in Northwest Tanzania.* Amsterdam: Rodopi.

Wijsen, Frans, and Sylvia Marcos, eds. 2010. *Indigenous Voices in the Sustainability Discourse: Spirituality and the Struggle for a Better Quality of Life.* Berlin: LIT Verlag.

Winzeler, Robert L. 2008. *Anthropology and Religion: What We Know, Think, and Question.* Lanham, MD: AltaMira Press.

Wiredu, Kwasi. 2002. "An Akan Perspective on Human Rights." In P. H. Coetzee and A. P. J. Roux, eds., *The African Philosophy Reader. Second Edition. A Text with Readings.* Cape Town: Oxford University Press of Southern Africa, 313-23.

Wrong, Michela. 2009. *It's Our Turn to Eat: The Story of a Kenyan Whistleblower.* London: Fourth Estate.

Zahan, Dominique. 1979. *The Religion, Spirituality, and Thought of Traditional Africa.* Chicago: University of Chicago Press.

———. 2000. "Some Reflections on African Spirituality." In Jacob K. Olupona, ed., *African Spirituality: Forms, Meanings, and Expressions.* New York: Crossroad, 3-25.

Zuesse, Evan M. 1979. *Ritual Cosmos: The Sanctification of Life in African Religions.* Athens: Ohio University Press.

Index